F O

# FORT SMITH

## Little Gibraltar on the Arkansas

Second Edition
By
EDWIN C. BEARSS
and
ARRELL M. GIBSON

UNIVERSITY OF OKLAHOMA PRESS
NORMAN AND LONDON

OTHER BOOKS BY EDWIN C. BEARSS:

*Decision in Mississippi* (Little Rock, 1962)
*Rebel Victory at Vicksburg* (Little Rock, 1963)
*Hardluck Ironclad Cairo* (Baton Rouge, 1966)
*Steele's Retreat from Camden* (Little Rock, 1967)
*Fort Smith: Little Gibraltar on the Arkansas* (in collaboration with Arrell M. Gibson, Norman, 1969, 1979)

OTHER BOOKS BY ARRELL M. GIBSON

*The Kickapoos: Lords of the Middle Border* (Norman, 1963)
*The Life and Death of Colonel Albert Jennings Fountain* (Norman, 1965)
*Fort Smith: Little Gibraltar on the Arkansas* (in collaboration with Ed Bearss, Norman, 1969, 1979)
*The Chickasaws* (Norman, 1971)
*Wilderness Bonanza: The Tri-State District of Missouri, Kansas, and Oklahoma* (Norman, 1972)
(editor) *Frontier Historian: The Life and Work of Everett Dale* (Norman, 1975)
*The Oklahoma Story* (Norman, 1978)

LIBRARY OF CONGRESS CATALOG CARD NUMBER: 68-31377

ISBN: 0-8061-1232-8

# Contents

# Illustrations

# Maps

# FORT SMITH

# CHAPTER ONE

# Introduction

THE UNITED STATES ARMY was a primary force in opening the Southwestern wilderness. By 1817, a pattern of military settlement had developed which was repeated with increasing regularity. Detachments, often no larger than a company of troops, entered the wilderness to construct forts at strategic spots on waterways and athwart Indian trails. The log palisade military posts were, except for occasional trader establishments, the first settlements. The life of each of these harbingers of civilization was brief—rarely more than twenty years, usually less. When the area was safe for pioneer farmers and townsmen, the soldiers moved on to open new frontiers.

But each post, while in operation, played a determinative role in local development. The most obvious duty was military—guarding the United States when the Southwest was shared with Spain and Mexico. An extension of the military role was pacifying the Indian tribes upon whose hunting range the military settlement intruded. Post officers often hosted councils where federal officials negotiated cession treaties with tribal leaders which opened new areas to civilian settlement.

In a broad sense, the post garrison pioneered in that it was the first to bring formal United States dominion to a new frontier area. Besides providing protection and pushing back obstacles to civilian settlement, soldiers based at Southwestern posts laced the wilderness with its first roads and established communication systems. Military detachments explored, surveyed, and mapped the unknown regions.

Almost every Southwestern military station provided urban impetus. Near each post there grew up a crude civilian settlement consisting of shops and stores for traders and tavern keepers, and residences for the wives and families of the men at the post. Thus the station's presence generated a satellite settlement which eventually became a town. The legacy of the old fort is preserved in the name the town now bears. The earliest social life for Southwestern frontier zones can generally be traced to the interaction of military and civilian at these remote stations. Post personnel often added to the satellite community's population when discharged soldiers took up permanent residence there.

Just as the military settlement generated urban development, it also seeded the local economy. Often the only source of money for a wilderness region was the soldier's pay freely spent in the town taverns, bawdy houses, and stores and the purchases from local farmers by post commissary officers who bought grain, livestock, and vegetables to add variety to the usual monotonous salt pork and beans fed to the troops. Thus by the time that War Department officials regarded a particular Southwestern post's function as fulfilled and were ready to close it and order the garrison into the wilderness, the military settlement had served several local nonmilitary purposes—economic, social, and demographic.

In its early years, Fort Smith was a typical Southwestern military settlement. From 1817 to 1824 it followed the emerging pattern of the army post as the forerunner of civilian settlement and civilization. Established by Major William Bradford and a company of the Rifle Regiment in 1817 on Belle Point, at the junction of the Poteau and Arkansas rivers on the present Arkansas-Oklahoma border, Fort Smith was the first United States military installation in a raw Southwestern wil-

derness. Its troops guarded United States interests in the Southwest and contained the fierce border struggle between the
Osages and the Cherokees. In 1824, War Department officials
decided that the original function had been fulfilled and ordered the garrison west to build two new posts—Fort Gibson
and Fort Towson.

But Fort Smith refused to die, and its periodic regeneration
gave it an unusual quality of longevity which provides additional justification for more detailed attention. Its useful life
to the federal government spanned a longer period—1817 to
1896—than most frontier military settlements. Time and again,
War Department officials were ready to close the post and
relocate the garrison at a new Western station, but they succumbed to intense pressures and found new functions for the
post. Eventually, Fort Smith became the mother post for the
Southwest. Fort Smith's longevity was due largely to the energy and resourcefulness of the local residents, who derived
economic benefits from the presence of this income-producing
federal installation in their midst. A study of the vicissitudes
of Fort Smith and the vigorous, sustained local civilian pressure to keep it operational gives lie to the cliché of the hardy
frontiersman, the epitome of self-reliance and individualism—
perhaps he was just as dependent upon federal pap as his twen-
tieth-century counterpart.

An examination of the history of Fort Smith yields useful
knowledge concerning the soldier as a pioneer. He had to have
those hardy, tough qualities generally attributed to the American pioneer. The soldier did not have the benefits of complete
freedom enjoyed by his civilian counterpart—he was constantly subject to stern discipline and cruel punishment if he
faltered. As a pioneer in the Southwestern wilderness, he had
to be versatile. At once he was an engineer, builder, farmer,
and guardian of United States interests. He cleared the land,
cut and dressed timbers from the forest, built walls for bar-

racks and storehouses, and raised a palisade. He surveyed and built the system of federal roads radiating west of Fort Smith. Congressional parsimony forced him to be a farmer, too. He cleared the land, plowed the fields, sowed corn and other vegetables for his mess. The Fort Smith trooper rode dim express trails carrying letters and military papers to command centers on the Missouri and the Mississippi. He patrolled a bloody border separating vengeance-driven Cherokee and Osage war parties. Occasionally, he marched to the very borders of the United States to watch for intruding Spanish patrols. And often, he died in this wilderness, his monument a humble headstone in the post cemetery or an unmarked grave in the Kiamichis.

A case study of Fort Smith yields also useful knowledge concerning United States military and Indian policy in the Southwest. Its founding in 1817 provided the nation a forward station thrusting into new territory claimed by both the United States and Spain. The boundary settlement with Spain in 1819–21 set the Red River and the 100th meridian as the segment of the international boundary closest to Fort Smith. Major William Bradford and Colonel Mathew Arbuckle watched this border for intruders. General Edmund Gaines, commanding officer of the Western Military Department, inspected Fort Smith in 1822 and declared that "in case of war in the West, it would become the Depot of the army in the field." As the military frontier advanced into the Southwest, Fort Smith, at the head of effective navigation on the Arkansas, became the commissary and quartermaster depot for the region, its constituency extending far into the Kiowa and Comanche country at Fort Cobb, and for a time to the military stations on the Brazos. As for Fort Smith's role in Indian policy—from the beginning, its officers and men supervised border tribal relations. The post commandant hosted several important intertribal councils. In the time of Indian relocations, Fort Smith served as a major supply depot and relocation center for emigrating tribesmen. The Belle Point station was headquarters for the 1825 boundary survey which ran the line separating Arkansas Territory and the Choctaw Nation. For a time the superintendent of Indian affairs had his headquarters at Fort Smith. Patrols from Fort Smith ranged eastern Indian Territory, removing squatters and clearing the lands for settlement by the Five Civilized Tribes. And at the close of the Civil War, a grand council of Confederate Indian leaders met with Union officials at the old post to negotiate the Reconstruction settlement.

Certainly one of Fort Smith's most conspicuous and enduring functions was that of establishing order in the Southwestern wilderness. From 1817, its presence was notice to the lawless that United States dominion had come to this frontier. Fort Smith troops reduced the turbulence created by the Osage-Cherokee vendetta. In later years, when the Five Civilized Tribes had relocated west of Fort Smith, the post was a contraband checkpoint to thwart smugglers and whisky runners who flourished on the Arkansas–Indian Territory border. Fort Smith's most dramatic role as a center of law and order came in the post–Civil War period when it served as headquarters for Judge Isaac Parker's federal district court. The "hanging judge" curbed the rampant lawlessness of Indian Territory. His gallows at old Fort Smith claimed their criminal tribute until 1896.

Through the portals of Fort Smith, one can see the panorama of Southwestern history unfolding. Like a funnel, the Belle Point station fed into the wilderness the soldier, trader, trapper, government explorer, the Texas-bound immigrant, mail and passengers on the Butterfield Overland stage, and argonauts bound for the Pacific shore.

# CHAPTER TWO

## Belle Point

BELLE POINT stood above the blending waters of the Arkansas and Poteau like a sentinel watching over the raw Southwestern wilderness. Its tawny bluffs, jutting fifty feet above the shoreline, were capped with a thick forest which flared into immense meadows, in spring "beautifully decorated with Painted Cup" and "occasional clusters of a white flowered . . . American primrose." According to tradition, *coureurs de bois* from their fur stations on the Nescatunga, Illinois, Verdigris, and Grand rivers rendezvoused here before advancing on Post of Arkansas and New Orleans for the annual exchange and frolic. An early-nineteenth-century visitor described this handsome crag as "more commanding and picturesque than any other spot of equal elevation on the banks of the Arkansas."[1]

Belle Point became the focal point of the Anglo-American Southwest in 1817 when it was selected as the site for Fort Smith. The genesis of this pioneer post courses into the nation's policy on land and the Indian.

Soon after 1800, the federal government began relocating the Cherokees and other Eastern tribes in order to provide new lands for expanding United States settlements. The Indian colonization zone most favored by the United States was

---

[1] Thomas Nuttall. *A Journal of Travels into the Arkansa Territory during the Year 1819* (vol. XIII of *Early Western Travels*, 1748–1846, ed. by Reuben G. Thwaites), 201.

on the lower Arkansas River. Because the Osages claimed this
region, federal officials negotiated treaties with tribal leaders
during councils held at St. Louis in 1808 and 1809 providing
for the cession of all lands east of a line extending south from
Fort Osage on the Missouri River to the Arkansas.[2]

After the St. Louis councils, President Thomas Jefferson
authorized the Cherokee Nation to send parties west of the
Mississippi to explore that part of the Osage cession bordering
the White and Arkansas rivers. Favorable reports on the new
colonization zone resulted in nearly two thousand Cherokees
abandoning their settlements in Georgia and Tennessee and
moving to the Arkansas. Cherokee Agent Return J. Meigs
sent William L. Lovely to establish a subagency among the
Arkansas Cherokees, and United States commissioners surveyed boundaries for their Western domain.[3]

Hardly had the Cherokees become established in their new
homeland when trouble developed. New settlers encroached
on their lands, stealing horses and slaughtering buffalo for
tallow and hides, leaving the carcasses to rot, and killing bears
solely for oil. Cherokee leaders protested that renegade traders
pandered "rotgut" frontier whisky to their warriors and that
squatters built cabins on Cherokee land, burned the timber,
and opened fields. The Verdigris Osages, the southern segment
of this powerful tribe, numbering about fifteen hundred and
led by the famous Clermont, were the chief tormentors of the
Cherokees. Although the Arkansas Cherokees increasingly
subsisted by farming, they continued to hunt and traffic in
furs and hides, and a principal inducement for them to move
west had been reports of abundant game in the new country.
As game and fur-bearing animals became scarce in their own

[2] Charles J. Kappler (comp. and ed.). *Indian Affairs: Laws and
Treaties*, II, 95–99.

[3] Lovely to Clark, August 9, 1814. National Archives, Office of Indian Affairs, Letters Received File.

territory, Cherokee hunters pushed west of the Osage cession and established hunting camps on the Canadian and Cimarron.[4]

Osage war parties ambushed Cherokee hunting camps, plundered their traps and furs, and ran off Cherokee horses. After several Osage raids, Cherokee hunting parties became war parties, more interested in Osage scalps than in furs and hides. Incidents mounted, each raid requiring its revenge, with the result that by 1814 life and property, white as well as Indian, were in great peril on the Arkansas.

Agent Lovely worked faithfully and diligently to abate this turmoil. He regularly reported on the explosive state of affairs in his jurisdiction to William Clark, governor of Missouri Territory and superintendent of Indian affairs with headquarters at St. Louis. As early as 1814, Lovely urged Clark to recommend to the secretary of war that a military post be established in the troubled zone. He pointed out that although the Indians, both Cherokees and Osages, were culpable, of equal blame for the troubled condition on the Arkansas were "some whites of the Worst Character in this Country whose influence with the Indians is dangerous to the peace," and that all parties required the restraining influence a military post would provide.[5]

Lovely also kept Cherokee Agent Meigs informed on the Cherokee border difficulties, and asked him to add his influence to the request that the secretary of war establish a military post on the Arkansas. Meigs strongly seconded Lovely's recommendation because he was interested in relocating the remainder of the Eastern Cherokees on the Arkansas in order to make their lands available for the settlers. A common excuse used by Eastern Cherokee leaders when Meigs encouraged

[4] Ibid.
[5] Lovely to Clark, October 11, 1814. *Territory of Louisiana-Missouri, 1815-1821* (vol. XV of *Territorial Papers of the United States*, ed. by Clarence E. Carter), 55.

them to move West was that vicious whites and Osages made life and property unsafe in the wilderness.[6]

To strengthen his appeal for military assistance on the Arkansas, Lovely sent a number of Cherokee delegates to St. Louis for councils with Governor Clark. At the April, 1816, council, Cherokee Chief John Chisholm presented Clark a letter from Agent Lovely reiterating the need for military occupation of the Osage-Cherokee border. Chisholm added his comments on the need for protection and denounced the Osages.[7]

After two years of waiting without avail for military assistance, and because of the intensifying struggle for control of the border region, Lovely made one last attempt to quiet the belligerents by removing the chief source of trouble. Soon after the Chisholm delegation returned from St. Louis, he asked Osage and Cherokee chiefs to meet with him at the mouth of the Verdigris. During the Verdigris council, Lovely pointed out that the principal Osage excuse for continuing the border strife was that Cherokees had trespassed on their land. The agent proposed that the Osages cede to the United States a tract bounded on the east by the 1808 Osage boundary, thence up the Arkansas to the mouth of the Verdigris, up the river to the falls, northeast to the saline spring on Grand River, and due east to the Osage boundary. The Osages agreed to cede the land. Known as Lovely's Purchase, this area would provide the Cherokees a hunting outlet.[8]

Before Lovely could know the results of his efforts on behalf of peace on the Arkansas frontier, he died. Clark appointed Reuben Lewis, a frontier trader, to replace him as Cherokee subagent.

Clark was not indifferent to Lovely's pleas for military

[6] Meigs to Secretary of War, February 17, 1816. In *ibid.*, 121.
[7] Clark to Lovely, May 2, 1816. In *ibid.*, 134–35.
[8] Grant Foreman. *Indians and Pioneers*, 46.

assistance. He wrote a number of letters to the secretary of war between 1814, when Lovely first broached the proposal, and 1817. He pointed out that a military post on the Arkansas was essential, not only to force an end to Osage-Cherokee hostilities but also to detect illicit trade on the Arkansas, thwart the extension of settlements above the Osage boundary, watch over bands of wild Indians residing high on the Arkansas, and generally protect the interests of the nation against domestic and foreign threat.[9]

The year 1817 saw a number of significant developments on the Arkansas frontier. During the summer, Eastern Cherokee chiefs and a delegation of Arkansas Cherokees met at Cherokee Agency, Tennessee, to negotiate a cession treaty with United States commissioners. The government agreed to provide the Cherokees land on the Arkansas equal in extent to an area ceded to the United States in the Southeastern states. The treaty promised supplies, equipment, and provisions for each emigrating warrior and his family, and assured military protection for all who moved to the Arkansas. At the time of the 1817 treaty, two thousand Cherokees resided in the West; in less than two years, the Western Cherokee population increased to nearly six thousand.[10]

Also in 1817, the Cherokee-Osage vendetta intensified, and augured total war. This threat grew out of an incident on the Canadian during the autumn of 1816. A Cherokee hunting party came upon an Osage camp, routed the warriors, and made off with several horses. An Osage relief party overtook the raiders, killed and scalped a Cherokee, and recovered the horses. The Cherokee council in January, 1817, noted this incident and voted to wage a campaign of annihilation against the Osages. A message was sent to the Cherokees in Tennessee

9 Clark to Secretary of War, September 30, 1816. *Territory of Louisiana-Missouri*, 177.
10 Kappler. *Indian Affairs: Laws and Treaties*, II, 141–44.

inviting adventure-seeking warriors to join their tribesmen for the Osage campaign. Cherokee war leader Tick-e-Toke planned to begin the action in the spring as soon as the grass was high enough to sustain the horses.[11]

Both Meigs and Clark were informed of the Cherokee offensive. Meigs intercepted most of the Cherokee volunteers en route to the Arkansas, but several warriors slipped away. Clark doubted that the conflict would erupt before autumn, because the Osages left their villages in May to hunt buffalo on the plains, but he admitted to the secretary of war that he favored the Cherokee action because it would reduce Osage power. He declared that the Osages were "more vicious than they formerly were. They have killed our Citizens and frequently whip, and plunder them. . . . The war which the Cherokees & Osage are now engaged in . . . may produce . . . a favourable effect."[12] Before Tick-e-Toke's army could get under way, certain tribal leaders were called to Cherokee Agency in Tennessee to participate in the council which resulted in the 1817 cession treaty.

The year 1817 also marked the founding of Fort Smith. The military directive which brought this about was issued by Acting Secretary of War Richard Graham on July 30, 1817. He advised General Andrew Jackson, commanding the Southern Department with headquarters at Nashville, that an army post was to be erected at or near the point where the Osage boundary crossed the Arkansas River. Graham instructed Jackson to see that the new station was garrisoned by one company "under a skilful and experienced officer, in whose discretion confidence can be placed" and whose chief assignment was "to take all proper measures for the restoration of

[11] Graham to Clark, April 1, 1817. National Archives, Office of Indian Affairs, Letters Sent File.
[12] Clark to Secretary of War, May 15, 1817. *Territory of Louisiana-Missouri*, 260–62.

peace, and the preservation of harmony between the Osage and Cherokee tribes." Graham pointed out to Jackson that the increase in the Cherokee population on the frontier due to the recent treaty would escalate tension among both the Osages and the expanding white settlements in that area. The Acting Secretary of War added that to avoid a clash between whites and Indians it would be necessary to prevent citizens from hunting and trespassing on Indian lands.[13]

Troops for the new post were to come from the Rifle Regiment, rated the crack infantry unit of the army. This regiment had its origin in a law passed by Congress in 1799 authorizing formation of a battalion of riflemen. A full regiment was authorized in 1808, and six years later three additional such regiments were formed. With retrenchment following the War of 1812, the four regiments were consolidated into a single force. Rifle Regiment troopers were specialists in scouting and patrol duty. They were required to fire without rests, and recruits were admitted to this select unit only after perfecting marksmanship on targets set at from fifty to one hundred twenty yards. Their uniforms were gray, cut in a pattern similar to that of the dress uniform of West Point cadets.[14]

Jackson relayed Graham's order concerning the new post to General Thomas A. Smith, commander of the Ninth Military Department with headquarters at Belle Fontaine on the Missouri River fifteen miles north of St. Louis. Smith selected Major William Bradford, a veteran of the War of 1812, to command the new fort on the Arkansas. Major Stephen H. Long of the Topographical Engineers and a five-man engineering party were to accompany Bradford, select the site

---

13 Graham to Jackson, July 30, 1817. Jackson Papers, Library of Congress.
14 Francis B. Heitman. *Historical Register and Dictionary of the United States Army*, I, 141.

for the post, and sketch the construction plans. About half of Bradford's company was at Belle Fontaine. It was to be brought to full strength from Rifle Regiment detachments on duty at Baton Rouge and Natchitoches under the command of Major Joseph Selden, presently en route by keelboat up the Mississippi.[15]

Bradford drew ordnance, commissary, and quartermaster supplies for the new post from stocks at Belle Fontaine. Among the items troops stowed aboard a large keelboat were two six-pound cannon mounted on carriage, two sets of harness for four-horse teams to pull the artillery, and more than half a ton of pig lead for casting bullets.[16]

By formal orders, General Smith directed Major Bradford to

... ascend the Arkansaw river to the point where the Osage boundary line Strikes that river, with the advice of Major Long, select the best site to be found upon it near to that line and thereon erect as expeditiously as circumstances will permit a Stockade most sufficient for the comfortable accommodation of one company, with necessary quarters, Barracks, Store houses, Shops, Magazines, and Hospital, conformable to the plan furnished by Major Long, which he will adapt to the nature of the position.

The department of War having ordered the establishment of a Post on the Arkansaw with the men to prevent the Indian Tribes in that quarter continuing hostilities with each other, you are required to represent to the Chiefs and warriors of those Tribes the wish of the President on this Subject and use every legal means in your power to restore tranquility among them. Should the executive of this Territory call upon you to remove any portion or all of the Intruders from the Indian or public lands in that Section of

[15] *Ibid*, 238, 640.
[16] Return of Ordnance at Fort Belle Point. Jackson Papers, Library of Congress.

the country you will take suitable measures for its accomplishment.

In consequence of the remoteness of your post, much will depend upon your own activity, economy and arrangement, to these you must have recourse for supplies of every kind which may be necessary beyond what you can take with you.[17]

Major Bradford's transport, laden with supplies, ordnance, and troops, slipped from its berth into the Missouri River current in mid-September, 1817. On October 1, his craft rendezvoused with Major Selden's transport near the mouth of the Ohio. Crewmen lashed the two keelboats side by side, and Selden's Rifle Regiment contingent boarded the Arkansas-bound vessel. Boatmen cast the fasts loose; Selden continued toward Belle Fontaine, and Bradford resumed his run down the Mississippi.

Bradford was distressed to find that at least twenty-four of Selden's men transferred to his command were so ill that they required medical attention. Having neither surgeon nor subaltern, Bradford and Major Long themselves nursed the sick. All men capable of working were formed into fatigue parties. The run to the mouth of the Arkansas was unusually slow because of the care and attention required by the seriously ill, and Bradford's keelboat did not reach Post of Arkansas until October 15. Cooler weather hastened the recovery of most of the ailing; each day several men were restored to duty, although three died on the Mississippi.

To allow his troops additional time to recuperate and to take on fresh provisions, Bradford decided to lay over at Post of Arkansas a few days before pushing up the Arkansas, but he directed Major Long to proceed at once and to reconnoiter

[17] O'Fallon to Bradford, September 15, 1817. Smith Collection, Missouri Historical Society.

the river to the mouth of the Verdigris. With a small detachment and provisions for twenty-four days, Long ascended the Arkansas in a skiff.[18]

As Long approached the estimated position of the Osage line, he carefully examined the river bank for a site on which to erect the new post. Belle Point loomed conspicuous and superior over all other considered locations. After recording astronomical observations at the mouth of the Verdigris, Long returned to Belle Point.

On December 1, Long made a thorough reconnaissance of the headlands above the point and found everything favorable from a military engineering view, thus confirming his initial judgment that Belle Point surpassed all other locations as a site for the new post. While his men constructed rude shelters, Long surveyed the site and sketched building plans to guide Bradford's men in erecting the fort. Long gave the name Camp Smith to the cluster of primitive shelters erected by his men.[19]

While awaiting Bradford, Long decided to explore the rough mountain country south of Belle Point. Before departing, Long directed two of his men to remain at Camp Smith and deliver the fort plans to Major Bradford. He obtained horses from the Cherokees and set a course to the southwest. Ascending the Poteau, he led his patrol across the San Bois, Winding Stair, and Kiamichi mountains to the headwaters of the Kiamichi, which he followed to the Red. He followed the north bank of the Red until he crossed a heavily traveled Indian trace leading in a northeasterly direction. On December 31, the explorers reached an area containing "thirty thermal springs." Continuing north, Long forded the Arkansas River near present Little Rock, came to the Mississippi at

[18] Long to Smith, October 15, 1817. Smith Collection, Missouri Historical Society.

[19] Long to Smith, May 12, 1818. National Archives, War Department, Western Department, Letters Sent File.

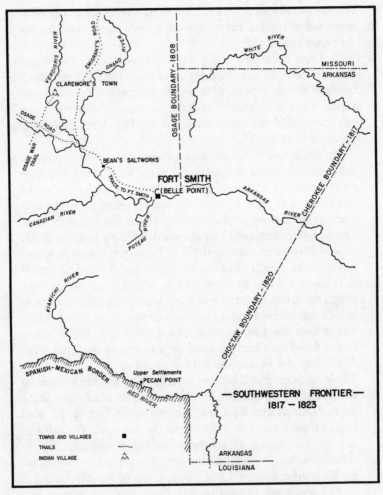

THE SOUTHWESTERN FRONTIER, 1817–1823.

Herculaneum, and reached Belle Fontaine at the end of January, 1818.[20]

On Christmas, 1817, as Major Bradford's keelboat struggled off Belle Point in the combining currents of the Arkansas and the Poteau, he was hailed to shore by the two-man detachment from the engineering party left at Camp Smith by Major Long. They gave Bradford the construction plans, pointed out the site location atop Belle Point, and then boarded the skiff and prepared to rendezvous with Long on the lower Arkansas. Bradford was impressed with Long's selection, observing that it was well watered and looked "healthy," and agreed that the spot between the Poteau and the Arkansas was superior to all others on the river "calculated for a military post."

The slow trip up the Arkansas had brought almost complete recovery to Bradford's ailing troops. When they reached Belle Point, only four men were still seriously ill and six were classed as convalescent. Bradford drove his men hard. Working parties unloaded the keelboat, pitched tents around the crude brush shelters, and cut logs from the thick forest atop Belle Point. On New Year's Day, 1818, Bradford wrote General Jackson on the progress his Rifle Regiment detachment had made in the week since landing at Belle Point. "I have them all comfortably situated together with a hospital for the sick, a Store house for the Public, a Provision house for the contractor, and am about a hut for myself."[21]

[20] Long to Smith, January 30, 1818. Smith Collection, Missouri Historical Society.

[21] Bradford to Jackson, January 1, 1818. Jackson Papers, Library of Congress.

# CHAPTER THREE

# War Drums on the Verdigris

THE FIRST YEAR AT BELLE POINT was probably the busiest for any company in the history of the Rifle Regiment. Bradford's troops worked at a variety of tasks. One party cut a road through the wilderness to provide military couriers an overland route between Fort Smith and Belle Fontaine. Another stayed in the field almost continuously, patrolling the Osage line to intercept Cherokee and Osage war parties. A survey detail mapped the country adjacent to Belle Point. But that first year at Camp Smith, most of the seventy-man company did construction work. Some went into the forest to fell trees and dress timbers; others raised walls and erected buildings.

Major Long's construction plans called for a stockade wall ten feet high and eight and one-half inches thick, the garrison to be placed in a hollow square each side of which was 132 feet long. At opposite corners, one fronting the river, the men erected blockhouses, twenty-eight feet square, extending ten feet beyond the garrison walls, and topped with a cupola eight feet square.

On the inner stockade wall, Bradford's men constructed sentinel platforms six feet above the ground providing a walkway three feet wide. Within the garrison square, the building plan called for a commanding officer's quarters, subalterns or junior officers and surgeon's quarters, soldiers' barracks, guard and musicians' quarters, provision house and carpenter shop, saddle and tailor shop, a sutler's room and hospital, a kitchen, and a magazine. A moat four feet deep and flaring from a base of six feet to eight feet at the top was to surround the post, its inside wall or scarp to be paved with stone to serve as a foundation for the outer garrison walls. Entrance was to be by a main gate ten feet wide and eight feet high. In 1818, the War Department designated the works at Belle Point a permanent post in the system of Western defenses with the name Fort Smith.[1]

Bradford was never able to make the construction progress expected of his company, because each succeeding month the Arkansas frontier became more turbulent and he had to assign an increasing number of troops to peace-keeping functions. Thus an 1821 inspection of Fort Smith revealed that three years of intermittent work on the Belle Point defenses had produced two sides of the garrison square next to the land, the two blockhouses, and most of the interior buildings. Despite many interruptions, Bradford's men had cut, hewed, and dressed the timbers for the walls next to the water.[2]

The major problem of Fort Smith's first garrison was to restore peace between the Cherokees and Osages. Even as the Rifle Regiment decended the Mississippi in October, 1817, en route to the Arkansas, the vaunted Cherokee offensive led by Tick-e-Toke, Taluntuskey, the Bowl, and Black Fox was launched.

Tick-e-Toke's scouts found the Verdigris villages empty of warriors. Most of Clermont's people were on the Cimarron and Salt Fork hunting buffalo. Elderly men and women and

---

[1] A Plan of the Garrison at Belle Point, Arkansas Territory as Furnished Major William Bradford by Major Long, Corps of Engineers. National Archives, War Department, Plans and Sketches of Early Posts and Harbors.

[2] John R. Bell. *The Journal of Captain John R. Bell* (vol. VI of *Far West and Rockies Series*, ed. by Harbin M. Fuller and LeRoy R. Hafen), 283.

several young mothers and their children had remained in the village.

Squads of Cherokee horsemen struck the undefended Osage community from all sides. The fury of their attack was certain and deadly. An estimated sixty-nine Osages were slain; countless old men, women, and children suffered wounds; and one report claimed that the older boys were brutally emasculated. Tick-e-Toke's warriors captured more than a hundred prisoners, mostly younger women and children, and plundered great quantities of corn, pumpkins, squash, lotus roots, jerked meat, buffalo robes, deer skins, furs, pots, and kettles. The raiders loaded the captives and booty on captured horses, burned the lodges, and returned to their towns on the Arkansas.[3]

Major Bradford learned of the so-called Battle of Claremore Mound soon after arriving at Belle Point. On separate occasions he visited the leaders of both tribes and urged a truce until he could investigate and satisfy himself as to the conflicting claims and charges. From War Department instructions it was apparent to Bradford that the Cherokees were favored by the federal government in this border contest. Secretary of War John Calhoun was anxious that Bradford exert himself to protect the Cherokees from Osage retaliation.

Soon after the Claremore Mound affair, a Cherokee delegation traveled to Washington for the purpose of appealing to the president to grant them the Osage lands west to the Verdigris. The delegates claimed that this area properly belonged to the Cherokees as the fruits of conquest, and said that it was essential as a hunting outlet to the western hunting grounds.

Both President Monroe and Secretary Calhoun were sympathetic to the Cherokees, and thought that the Osages should yield part of their land so that the Cherokees could reach the

[3] Bradford to Jackson, January 1, 1818. Jackson Papers, Library of Congress.

buffalo range undisturbed. Calhoun admitted that the president was "anxious to hold out every inducement to the Cherokees . . . to emigrate to the West of the Mississippi," and a first step in accomplishing this was to placate the Arkansas Cherokees even at the sacrifice of justice for the Osages.[4]

The fact that the Arkansas Cherokees had the ear of the president and the secretary of war made them more arrogant and demanding than ever. The assurance that their interests would receive unqualified support and protection undoubtedly explained the heavy migration of Eastern Cherokees to the Arkansas during 1818. Although the increased Cherokee population near Fort Smith aggravated border tensions and added to Major Bradford's problems, it had one good result. Among the recent Cherokee immigrants was Taluntuskey's brother John Jolly.

Unlike Taluntuskey, a leader of the war faction among the Western Cherokees, Jolly was interested in the orderly, peaceful development of the Western Cherokees and became the leader of a peace faction. Soon after his arrival on the Arkansas, Jolly and other Cherokee headmen in company with Cherokee Agent Reuben Lewis traveled to Fort Smith to ask Major Bradford to assist them in ending the Cherokee-Osage vendetta. Bradford communicated to the Osages the Cherokee interest in peace. Tribal leaders agreed to a council, and asked Bradford to arrange for a meeting at Fort Smith. The lower Arkansas region was still a part of Missouri Territory, administered by Governor William Clark, who doubled as regional supervisor of Indian tribes as superintendent of Indian affairs. When Bradford submitted the request for authority to hold a tribal council at Fort Smith, Clark refused, insisting that the tribes send delegates to a council at St. Louis and saying that

[4] Calhoun to Clark, May 8, 1818. *Territory of Louisiana-Missouri, 1815–1821* (vol. XV of *Territorial Papers of the United States*, ed. by Clarence E. Carter), 390–91.

it was "thought by both parties that no treaty they could make would be considered as reciprocally binding upon them, unless it should be ratified and confirmed in my presence."[5]

During the late summer of 1818, Osage and Cherokee headmen gathered at St. Louis. The Osage leaders were in an especially difficult position. Their warriors were charged with numerous attacks on the Missouri settlements. Settlers' claims lodged with the United States government against the Osages for horses, firearms, and other property stolen or destroyed in raids exceeded the value of the annuity due that tribe. Clark assured the Osages that in exchange for a land cession the United States government would assume the settlers' claims against the tribe. Thus, on September 25, the Osages ceded Lovely's Purchase to the United States. Eleven days later, Osage and Cherokee headmen signed a treaty pledging their tribes to "perpetual peace." The Cherokees promised to return captives taken in the Claremore Mound raid, and the Osages assured the Cherokees "undisturbed passage to the hunting grounds" west of their villages with permission to hunt on land claimed by the Osages south of the Arkansas. The captives were to be surrendered at Fort Smith.[6]

The pledge of "perpetual peace" was broken by the Cherokees on the way home from St. Louis. Stragglers from the Cherokee delegation came upon an Osage hunting camp at the Batesville crossing on White River and made off with forty horses. In reprisal, the Osages looted several Cherokee hunting camps of a large quantity of furs.

Nathaniel Pryor, an Osage trader, informed Bradford of the Cherokee raid on White River and warned that the Osages were again preparing for war. Bradford rode to Clermont's village and assured the Osage leader that he would use his in-

[5] Clark to Calhoun, October, 1818. *Ibid.*, 454.
[6] Charles J. Kappler (comp. and ed.). *Indian Affairs: Laws and Treaties*, II, 167–68.

fluence to recover the horses stolen on White River and to force the Cherokees to return the Osage captives as promised in the recent treaty if Clermont would hold his warriors in check. Clermont assented and pledged that the Osages would not trade the Cherokee furs until he had heard from Bradford.[7]

Next, Bradford sent for Reuben Lewis, who reported that he had seen the stolen horses and would do his utmost to have the animals restored to the Osages. But the Cherokees deliberately delayed returning the horses and refused to discuss restoring the Osage captives, explaining to Lewis and Bradford that they wished first to meet with Governor Clark at St. Louis. This demonstrated Bradford's anomalous position; although he was responsible for maintaining peace on the Arkansas frontier, he was thwarted in discharging this responsibility because of the favored position of the Cherokees, who knew that Clark was the voice of the secretary of war and the president and would support them in their contest with the Osages.

Bradford's role in frontier affairs improved in March, 1819, when Congress detached the southern half of Missouri Territory and created the Territory of Arkansas. James Miller of New Hampshire was named governor, and Robert Crittenden of Kentucky became territorial secretary. These events had a twofold effect on Fort Smith. As a territory of the first class, Arkansas underwent a population boom, and the expanding settlements soon placed an inexorable pressure on the Western Cherokees, making them more restive and thus adding to the peace-keeping problems facing the troops at Belle Point. But it enabled Bradford and the Rifle Regiment company at Fort Smith to deal more directly with the Cherokees, for Miller was also appointed superintendent of Indian affairs for the

---

[7] Bradford to Calhoun, February 4, 1819. *Territory of Arkansas, 1819–1825* (vol. XIX of *Territorial Papers of the United States*, ed. by Clarence E. Carter), 33–34.

territory. Miller opposed Clark's laissez-faire policy toward the Cherokees and generally supported Bradford in a more direct line of action. Thus, soon after Miller's appointment, Bradford sent a sergeant and a squad of Rifles to the Cherokee villages with instructions to recover the Osage horses. The party returned with fourteen animals, which were delivered to Clermont with word from Bradford that the remainder would be restored when the Osages delivered the Cherokee furs to Fort Smith.[8]

Bradford urged the Cherokee chiefs to respect the St. Louis Treaty of 1818 and to return the Osage captives. Chief Jolly and the peace faction among the Western Cherokees favored such action, but Tick-e-Toke and his war faction were opposed. Finally, in July, 1819, word came to Fort Smith that the Cherokees were ready to meet their treaty obligation. Bradford alerted Clermont to have a delegation ready to meet at Belle Point. For most of July, the Osage leader, his headmen, and hundreds of Indian families anxiously waited for Bradford's messenger at the mouth of the Verdigris. Then word came to Fort Smith that the Cherokees were busy with the harvest and thus unable to journey to Fort Smith until September. Clermont, perplexed, led his people back to their villages.[9]

The Osages were eager to have the restoration accomplished so that they could be off for the autumn buffalo hunt on the Cimarron and Salt Fork, knowing that if they waited too long other tribes would drive the buffalo far to the south. Finally, Clermont and a large party rode to Fort Smith to plead with Bradford for action. Bradford's message to the Cherokees for prompt fulfillment of the terms of treaty was answered with

[8] Bradford to Calhoun, March 28, 1819. *Ibid.*, 57–58.
[9] Thomas Nuttall. *A Journal of Travels into the Arkansa Territory, during the Year 1819* (vol. XIII of *Early Western Travels, 1748–1846*, ed. by Reuben G. Thwaites), 201.

the statement that several Osage women had married Cherokees and "were happy and did not wish to come back and live
with savages." To this, the Fort Smith commandant answered
with the ultimatum to have the captives at the post in ten days
or he would send troops after them. On the evening of October 6, the Osages gave up and started for their Verdigris villages, but the next morning the Cherokees began arriving, and
Bradford sent for the Osages. When all but Clermont and his
principal headman Tallai returned, the Cherokees, headed by
Tick-e-Toke, refused to discuss repatriation of the captives
until the principal men of the Verdigris Osages were present.
Bradford sent for them, they arrived, and the council got
under way. After much talk, Tick-e-Toke ordered the captives brought into the council, and a Cherokee headman proposed that each be given the choice of remaining with the
Cherokees or of returning to the Osages. This point was not
pressed, and there followed touching scenes of joy mixed with
sadness in those families in which Osage women had married
Cherokees. One separation was so touching that it was noticed
by a visitor who attended the Fort Smith council.

> Their parting was a scene of sorrow; the Cherokee promised
> to go to the village, and ask her of her father, she also plead
> with the chiefs to stay, but . . . [Clermont] unmoved by her
> tears and entreaties, answered, "Your father and mother
> lament you; it is your duty to go and see them. If the Chero-
> kee loves you, he will not forget to come for you."[10]

The Fort Smith council of 1819 did not settle the Cherokee-
Osage controversy permanently, but it did produce a temporary lull in border action which enabled Major Bradford
to give attention to other pressing problems. One of these concerned Rifle Regiment personnel at Belle Point. The company
had been rushed off to the Arkansas frontier to deal with the

[10] *Ibid.*, 278–79.

border crisis, and at the time no surgeon or junior officers were available for assignment. In 1818, Lieutenant William Blair joined Bradford's staff; the next year, Lieutenant John Edmonson and Dr. Thomas Russell arrived at Fort Smith, the latter to serve as post surgeon.[11]

Keeping the enlisted ranks at full strength was a continuing problem for Bradford. The attrition in his company caused by death, expiration of enlistment, and desertion cut his roster at times to as few as forty men. His seventy-man enlisted complement was to consist of three sergeants, four corporals, one drummer, one fifer, and the remainder, privates.[12]

At times, 20 per cent of the company was confined to the post hospital or barracks, generally stricken with the "ague and bilious fever." The sickness was especially serious during 1819, when more than a hundred Cherokees died from its effects. At Belle Point, the "ague and bilious fever" hit with epidemic force, and at one time during the summer nearly a third of the company was either coming down with it, moving toward the crisis with high fever, or feebly approaching recovery. The treatment consisted of doses of laudanum to tranquilize the patient during raging fever spells, purges of castor oil, and confinement to post hospital or quarters. One of those who suffered through this ailment during the 1819 epidemic reported that it started with

> slight chills, and was succeeded by a fever, attended with unremitting vomiting, accompanied with blood and bloody faeces. Ejecting all medicine, it became next to impossible to administer internal relief. The paroxyms, attended with excruciating pain, took place every other day, similar to the

[11] Returns for the Troops Stationed at Fort Smith, October 31, 1819. National Archives, War Department, Western Department, Reports Received File.

[12] Returns for the Troops Stationed at Fort Smith, November 30, 1820. National Archives, War Department, Western Department, Reports Received File.

common intermittent. One of the soldiers . . . was afflicted in this way for the space of six days, after which he recovered. On the intermitting days he appeared perfectly easy, and possessed a strong and craving appetite.[13]

Bradford's company strength was further reduced by frequent infractions of military law—most commonly sleeping on watch, fighting, and drunkenness on the post—which resulted in loss of rank for many noncommissioned officers and stiff sentences in the stockade for private soldiers. The isolated location of Fort Smith prevented the occasional frolic which a nearby town would have provided. This isolation, combined with the heavy duty exacted by the post commander, caused many of the men to brood and eventually to desert. Many of these desertions were known to have been caused by homesickness. Furloughs for enlisted men were possible only in instances of dire emergency, generally connected with family affairs. Bradford had a three-man detail described as "excellent trackers" in the field most of the time, trailing errant soldiers. Bradford paid a thirty-dollar reward for each runaway restored to his command, and recovered this money by docking the offender's pay.[14]

The service hitch was for five years, and as an enlistment bounty each recruit was promised a warrant entitling him to free land on the public domain. The land warrant was delivered to the soldier at the end of his enlistment period. Bradford had little luck in persuading those soldiers with expiring enlistments to reenlist and remain under his command at Fort Smith—only about one in five staying. On several occasions as his ranks dwindled through expiration of enlistments, Bradford sent Lieutenant Blair with a five-man escort to the Mis-

---

[13] Nuttall. *Journal of Travels*, 279–80.
[14] Returns for the Troops Stationed at Fort Smith, November 30, 1820. National Archives, War Department, Western Department, Reports Received File.

sissippi River towns to seek recruits. Most replacements came from St. Louis and the army recruit depot at Philadelphia. The army was generally held in low esteem, and few ambitious and able youths would sign up. Thus recruiters usually filled enlistment quotas with misfits, derelicts, and unsuspecting foreign immigrants. During 1819, Bradford received several recruit contingents consisting largely of Germans, Hungarians, English, Poles, and Austrians. His top sergeant was Oliver Carter, an Irishman.[15]

Major Bradford, not indifferent to his men's morale, introduced a number of innovations to mitigate the tedium of service at this frontier military station. One was to authorize his company to have women at the post. From the earliest days at Belle Point, many soldiers had satisfied their hunger for female companionship by an occasional tryst with an Osage or Cherokee. Bradford's order of 1819 permitted married men to build cabins for their families on public land near the post. The major led the way by bringing Mrs. Bradford to Belle Point. As the post commandant's wife, she set the pace for other pioneer women at Fort Smith by having a garden and a cow, so that her table was well supplied with vegetables, milk, and butter. By 1820, there were fourteen white women at the post, nine of them the wives of officers and enlisted men; the rest were designated washerwomen, who drew rations with the troops.[16]

Another morale-improving change at Fort Smith was Bradford's authorization to establish a post store. Hugh Glenn, Fort Smith's first sutler, drew his supplies from Louisville and

[15] Returns for the Troops Stationed at Fort Smith, June 20, 1820. National Archives, War Department, Western Department, Reports Received File.
[16] Returns for the Troops Stationed at Fort Smith, August 31, 1819. National Archives, War Department, Western Department, Reports Received File. Although visitors wrote of a "Mrs. Bradford," it is suspected that this woman was the major's mistress rather than his wife.

Cincinnati. Later, he was succeeded by John Nicks and John Rogers, whose account books show that whisky was the most popular commodity stocked. Since at this time the Fort Smith post exchange was the only store within fifty miles, the sutlers also stocked those commodities and items which a trapper or frontiersman would require. Among the most popular were salt, sugar, coffee, flour, beans, rice, thread, needles, locks, flat steel, knives, gunlocks, powder, lead, tobacco (twist and cut), molasses, writing paper, combs, razors and straps, cloth wearing apparel, bacon, playing cards, cheese, files, shovels, hammers, saws, iron kettles, medicines—and green ribbon and lace for a Mrs. Loving.[17]

One morale factor which Bradford could not control was that of irregular pay periods. Pay rates began at five dollars a month for privates. The army paid the troops by means of traveling paymasters, and Fort Smith's isolated position made it an infrequent stop for these officers. Bradford's men had been paid in the late summer of 1817 before leaving Belle Fontaine for the Arkansas frontier. Paymaster Major John Hall reached Belle Point in June, 1818, and did not return until March of the following year. The post sutler extended credit to the soldiers, but there were limits to which he would go. Bradford, in his letters to the War Department, was highly critical of the "gross neglect" of his company in this regard.[18]

Army regulations made no provision for chaplains at the posts. The spiritual welfare of the troops, if regarded at all, was a local concern and generally of a casual nature. Even if there had been a formal religious program at Fort Smith, it is doubtful that any substantial number of Bradford's hard-bitten riflemen would have patronized it. In later times, itinerant

[17] Nicks-Rogers Sutler Account Book, Fort Smith, Arkansas Territory, 1821–22. Arkansas History Commission Files.

[18] Bradford to Parker, undated. National Archives, War Department, Western Department, Adjutant General Letters Received File.

preachers held occasional services at Fort Smith, but the first
opportunity for the Rifle Regiment company to develop a
spiritual life came in 1819 when the United Foreign Missionary Society of New York sent Epaphras Chapman and Job
Vinall to the Arkansas to select a mission station site. En route
to Belle Point they met with the Cherokees and were well received. At Fort Smith, Osage leaders invited them to establish
a mission in their country. Vinall died of "ague and bilious
fever" during his stay at Fort Smith and was buried in the post
cemetery. Chapman accepted the Osage invitation and returned to New York. His board selected seventeen workers—
nine men and eight women—to staff the Western mission,
appointed William Vaill superintendent and Chapman assistant, and chose the name Union Mission for the Osage station.[19]

Vaill's party came west by the way of Pittsburgh in 1820,
walking to the Ohio, then traveling by keelboat to the Mississippi and eventually the Arkansas. Bradford favored the mission on Grand River for several reasons. He hoped that the
Union Mission's program would reduce the Osages' war-
making propensities, and that the station would give him a
listening post among the Osages. Further, those few of his
men so disposed would have an opportunity to worship.[20]

Occasional visitors broke the military routines at Belle
Point. Thomas Nuttall, the distinguished natural scientist
sponsored by the American Philosophical Society and wealthy
patrons in Philadelphia, arrived at the post in 1819 to study the
flora and fauna of the Arkansas. His adventures and excursions, with Fort Smith as a base, furnished material for his *A
Journal of Travel into the Arkansa Territory, During the
Year 1819*. Nuttall made a reconnaissance of the mountains

19 William W. Graves. *The First Protestant Osage Missions, 1820–
1837*. Also Calhoun to Chapman, May 3, 1820. *Territory of Arkansas*,
XIX, 176–77.
20 Grant Foreman. *Indians and Pioneers*, 92–103.

southwest of Fort Smith to the headwaters of the Kiamichi, then south to the Red, and observed the pioneer settlements in that region. He also journeyed up the Cimarron, the Verdigris, and the Grand. That he was struck by the raw beauty of the country around Fort Smith is indicated by his *Journal*:

> Our route was continued through prairies, occasionally divided by sombre belts of timber, which serve to mark the course of the rivulets. These vast plains, beautiful almost as the fancied Elysium, were now enamelled with innumerable flowers, among the most splendid of which were the azure larkspur . . . fragrant phloxes, and the purple psilotria. Serene and charming as the blissful regions of fancy, nothing here appeared to exist but what contributes to harmony.[21]

Most of the traffic to Fort Smith came from the east, but in September, 1820, two exploring parties, separated detachments of the same expedition, arrived at Belle Point out of the west. In the preceding year, a twenty-man contingent of scientists and soldiers commanded by Major Stephen H. Long departed St. Louis via the Missouri on an extended Western reconnaissance. Long's column left the Missouri at the mouth of the Platte and penetrated the Rocky Mountain region, explored the valleys, and climbed several mountains. The expedition cartographer named one of the most conspicuous peaks for Major Long. On the upper waters of the Arkansas, Long directed Captain John R. Bell to proceed along that stream to Fort Smith with scientists and an armed escort.[22]

Bell's column began the descent of the Arkansas on July 19, 1820. Four days out of Fort Smith, three privates—Modica Nowland, Charles Myers, and Peter Bernard—slipped away

21 Nuttall. *Journal of Travels*, 208.

22 Erwin James. *Account of an Expedition from Pittsburgh to the Rocky Mountains* (vol. XIV of *Early Western Travels, 1748–1846*, ed. by Reuben G. Thwaites), I, 13–16.

with three horses and the party's valuables, including manuscripts by Thomas Say and Lieutenant William Swift on the
manners, customs, and languages of Indian tribes, notes on
flora and fauna, and valuable topographical data. Failing in his
attempt to overtake the deserters, Bell resumed his march. His
weary column straggled into Fort Smith on September 9.[23]

After seeing Bell's party off, Long turned his detachment
south to seek out the headwaters of Red River. Below the
Cimarron he came upon a stream which he believed to be
the main tributary of the Red and he followed it across the
plains. His error was revealed on September 10 when he arrived at the junction of the Arkansas and Canadian, and his
"disappointment and chagrin at discovering the mistake . . .
[he] had so long laboured under, was little alleviated by the
consciousness that the season was too far advanced" to begin
again.[24]

On September 13, Long's column arrived at Belle Point
and shared in the hospitality Major Bradford and his troops
had bestowed on Bell's recuperating party. Because their men
had suffered from intense summer heat, lack of food, and general hardship and were in a weakened condition, Long and
Bell decided to lay over at Fort Smith for a week to rest and
recover. Post officers assigned enlisted men to cook for the
explorers, and both Long and Bell were surprised at the variety
of food available at Belle Point. Expedition member Edwin
James wrote:

Our attentive host knowing the caution necessary to be
used by men of our situation, restrained us from a too un-
bounded indulgence in the use of bread, sweet potatoes,
and other articles of diet to which we had been long unac-
customed. The experience of a few days taught us that it

23 Bell. *Journal*, 275.
24 James. *Account of an Expedition*, III (XVI), 180.

would have been fortunate for us if we had given more implicit heed to his caution.

For several months the explorers had eaten nothing but meat, and now they feasted on "green corn, melons, sweet potatoes, and other esculent vegetables [which had for a] long time been untasted luxuries." The explorers did not exercise sufficient caution in eating the vegetables, because they "soon found their health . . . impaired."[25]

Long was generally impressed by Bradford's construction progress on the post in spite of the many interruptions caused by frontier turbulence and special duties assigned the post garrison. Bradford shared the expedition's concern for the loss of their manuscripts and instructed his patrols to watch for the deserters. Officers at Fort Smith sent a notice to the editor of the *Arkansas Gazette* offering a two-hundred-dollar reward for apprehension of Nowland, Myers, and Bernard and recovery of the manuscripts. Neither the men nor the papers were ever found. After a week's rest, Long's column departed Fort Smith for Cape Girardeau.[26]

Supply for remote Fort Smith was a major problem not only because of its isolation but also because of the changing rules issued by the commissary general's office. When Fort Smith was established in 1817, the system of subsisting military stations was based on annual contracts awarded by the commissary general to the civilian contractors who submitted the low bid for supplying each post. The civilian was resident at the post, and issued rations—usually salt pork, coffee, beans, flour, soap, salt, vinegar, whisky, and candles—to the troops. When Bradford's company was rushed away to the border in 1817, there were no junior officers, no surgeon, and no contractor. Bradford hauled his initial subsistence stores on the

---

[25] *Ibid.*, 187.
[26] *Arkansas Gazette*, October 7, 1820.

keelboat with his troops and detailed a sergeant to handle the issue of provisions. Finally, in the spring of 1818, General Smith advised Bradford that a civilian contractor, James Johnson, was on the way to supply subsistence stores.[27]

Colonel Johnson had hardly become established as subsistence contractor at Fort Smith when in 1819 the War Department, in an economy move, decided to abolish the practice of having its frontier posts supplied by civilians. Instead, the commissary general planned to assign to each post a junior officer to serve as assistant commissary. His duty would be to obtain through contracts with suppliers those staples required at his post, but insofar as possible the station was to become self-sufficient by producing its own food. Post commanders were to detail troops for agricultural duty, hunting, and other food-gathering assignments.

Bradford was asked to report to the commissary general on how Fort Smith would fit into this new system. The major responded that the post, situated five hundred miles by water and three hundred by land up the Arkansas, could receive staple requirements from towns on the Mississippi. Bradford added that during high water a fully loaded eighty-ton barge could ascend the Arkansas; keelboats of nine or ten tons capacity could reach Fort Smith at any stage of water; and river craft usually required about thirty days to reach the post. About the requirement that his post produce most of its subsistence locally, he said that it was impracticable to rely on rations of meat from the nearby woods, where game was becoming scarce; and, with post construction, peace-keeping duties, and a score of other special assignments, he was reluctant to draw on his men for agricultural duties. There were other drawbacks. Few of the men knew much about growing food crops; there were no horses or oxen for this purpose at

[27] Pentland to Bradford, May 1, 1818. Smith Collection, Missouri Historical Society.

the post; and, if Fort Smith did produce grain, there was no mill to grind it into flour or meal.

In spite of these obstacles, Bradford sent agricultural details to clear land and prepare fields, using his personal horses and oxen for the heavy work. Admitting his limitations as a husbandman, he requested the adjutant general to send him copies of the *American Gardener* with Fort Smith's allocation of seed. Fort Smith's first attempt at producing subsistence was a success. Good rains fell along the Arkansas during the growing season of 1819. The troops produced bumper crops in both cornfields and vegetable gardens. By August 10, Bradford reported that the contractor had liquidated his responsibility and that the post was on its own—there was "not one ounce of breadstuff here for our support, not an ounce of soap to wash the men's clothing nor one gill of whiskey," and the troops were "living on roasting ears and vegetables."[28]

Bradford secured a pair of millstones, and his men soon had a horse-powered grain mill in operation. During August, the mill delivered 476 rations of cornmeal to the post commissary.[29]

Lieutenant John Edmonson, Fort Smith's assistant commissary, arrived at Belle Point during the late summer on a keelboat laden with staples for the garrison—salt pork, flour, coffee, sugar, vinegar, salt, pepper, whisky, and soap. A noncommissioned officer reported that the twenty barrels of flour had an offensive odor, and Bradford ordered the casks opened. A survey board declared the contents not only "unwholesome and altogether unfit for use," but also short in weight. Bradford reported the flour's condition to Commissary General George Gibson and recommended that the supplier not be

[28] Bradford to Gibson, August 10, 1819. National Archives, War Department, Quartermaster General Letters Received File.
[29] Bradford to Gibson, August 26, 1819. National Archives, War Department, Quartermaster General Letters Received File.

paid. He added the assurance that his corn was "hard enough to grit, so we are not to starve."[30]

Lieutenant Edmonson's service as assistant commissary at Fort Smith only complicated the subsistence problem. Bradford complained to Gibson that Edmonson was seldom on duty, that he was often absent from the station for as long as ten days, and that he delegated his issuing function to a non-commissioned officer. Edmonson "scarcely ever goes into the issuing house," and Bradford "thought it a bad plan to confide the superintendence of issuing solely to non-commissioned officers." When Bradford admonished Edmonson for what he regarded as neglect of duty, Edmonson insolently retorted that he was responsible only to Commissary General Gibson. Bradford wrote to Gibson: "I will tell you one thing for all if you have such indolent and drunken men as Lieut. Edmonson in your employ, General, the U.S. will find the present plan of supplying the army a losing one, but with proper management, I can safely say this post can be supplied at one-third of the expense saved to the Government that has here-tofore been paid."[31]

During Edmonson's tenure at Fort Smith, the subsistence functions were gradually taken over by Bradford, who stressed production from the eighty-acre post farm and purchases of beef from the Cherokees at six cents a pound. Fresh beef three times a week provided welcome relief from the ubiquitous salt pork for the Belle Point garrison. When Bradford turned over the command of Fort Smith to Colonel Mathew Arbuckle in 1822, the commissary had accumulated a surplus of foodstuffs, including a thousand bushels of corn.

With the increasing burden of such purely local duties as

[30] Bradford to Gibson, August 26, 1819. National Archives, War Department, Quartermaster General Letters Received File.

[31] Bradford to Gibson, August 10, 1819. National Archives, War Department, Quartermaster General Letters Received File.

supervising production of foodstuffs for the garrison and continuing construction on the fort, it is surprising that Bradford could find the time, energy, and manpower to discharge the many additional and varied assignments the War Department thrust upon him. The Cherokee-Osage vendetta continued with undulating fury, requiring his constant attention as peacemaker, and settlers from the emerging Territory of Arkansas increasingly provoked frontier incidents.

The population influx after the organization of the new territory soon spilled over onto Indian land. First, the settlers squatted on Cherokee lands in northwestern Arkansas. Cherokee leaders protested to the president and secretary of war. Soon, orders came from Washington directing Bradford to send troops to assist Cherokee Agent Reuben Lewis in running a new survey of the tribe's domain between the White and Arkansas rivers and to eject all settlers found within the marked area.

Then, settlers turned up in Lovely's Purchase, incurring complaints from both Cherokee and Osage leaders. Bradford was instructed to send troops from Fort Smith to warn the intruders, but to allow them time to harvest their crops and round up their livestock before driving them out.[32]

Next, Bradford heard from the War Department concerning groups of Arkansas settlers west of the Kiamichi on Red River. He was instructed to force them east of the Kiamichi— the area occupied by their settlements was on land claimed by the Osages as a hunting preserve. On May 16, 1819, Bradford led a column out of Fort Smith bound for Red River. A seven-day march through punishingly rough country brought the troops to the mouth of the Kiamichi. They found several settlements where squatters had cleared considerable farms and were "ill prepared" and unhappy at being told that they

[32] Calhoun to Bradford, April 30, 1821. *Territory of Arkansas*, XIX, 286.

must move. Thomas Nuttall accompanied Bradford's Red River expedition and described the settlers "of worst moral character imaginable, being many of them renegadoes from justice, and such as have forfeited the esteem of civilized society. When a further flight from justice became necessary, they passed over into the Spanish territory."[33]

Territorial officials also added to the problems of the tiny garrison at Fort Smith. Major Bradford was required by general orders from the War Department to enforce federal laws regulating trade and travel in the Indian country. Entry of citizens without proper licenses and papers was strictly forbidden. Bradford and Governor Miller were authorized to issue credentials to applicants desiring to travel and trade in the Indian country, and both had been judicious in the number of permits issued. On one occasion when Miller was in the East, Acting Governor Crittenden issued some of his friends more than two hundred permits authorizing them to cross into the Indian country west of Fort Smith to hunt, trap, and trade with the Indians. Bradford's superiors ruled that Crittenden's action was excessive and illegal and that the two hundred were intruders. Bradford's troops had the difficult task of searching the wilderness for these citizens of Arkansas, confiscating their permits, and escorting them east of Fort Smith.[34]

Persistent uncertainty and anxiety existed about the largely undefined boundary separating Spain and the United States in the Southwest. Because Fort Smith occupied the United States' forward defensive position in that region, its garrison had the added responsibility of watching for illegal Spanish activity. In 1818, a party of trappers stopped at Fort Smith to inform Bradford that they had observed a Spanish column on the Canadian River. Bradford sent a patrol to check on this

[33] Nuttall. *Journal of Travels*, 222.
[34] Atkinson to Bradford, December 15, 1819. *Territory of Arkansas*, XIX, 128–29.

movement and also to investigate reports that Spanish traders from Santa Fe were plotting with unruly plains tribes on the Arkansas and Canadian. In 1819, the Adams-Onís Treaty established Red River and the 100th meridian as part of the southern and western international boundary between Spain and the United States. After this agreement was ratified in 1821, United States patrols had a definite boundary to guard.[35]

The lines of communication connecting Fort Smith, Eighth Military District headquarters, settlements on the Mississippi, and the War Department in Washington were ever changing. The first mail road between Fort Smith and Belle Fontaine was surveyed by Bradford's men in 1818. Express riders traveled from Belle Point to Cadron, up the valley of Black River to Cape Girardeau, then by boat on the Mississippi or along the river trace to St. Louis. Personal mail came by way of Cadron—the troops could expect a delivery about once each month.

In 1819, a post office was established at Franklin on the Missouri River. Eighth District headquarters directed Bradford to build a road from Belle Point to Franklin, because it was estimated that dispatch delivery time to St. Louis could be shortened by one-third on this route. For working on roads as well as on fortifications, surveys, and other constant labor assignments of not less than ten days, men of Bradford's company received a special payment of fifteen cents and an extra gill of whisky for each day so employed.[36]

Belle Point mail for Washington was often carried by officers en route to the nation's capital. A letter to or from the secretary of war often required six weeks for delivery. A harbinger of improved communication for the Southwestern frontier was the *Comet*, the first steamer on the Arkansas,

35 Bradford to Calhoun, March 28, 1818. *Ibid.*, 59–60.
36 Bradford to Jesup, March 4, 1820. National Archives, War Department, Quartermaster General Letters Received File.

which arrived at Post of Arkansas eight days out of New Orleans.[37]

For carrying official mail, Bradford relied on express riders drawn from the ranks. One incident involving a messenger revealed that even this generally reliable method of maintaining official contract between the wilderness post at Belle Point and headquarters had its hazards. After a long, tiring ride, the express rider lay down to sleep in the woods. During the night a spark from his campfire ignited dry leaves, and in a twinkling the flames spread to the mailbag. Charred beyond use were official letters and vouchers Bradford had prepared for the quartermaster general requesting reimbursement for personal funds he had advanced to the troops as pay for extra duty work on roads and fortifications and for beef and other items he had purchased locally to supply the garrison. He said that the vouchers were for about a thousand dollars—"too much for a man of my small purse to loose."[38]

[37] *Niles Register*, May 27, 1820.
[38] Bradford to Jesup, March 4, 1820. National Archives, War Department, Quartermaster General Letters Received File.

# CHAPTER FOUR

## Fort Smith's New Garrison

Each year seemed to bring fresh troubles to the Arkansas frontier and to place added responsibility on Major Bradford's hard-working Rifle Regiment company. In 1820, the United States government negotiated with the Choctaws in Mississippi the Treaty of Doak's Stand, granting this tribe a vast domain south and west of Fort Smith. The fact that the southwestern section of Arkansas Territory, already settled and organized into counties, was included in the Choctaw cession aroused loud and intense protest from Arkansas officials, citizens, and local newspaper editors, who charged that the federal government had given the Indians an overwhelming portion of the best lands in Arkansas Territory. James W. Bates, Arkansas' territorial delegate, argued in Washington that government commissioners proposed to "give to the Indians several of our organized Counties & a large proportion of our population—the whole of the County of Miller, the better part of Hempstead & portions of the Counties of Clark & Pulaski."[1]

Although no great number of Choctaws migrated west at this time to establish homes in the tribe's new domain, the prospect stirred up the settlers and made them anxious, belligerent, and more troublesome than ever. The garrison at Fort Smith noted an increased turbulence in frontier affairs after

[1] Bates to Calhoun, November 28, 1820. *Territory of Arkansas, 1819–1825* (vol. XIX of *Territorial Papers of the United States*, ed. by Clarence E. Carter), 237–39.

the Treaty of Doak's Stand, but their greatest problem continued to be the Osage-Cherokee vendetta.

Incidents during 1820 indicated a breakdown of Major Bradford's hard-won peace settlement. Renewed hostilities arose from an attempt by the Cherokees in February, 1820, to exercise their 1818 treaty privileges of hunting west of the Poteau.

Game was plentiful in that rough mountainous region southwest of Fort Smith, and February was the best season for hunting bears. The fur was in prime condition then, and the males were easily distinguished from the females because the cubs, born in December, were with their mothers. The Cherokees were having great success on their bear hunt until Bad Tempered Buffalo and his Osages came upon the Cherokees, struck from ambush, killed three, and took the furs they had with them.[2]

The Cherokee council met and drafted a memorial to Major Bradford protesting the ambush and demanding that he force the Osages to surrender three Cherokee warriors. If no satisfaction had been obtained in two months, the Cherokee chiefs threatened to turn their warriors loose on the Osage towns. Bradford urged the Cherokees to abstain from hostilities until he could investigate and report to Secretary of War Calhoun. His findings indicated that the Osage raid was to avenge Cherokee provocations, and he defended the Osages in his report to Calhoun. Calhoun continued to champion the Cherokees, but he instructed Bradford to warn them to keep the peace, suggesting that Bradford might use the offices of Governor Miller and newly appointed Cherokee Agent David Brearley to avert a full-scale border war.[3]

Miller asked Bradford to convene a council of Cherokee

2 Miller to Calhoun, June 20, 1820. *Territory of Arkansas*, XIX, 191.
3 Calhoun to Bradford, May 12, 1820. *Territory of Arkansas*, XIX, 181–82.

and Osage leaders at Fort Smith during the late summer, but he was delayed by business with the territorial legislature and did not meet with Brearley until October. Miller's Fort Smith council was finally scheduled to convene in December. The Cherokee delegation was present before the appointed day, and Bradford had assurances that the Osages would be represented. At the last minute, however, Osage leaders refused to journey to Fort Smith, and so Miller, Bradford, and a column of Rifles marched to the Verdigris. The Osages, surprisingly conciliatory, offered to abandon their demand that the Cherokees restore those few Osage captives still remaining with them in return for the Cherokees' withdrawing their requirement that the Osages surrender certain warriors to the Cherokees.[4]

Miller hastened to the Cherokee villages to present the Osage proposition. When the council rejected it, the governor in a burst of exasperation declared he was "washing his hands of the whole affair; either make peace in your own way or get satisfaction" as long as they did not "interfere with persons or property of white people."[5]

The Cherokee-Osage feud smoldered for several months, the war faction in each tribe agitating for a showdown. The Osages, led by Bad Tempered Buffalo, were the first to take the initiative. The teachers at Union Mission learned that this uncompromising leader of the war faction was making preparations to attack the Cherokee settlements and sent Mark Bean, a settler who operated a salt works in Lovely's Purchase, to spread the alarm. Bean hurried to Fort Smith, alerted the garrison, and then rode downriver to warn the Cherokees.[6]

[4] Miller to Calhoun, June 20, 1820. *Territory of Arkansas*, XIX, 191–93.

[5] Miller to Cherokee Indians, March 20, 1821. *Territory of Arkansas*, XIX, 335.

[6] An Account of the Cherokee War, April 8, 1821. *Territory of Arkansas*, XIX, 343.

On April 9, sentries at Belle Point sighted a large body of horsemen bearing down on the Arkansas River landing opposite the post. Major Bradford was in St. Louis raising recruits to fill his depleted company, which at the time contained only forty men. Lieutenant Martin Scott, acting commander, saw that the party was Osage, in war paint, heavily armed, and numbered more than two hundred. When Bad Tempered Buffalo gestured that he wished to visit the fort, Scott sent a boat, manned by a sergeant and crew, with instructions to allow only chiefs to board. The boat brought back Bad Tempered Buffalo and seven war chiefs, who, through post interpreter Joseph Duchassin, demanded powder and permission to camp and hunt below the fort. Scott refused both demands. Bad Tempered Buffalo persisted and made threatening gestures. Scott answered by ordering his men to wheel out the two artillery pieces and prepare for action. The intimidated Osage leaders were then returned to the north bank.

While their chiefs were at Belle Point, the warriors were active. A soldier's family who lived in a log farmhouse across the river near the north-bank landing had a terrifying afternoon. The Osages drove the mother and children into a corner of the cabin, flashed cocked firearms, tomahawks, and knives in their faces, and threatened to kill and scalp them. The waiting Osages also captured a hunting party—four Quapaws, a Cherokee, and Ettienne Vaugine, a trader—camped on the Poteau opposite the fort.

Soon after the Osage leaders rejoined their warriors on the north bank, Lieutenant Scott noticed that the Indians were felling trees and constructing rafts. He yelled a warning across the river, ordering them to abandon their rafts and disperse. When they ignored him, Scott returned to the fort, ordered the cannons charged with canister, and placed a gunner with lighted match by each piece. The invaders took to the woods.

Thwarted in their attempt to obtain powder to arm their

Cherokee offensive, the frustrated Osages fell upon the captured hunting party. Shots rang out of the woods. Three of
the prisoners—the Cherokee, Vaugine, and one of the Quapaws—escaped by swimming the river under the cover of the
guns of Fort Smith. When the firing began, Scott rushed
squads of Rifles across the river. The soldiers found three dead
Quapaws, and rescued the terrified mother and her children
and delivered them safely to the post.

Short on powder, the Osages were unable to carry their
war to the Cherokee country, and contented themselves with
raiding hunting camps and robbing settlers of guns, provisions,
and horses. Frightened families fled to Fort Smith and remained there for several weeks.[7]

As soon as Bradford returned from St. Louis with reinforcements for his Rifle Regiment company, he immediately
increased the strength and number of patrols on the Osage
line. His border guards intercepted both Osage and Cherokee
raiders and turned them back, but a war party occasionally
managed to slip through.

In June, 1821, the Cherokee Wat Webber eluded Bradford's patrols and led a foray into Osage country while most
of Clermont's warriors and their families were on the western
prairies hunting buffalo. Webber's raiders cut a bloody course
along the Grand and Verdigris, preying on Osage mixed-
blood families, the protégés of Union Mission teachers. Fifteen miles above Union Mission, the Cherokees shot and killed
Joseph Revoir, plundered his trading house, and made off with
fourteen horses.[8]

Governor Miller, having declared that it was futile to attempt to achieve border peace, had detached himself from any
substantial contact with the tribes, and gave most of his atten-

[7] *Arkansas Gazette*, May 12, 1821. *Niles Register*, June 30, 1821.
[8] Bradford to Calhoun, August 10, 1821. *Territory of Arkansas*, XIX,
308–9.

tion to administrative and political affairs for Arkansas Territory. Miller's virtual abandonment of his function as superintendent of Indian affairs for the region increased Bradford's
responsibility proportionately. The major continued to make
periodic visits to the Osages and Cherokees, admonishing tribal
leaders to control their warriors and to leave the settlers alone
or his troops would desolate their villages. He also worked to
recover property stolen from the settlers.

During the summer of 1821, Richard Graham, agent from
St. Louis, visited the Arkansas frontier to assist Bradford in
dealing with the tribes. He won from both the Osages and
Cherokees a promise that they would send delegations to St.
Louis for a major peace council. At the appointed time only
the Osages appeared. Bradford became even more cynical
about Cherokee intentions, and more and more he used his
troops to protect settlers and left the Indians to their own
devices. Two months earlier he had confided to Secretary of
War Calhoun that it might serve the government's purpose to
let the Osages and Cherokees fight. Their wars were of short
duration, only a few lives would be lost, and the conflict would
"end as it began in Stealing horses—and killing" stragglers.
Bradford considered the warriors of both tribes congenital
cowards, willing to attack the other only when the odds were
substantially favorable and victory a certainty.[9]

In late September, 1821, the Osages left their Verdigris villages for the autumn buffalo hunt on the plains. A Cherokee
force of three hundred warriors slipped past Bradford's patrols and picked up the broad Osage trail. Near the mouth
of the Cimarron, Cherokee scouts noted that the trail divided.
Expedition leaders detached a sixty-man column to follow one
fork while the rest continued on the principal Osage trace.
After a short ride, the smaller Cherokee force sighted women
gathering cattail stems and lotus roots. Survivors claimed that

[9] *Ibid.*

not even the dogs acknowledged danger as the enemy crept forward. At a signal the Cherokees swept into the defenseless camp, killed and scalped twenty-nine, captured thirty women and children, and took great quantities of furs, utensils, and other plunder, burning what they could not carry away. A woman who refused to accompany the Cherokees was shot and her body thrown onto the fire. The Cherokees returned by way of Fort Smith and flaunted their captives and plunder before Bradford and the troops. The major insulted the expedition leaders by observing that he saw no warriors' roaches among the scalps but only the long-haired tresses of squaws.[10]

The principal Cherokee force finally found the Osage hunting camp in November, but the alert Osages discovered their danger in time and attacked the unsuspecting invaders during the night. The surprise attack discouraged the Cherokees who slipped away at dawn. They passed Fort Smith on November 17, and Bradford laconically observed that "they have got floged."[11]

One effect of this Cherokee campaign was to ruin the Osage hunt and cause hunger and suffering among Clermont's people during the winter. The teachers at Union Mission helped them, but the missionaries were unable to believe that the design of the government was "to send the Indians from the east of the Mississippi river to carry on perpetual war with the natives of this country who have an inherent right to the soil."[12]

Another effect of the 1821 Cherokee invasion of the Osage country was to push the government to a decision it had been considering for more than a year—to increase military strength at Fort Smith from a token force to one of sufficient size to

[10] Bradford to Calhoun, November 20, 1821. *Territory of Arkansas*, XIX, 356. *Arkansas Gazette*, December 29, 1821, February 19, 1822.
[11] Bradford to Calhoun, November 18, 1821. *Territory of Arkansas*, XIX, 355.
[12] William W. Graves. *The First Protestant Osage Missions, 1820–1837*, 51–53.

overawe the perpetrators of border trouble. The War Department turned to Fort Scott, Georgia, for the means to bolster its defensive position on the Arkansas. Fort Scott was a link in the chain of military stations connecting General Andrew Jackson's army on the Florida frontier with its supply depots in the mid-Atlantic states. The 7th United States Infantry Regiment, commanded by Colonel Mathew Arbuckle, garrisoned this post.[13]

The Adams-Onís Treaty, negotiated in 1819 and ratified in 1821, which provided for the transfer of Florida from Spain to the United States, reduced the necessity of a military concentration in the Southeast. In mid-1821, the secretary of war alerted Colonel Arbuckle to be ready to move his regiment to the Southwest. Originally, the War Department planned to assign five companies of the 7th Infantry to Fort Selden on the Red River in Louisiana, where Arbuckle was to establish regimental headquarters. The other 7th Infantry companies were to proceed to Fort Smith.

The adjutant general directed Arbuckle, before leaving Fort Scott, to work with his regimental surgeon in classifying the enlisted men according to moral and physical qualifications. Arbuckle was to discharge those men found least qualified for military service and those with less than eighteen months left on a five-year enlistment. In no instance were the companies to be reduced below fifty-six officers and men. The commander was to detach 150 men for duty with the 4th Infantry at Pensacola. His own regiment was to be replenished with troops from the 8th Infantry Regiment who had remained in service after the liquidation of that unit and who were to rendezvous with the 7th at Pass Christian, Mississippi; to these were to be added men from the Rifle Regiment at Fort Smith.[14]

[13] Francis B. Heitman. *Historical Register and Dictionary of the United States Army*, I, 168.

Arbuckle was immediately faced with the problem of officer morale, which declined noticeably when the regiment was directed to prepare for a move to the Arkansas frontier. He informed the secretary of war that he was deluged with resignations of commissions and requests for transfer by company commanders and junior officers. Arbuckle pointed out that his regiment had been "stationed at Posts in the Wilderness, bordering on the Florida line" for six years. His officers believed that they were entitled to an interior post assignment, and were resentful that they were now to occupy the most remote Western station in the United States.[15]

The loss of officers did not slow Arbuckle in his preparations for the westward move. He wrote Captain Thomas Hunt, officer in charge of the New Orleans Quartermaster's Depot, asking him to charter enough light vessels to transport the 7th Infantry Regiment and saying that his unit would travel on flatboats to the Gulf via the Flint and Apalachicola rivers. The sloops should meet the regiment at Apalachicola Bay and carry it either to Pass Christian or to Bay St. Louis, where Lieutenant Colonel Zachary Taylor and three companies would join the regiment.[16]

In a broad reorganization, the War Department placed General Edmund P. Gaines in charge of the Western Military Department. He established headquarters at Louisville, and issued orders to strengthen the Fort Smith garrison. In late September, 1821, the 7th Infantry Regiment boarded flatboats for the descent to the Gulf. Colonel Arbuckle was snugly settled on the *Support* in the pleasant company of Mrs. Ruth Ellis. A fellow officer, Regimental Surgeon Thomas Lawson,

[14] Parker to Arbuckle, May 31, 1821. National Archives, War Department, Adjutant General Letters Sent File.

[15] Arbuckle to Kirby, July 2, 1821. National Archives, War Department, Adjutant General Letters Received File.

[16] Arbuckle to Hunt, July 26, 1821. National Archives, War Department, Adjutant General Letters Received File.

subsequently reported, in circumstances less pleasant for Arbuckle, that the Colonel was overfriendly with Mrs. Ellis— identified as an officer's mistress—that the two were disturbingly intimate and traveled together on the quarterdeck of the *Support* under an awning throughout the rain-drenched trip down the Flint and Apalachicola.[17]

Arbuckle's transports arrived on October 4 in Apalachicola Bay, where six schooners chartered by Captain Hunt were standing by. At Bay St. Louis, the convoy picked up Taylor and his three companies and proceeded to New Orleans. While Hunt arranged for river steamers, the troops camped on Bayou St. John. After eight days, dysentery had incapacitated so many men that Arbuckle ordered the regiment to a more healthful spot.

During the wait at New Orleans, orders arrived from the adjutant general which had important consequences for Fort Smith. The regimental command post was to be situated at Belle Point on the Arkansas rather than at Fort Selden on the Red. Consequently, Arbuckle was to go to the former station.[18]

It took Captain Hunt seven weeks to arrange steamboat transportation for the 7th Infantry. Finally, on November 6, 1821, the regiment departed New Orleans. Arbuckle and five companies were aboard the steamer *Tennessee* bound for Fort Smith. The rest of the regiment, under Lieutenant Colonel Taylor, had passage on the *Comet* and the *Arkansas* for the run up the Red. Heavy rains fell on the Mississippi, and the soldiers suffered "very much from wet and cold weather particularly those on deck." The *Tennessee* was "so much loaded that but few could find shelter from the weather under deck and a number died on the passage."[19]

[17] Colonel Mathew Arbuckle's Court-Martial. National Archives, War Department, Judge Advocate General Files.

[18] Gadsden to Arbuckle, November 29, 1821. National Archives, War Department, Adjutant General Letters Sent File.

Arbuckle's transport arrived off the mouth of the Arkansas in late November, 1821. Low water kept it from entering the river, and so the troops camped in tents while Arbuckle negotiated for keelboats to carry his battalion and gear up the Arkansas. The men had not completely recovered from their ordeal of the run from New Orleans, and at this temporary base many more were stricken and several perished. By late December, the regiment was waterborne on the Arkansas, and the troops worked in shifts with long poles thrusting the clumsy vessels upriver. Low water slowed the convoy for several weeks; but in mid-January, a rise in the river eased travel; in early February, the regiment passed Little Rock; finally, on February 26, 1822, the 7th Infantry reached Fort Smith.[20]

The garrison flag of the 7th Infantry Regiment was raised over Belle Point. Major Bradford was officially relieved as post commandant and with little reluctance turned the station over to Colonel Arbuckle. Besides opening roads, establishing communications, leading survey and mapping details, guarding a turbulent border, and inspecting westbound trade expeditions, Bradford had nearly completed construction on the post as directed by Major Long's building plans. Bradford had, through his tenacity and high sense of responsibility, created a nucleus for law, order, and the vanguard of a community and ultimate civilization. He had protected the interest and integrity of the United States on its farthest frontier, and his small force had served as at least a deterrent to mounting Cherokee-Osage savagery. But it was time for him to move on. He had become a *persona non grata* with the Osages and Cherokees, each blaming him for failing to hold the other at bay. He

[19] Colonel Mathew Arbuckle's Court-Martial. National Archives, War Department, Judge Advocate General Files.

[20] Elmer E. Swanton, "History of the United States National Cemetery and Military Occupation of Fort Smith, Arkansas." Unpublished manuscript in the library of the National Archives.

had angered settlers by obeying military orders for their expulsion from the Indian country. He had annoyed high officials in the Arkansas territorial government by his determination to enforce rules rather than to look the other way and extend special privilege. Even his junior officers were arrayed against him—one of them was already preparing court-martial charges—and threatened a minor revolt because of his strict requirements for attention to duty.

Bradford was ordered to report to Lieutenant Colonel Zachary Taylor's 7th Infantry battalion at Fort Selden. Before leaving, he did three things. First, he briefed Colonel Arbuckle on the special problems—especially the Cherokee-Osage trouble—he would face as post commandant. Next, he showed Arbuckle the ordnance and commissary reports of the stores on hand. He pointed out that when the adjutant general informed him of the plan to increase the Fort Smith garrison from company to battalion strength he had ordered commissary stores commensurate with the needs of a larger garrison. These included 300 barrels of salt pork, 625 barrels of fine flour, 3,500 gallons of whisky, 275 bushels of dried beans, 4,400 pounds of good hard soap, 1,650 pounds of good hard candles, 1,200 gallons of vinegar, and 70 bushels of salt. Finally, Bradford mustered his Rifle Regiment company for the last time. The major, described by a fellow officer as a "small, stern-looking man, an excellent disciplinarian, and a gallant officer," softened his taciturnity to express gratitude and farewell to his men. Before dark on February 26, 1822, Bradford's seventy officers and men were absorbed into understrength companies of the 7th Infantry Regiment, and the last company of the proud Rifle Regiment was no more.[21]

Arbuckle inspected the works at Belle Point and praised

21 Inspection Returns for the 7th Infantry Regiment, Fort Smith, February 28, 1822. National Archives, War Department, Western Department, Reports Received File.

Bradford's five years of work. He wrote the War Department that the fort was "nearly Completed and in a good state for defense." This, along with "the large Quantity of improved land, Under good fence, and other useful labor done at the Post, together with the good appearance of the Command affords satisfactory Evidence that there has not been a want of skill or industry on the part of the Commanding officer."[22]

Colonel Arbuckle's first inspection of the troops at Fort Smith revealed the toll taken by the transfer of his command from Fort Scott to Belle Point. Captain Granville Leftwich's Company B had lost three privates by death on the Arkansas, and nine men were too ill to stand muster. Lieutenant Richard Wash had worked over Surgeon Lawson in a bloody fist fight and was confined to quarters under arrest. Seven men from the disbanded Rifle Regiment company were assigned to Leftwich's company.

Company C had begun the trip understrength, lost four men by death en route, and was assigned thirty Rifle Regiment men. Of its officer corps, company commander Captain Daniel Burch was deathly ill in the Fort Smith hospital, and Lieutenant Benjamin Bonneville was on detached duty at Fort St. Philip. Lieutenant Pierce Butler was acting commander of this unit.

Captain Nathaniel Young was the only officer present, for Company G. Lieutenant Nathaniel G. Wilkinson was on detached duty at Natchitoches, and Lieutenant William L. Colquhoun had remained at New Orleans. Young reported that Private James French fell from a keelboat on the Arkansas and drowned. Because Company G was the best-manned, it received only six Rifle Regiment men.

Company H received fourteen men from Bradford's old company. Of these, four were ill, and Private William Stubbs was confined to the guardhouse for desertion. Private Peter

[22] *Ibid.*

Glover had died at Post of Arkansas on January 22, Lieutenant John Philbrick had been detailed as post commissary, and Lieutenant Edgar S. Hawkins had not reported.

Arbuckle's inspection of K Company revealed that because its officers were confined to the post hospital the unit was formed for inspection by Sergeant Hirum Riley. Six Rifles, including Sergeant Riley, joined K Company.

The Colonel's first inspection report disclosed that eight women had accompanied the 7th Infantry Regiment from Fort Scott, were married to or living with soldiers at the post, and were permitted to draw rations from the commissary because they were classed as laundresses. Arbuckle's inspection also showed that he considered the subsistence stores at Fort Smith "generally of good quality and abundant" and that all five companies were well supplied with clothing and camp equipment. He rated the arms, accouterments, and ammunition "tolerable"; those men able to stand muster, "generally stout and effective soldiers."

An alarming number of troops were confined to the post hospital or barracks with sundry ailments. Men of the 7th Infantry Regiment, knowing that they were going to the nation's most remote post and that it would be their last chance for a long time for a spree, had dissipated almost with a vengeance at New Orleans. Weakened by their extended frolic, then punished by harsh travel conditions on the Mississippi, Arbuckle's troops were ill prepared for the rigors of frontier life. The extended wait for transportation at the mouth of the Arkansas had further reduced the number of effective soldiers. Dysentery and pneumonia were the most serious complaints, but several men were on limited duty because of various venereal diseases. Mild weather and the approach of spring seemed to hasten recovery of the ailing troops, and by late March most of them were on full duty.[23]

23 *Ibid.*

Fort Smith had been constructed to accommodate one company of troops. Arbuckle's battalion contained five companies; at Belle Point, most of the men were first sheltered in tents. The most pressing need was to enlarge the post. Arbuckle pointed out to the War Department that the land question would first have to be settled because settlers of Arkansas Territory were pushing closer to Belle Point and occupying public land. He recommended that he be authorized to lay out and withdraw from settlement a military reservation with a perimeter of at least five miles of land fronting the Arkansas and a like amount on the Poteau. In addition to pointing out the need for more space to expand the military fortifications, he also proposed enlarging the post farm. The quartermaster general expected the garrison at Fort Smith to continue to raise most of its food, and the eighty-acre farm opened by Bradford's men was now inadequate. Additional land was needed also to pasture the cattle and hogs which were being added as a subsistence source.

The government allowed Arbuckle additional land only for the military reservation. He did receive authorization from the secretary of war to construct sufficient buildings to accommodate the increased force. On March 16, 1822, he wrote Calhoun that he would require a supply of "plank," "a small additional supply of Iron, Nails, &c.," and fifteen or twenty artisans as extra-duty men for the construction. He estimated that the expense would not exceed five hundred dollars.[24] Six weeks later, he received Calhoun's letter authorizing him to proceed. The Secretary of War directed that the "Barracks and Quarters be strong & comfortable, but plain, and erected at the least possible expense."[25]

[24] Arbuckle to Calhoun, March 16, 1822. *Territory of Arkansas*, XIX, 417–18.
[25] Calhoun to Arbuckle, May 4, 1822. National Archives, War Department, Quartermaster General Letters Sent File.

Arbuckle sent timber-cutting details into the forests and put a crew to work cutting limestone for foundations and chimneys. In March, he left for New Orleans aboard a keelboat to purchase the hardware, nails, and iron required in the post expansion. Before the first snow, the new Fort Smith garrison was housed in plain but cozy barracks. It was well that Arbuckle had pushed the enlargement of the post, for winter came early in 1822 and was unusually severe. On December 1, the temperature fell to six degrees below zero. Extended cold and deep snow drove game far down the valley of the Arkansas, and Arbuckle's men killed buffalo only fifteen miles west of the post.[26]

The year 1822 was a busy one at Belle Point. The post surged with industry. Artisans drawn from the ranks of the 7th Infantry constructed new barracks. An agricultural detail under Lieutenant Bonneville expanded the garrison farm. His careful management of the crops and livestock produced a bountiful and varied table for the troops; in his laconic style, he reported that rations had been "issued regularly with no complaints as to their quality."[27]

But there were complaints about the source of these rations Several officers were especially sensitive about their periodic assignments to lead details to herd the post livestock. About eight hundred hogs and more than a hundred cattle comprised the commissary herds. The hogs were especially troublesome. They foraged in the canebrakes bordering the Arkansas, wandered into the forest, and became wild. From time to time, an officer and a detail of enlisted men were assigned to round them up. Captain William Davenport had special contempt for this type of duty:

Raising and herding Cattle and Hogs is altogether foreign to

[26] Grant Foreman. *Indians and Pioneers*, 143.
[27] Bonneville to Gibson, July 22, 1823. National Archives, War Department, Quartermaster General Letters Received File.

the profession of army and it has always been a matter of surprise to the thinking part of the army, what could have induced the Govt. to undertake it. The same may be said of the cultivation of land by the soldiers. No advantages accrues to the U. S. from it, and very little to the soldiers employed, further than to give them wholesome exercise, and all that are acquainted with our frontier states, know we do not lack for that. It is in the interior when something of that kind is wanting to arouse our soldiers from a state of lethargy which they can not afford to fall into from idleness that the cultivating system should be pursued.[28]

There was much coming and going as company commanders scattered their men in special missions across the frontier, mapping, surveying, guiding travelers, inspecting traders' permits and cargoes, and patrolling the Osage line. Outposts—small military camps—were established on the Cimarron, Canadian, and White rivers and Piney Creek to watch for outbreaks of Osage-Cherokee trouble and to keep restless settlers off Indian lands. Company C was composed mainly of former Rifle Regiment personnel, who were the acknowledged aristocrats at the post and a ready reserve on which to draw for special frontier missions. Its favored status caused much rivalry with other companies.[29]

In 1822, the first river steamer reached Fort Smith. On March 17, the *Robert Thompson* had cast off from Pittsburgh towing a keelboat containing commissary supplies for Fort Smith. Major Asher Phillips of the Paymaster Corps was aboard the steamer bound for Belle Point with the garrison payroll. The *Robert Thompson* reached Little Rock on April

[28] Davenport to Hook, August 28, 1823. National Archives, War Department, Quartermaster General Letters Received File.

[29] Inspection Returns for the 7th Infantry Regiment, Fort Smith, April 30 and June 30, 1822. National Archives, War Department, Western Department, Reports Received File.

9 and arrived at Fort Smith landing eleven days later. The conquest of the Arkansas to Belle Point by steam navigation assured more rapid contact with the East, brought this wilderness outpost closer to civilization, and made possible more rapid delivery of mail, dispatches, and supplies.[30]

Also in 1822, Fort Smith received its first important inspection. Colonel Arbuckle had been advised that General Edmund Gaines, commanding officer of the Western Military Department, would arrive at Belle Point in late June on the final stop of an inspection tour of posts in his jurisdiction. Arbuckle went to New Orleans to collect hardware and other materials for the Fort Smith expansion project with the certainty that he could transact his business and be back at Belle Point well before Gaines arrived. But the general surprised everyone by beginning the inspection earlier than the announcd date and moving quickly from station to station. Thus he reached Mobile from Pensacola on February 19, moved to New Orleans, up to Baton Rouge, and to Fort Selden. From this post he moved to the Kiamichi River, traveled horseback to the headwaters of the Poteau, which he descended, to enter Fort Smith at five-thirty on the morning of April 22. A surprised garrison rolled out for an inspection and review. Major Abram R. Woolley, ranking officer in Arbuckle's absence, conducted the general about the post. Gaines was pleased with the conditions he found. His one criticism was the lack of proper storage for commissary stores, and he directed immediate construction of a suitable storehouse. He ordered the supplies to be temporarily stored in the two blockhouses. The general was at Fort Smith for twenty-three hours. At four-thirty on the morning of April 23, he was in the saddle rushing downriver to catch the *Robert Thompson*, which had left the preceding day and which he overtook twenty miles below Fort Smith and boarded for the return trip to his Louisville

[30] *Arkansas Gazette*, April 9, 1822.

headquarters. General Gaines' favorable impression of Fort Smith was reflected in his report to the secretary of war and his instructions to Colonel Arbuckle. He rated the Belle Point station of vital significance to United States defenses in the West, and wanted it "kept in high order of repair, and readiness with special attention to storage of ammunition and subsistence, for in case of war in the West, it would become the Depot of the army in the Field."[31]

Perhaps the most important event during 1822 at Belle Point in terms of frontier peace was the Fort Smith council, which convened on July 20. The efforts of several men had gone into arranging this meeting. Its origins ran back to February when Colonel Arbuckle, en route with his 7th Infantry troops for Belle Point, stopped at Little Rock for several days to discuss the Cherokee-Osage problem with Governor Miller. Arbuckle was briefed on the subject also by Major Bradford before the latter left Fort Smith for Fort Selden.

Miller was cynical of the chances for an enduring settlement, and believed that with greater military strength at Fort Smith the government should warn the tribes. If this failed to halt their marauding, killing, and general disturbance of frontier peace, then the power at Belle Point should be turned on them. This policy of force was advocated also by General Gaines, who announced at Fort Smith that he favored United States intervention as the means of pacifying the region. After returning to Louisville, he wrote both Arbuckle and Secretary of War Calhoun that undoubtedly the president had the authority to use force to stop a war carried on within the territorial limits of the United States.[32]

Calhoun explained to Miller, Arbuckle, and Gaines that

[31] Gaines to Arbuckle, May 15, 1822. National Archives, War Department, Western Department, Letters Sent File.
[32] Gaines to Calhoun, June 24, 1822. National Archives, June 24, 1822. War Department, Western Department, Letters Sent File.

although such a step had been considered by the War Department, government leaders believed that the president lacked this authority. A bill had been introduced into the first session of the 20th Congress to give the War Department the necessary authority, but it had failed to pass. Calhoun hoped the bill would be enacted during the second session; meanwhile, the principals should continue to use negotiations as the means of abating the border struggle.[33]

Consequently, Colonel Arbuckle began to make arrangements for a general council to convene at Fort Smith during the summer. General Gaines, after returning to his Louisville headquarters from Fort Smith, had written letters to the Cherokee and Osage chiefs urging them to cease their wars and join in a peace conference. He told them he would return to Fort Smith in August and sit on the council, and added: "The War in which you are engaged against . . . [the president's] other Red children, shall continue no longer. He [the president] requires and directs that both nations shall desist from further hostilities, bury the hatchet, and make peace upon just principles without delay."[34]

The most diligent worker for border peace was Nathaniel Philbrook, recently appointed subagent for the Verdigris Osage, who earnestly sought to win the confidence of Clermont, Tallai, and Bad Tempered Buffalo. Finally, he was requested by these leaders to visit the Cherokees and inquire about the Osage captives. Philbrook traveled to the Cherokee country and found the war faction and Tick-e-Toke insolent and arrogant. He reported that when General Gaines' letter was read before the Cherokee council, Tick-e-Toke asked to see it, seized the document, spat on it, and ground it into the dirt. Also in his presence, several Cherokees boasted that they

[33] Calhoun to Miller, June 22, 1822. *Territory of Arkansas*, XIX, 440.
[34] Gaines to Cherokee and Osage Chiefs, June 24, 1822. *Territory of Arkansas*, XIX, 442–43.

had slain 103 Osages during the past campaign. Philbrook was permitted to visit the captives, and found them well.[35]

In April, 1822, Philbrook returned to the Verdigris, and reported that the captives were healthy but homesick for their people. One mighty warrior wept with relief when told that his wife and children were well. Philbrook assured the Osages that he was working for the welfare of their people, and proposed that the chances would be improved if they attended the peace council at Fort Smith in July and if meanwhile they refrained from hostile actions. He persuaded them to place their marks on an armistice agreement, which he then carried to the Cherokees and which they too signed. By its terms, neither belligerent was to send war parties into the country of the other for twenty days after the Fort Smith council. If either violated the armistice, the United States would punish the offender.[36]

Colonel Arbuckle also worked to make the council a success. He sent regular messages to the leaders of both tribes urging participation in the conference and admonishing each to keep the peace, and was especially attentive when the leaders of either tribe called at the post. He took the time to show his visitors the troops in military formation, the new guns, and the vast buildup in military power at the post, hoping to intimidate them into peace by this show of force.[37]

During July, an extended drought settled over the lower Arkansas valley. Daily temperatures ranged up to ninety-five and on some days passed one hundred degrees. Drying south winds seared the grass and parched the land. Colonel Arbuckle was concerned that the discomfort from high temperature and lack of grass for Indian ponies might dissuade the tribes from

[35] Miller to Calhoun, March 1, 1822. *Territory of Arkansas*, XIX, 410–11.

[36] Miller to Calhoun, May, 1822. *Territory of Arkansas*, XIX, 437–38.

[37] Arbuckle to Calhoun, March 16, 1822. National Archives, War Department, Western Department, Letters Received File.

attending the council. Governor Miller, Cherokee Agent
Brearley, and Osage Agent Philbrook arrived several days before July 30 to make final arrangements for the council. General Gaines was delayed, and did not reach Belle Point until
after the conference closed. On the appointed day, delegations
from both tribes arrived, the Osages represented by 150 warriors led by Clermont, Tallai, and Bad Tempered Buffalo. The
smaller Cherokee delegation included Chiefs Wat Webber,
Waterminnow, Thomas Maw, John Martin, Young Glass, and
James Rogers.[38]

Colonel Arbuckle and Governor Miller convened the council on the morning of July 30, and the sessions extended over
eleven days. On August 9, the Osage and Cherokee chiefs
signed the Treaty of Fort Smith, an agreement drafted by
Brearley and signed also by Miller, Arbuckle, Leftwich,
Brearley, Philbrook, and Epaphras Chapman (for Union
Mission).

The Treaty of Fort Smith provided for restoring peace
between the two nations. The Cherokees surrendered eight
captives on the spot and promised to deliver the rest at Fort
Smith on September 20. If any wished to stay with the Cherokees, they could do so if the number did not exceed three.
The Osages pledged to permit unmolested Cherokee crossings
into their country and hunting south of the Arkansas. In return, Osages were assured that they could cross the Cherokee
line and hunt. Depredations were not to be settled by private
revenge but by appeal to the agents.[39]

Agent Brearley held the Cherokees to their pledge to restore all the captives, which was accomplished at Fort Smith
on September 29. Arbuckle observed that both parties reported to be satisfied. Even the cynical Miller was enthusiastic

[38] *Arkansas Gazette*, August 20, 1822.
[39] Cherokee-Osage Treaty, August 9, 1822. National Archives, Office of Indian Affairs, Treaty File.

over the results of the Fort Smith council, and wrote Secretary of War Calhoun that the Treaty of Fort Smith was expected to provide a permanent and peaceful settlement of the border war.[40]

[40] Arbuckle to Nourse, September 30, 1822. *Territory of Arkansas,* XIX, 462–63, and *Arkansas Gazette,* October 22, 1822.

CHAPTER FIVE

## Little Gibraltar on the Arkansas

THE FORT SMITH COUNCIL marked a change in the status of
the Belle Point outpost. In less than five years Fort Smith had
evolved from a primitive military station to a fort of the first
order, and the tidy log and rock buildings, expanded palisade
walls, and enlarged garrison elicited respect for United States
authority and an acknowledgment of its determination to
achieve border peace.

After the 1822 pact, Cherokee and Osage bands occasionally plundered when one caught the other in a vulnerable position, but the leaders of both tribes, fearful of the wrath of the
"heavy eyebrow soldiers" from Belle Point, did not approve
of these actions, declared the raiders renegades, and seemed
committed to peace. Old and irreconcilable Tick-e-Toke was
so distressed by this growing tendency toward border peace
that he seceded from his nation and led a band of fifty diehard
followers southwest of Fort Smith to live a life of wandering
protest.[1]

As the border feud cooled, Arbuckle reduced the number
of patrols on the Osage line to intercept intruders and turned
an increasing number of his men to more local details about
the post. Inspections became more penetrating, and company
officers made drill a daily affair. Arbuckle's ratings of "good,

[1] Arbuckle to Nourse, September 3, 1823. *Territory of Arkansas,
1819–1825* (vol. XIX of *Territorial Papers of the United States*, ed. by
Clarence E. Carter), 545–46.

sufficient, indifferent, tolerable, or deficient" for the company inspections became noticeably more discriminating. He frequently ordered a company mustered and examined by a disinterested officer, who reported to the colonel on the unit's discipline, quality of instruction, military appearance, and condition of weapons, accouterments, and clothing.[2]

The reduction in frontier details and the increase of local military routines about the post affected morale for both enlisted men and officers. With more leisure, Arbuckle's troops had time to indulge in the few crude pleasures available at the post and to contemplate their miserable assignment on this remote Southwestern frontier. Much of the officers' duty time, formerly taken up in leading patrols and other rugged frontier assignments which sapped the men and made them more amenable to military law, was increasingly taken up in holding company and regimental courts-martial conducted to try enlisted men for violating military regulations. Principal offenses were drunkenness, fighting, desertion, sleeping on guard, striking an officer, theft, and—on one occasion—homicide.[3]

Arbuckle's officer corps became increasingly restive and troublesome as the Arkansas frontier became quiet and their duties took on more and more of a garrison housekeeping character. Most 7th Infantry officers believed that the War Department was generally ill-using their talents, but their one continuing and special grievance was being shunted off to a frontier post isolated from towns and sources of culture and recreation. They found some entertainment locally in drinking bouts, competing for the few women at the post, gam-

[2] Inspection Returns for the 7th Infantry Regiment, Fort Smith, April 30, 1822. National Archives, War Department, Western Department, Reports Received File.

[3] Inspection Returns for the 7th Infantry Regiment, Fort Smith, August 31 and October 31, 1822. National Archives, War Department, Western Department, Reports Received File.

bling, and an occasional leave. But with limited recreation
outlets, they spent most of their off-duty time in barracks
politics. Jealousy, intrigue, and petty deception, common in
the officer corps in all ages, was rampant at Fort Smith. Arbuckle's officers, excessively ambitious, were obsessed with
rank consciousness, desire for promotion, and generally
anxious about their professional status.[4]

Officers were being stymied because regular cuts in army
strength by an economy-minded Congress caused a conges-
tion in field-grade officer positions. Officer appointments and
promotions were sensitive matters, and no vacancies could be
expected except those caused by resignation, death, or the
creation of new military units. Vacancies created by resignation and death all too often were filled with civilians rather
than with career soldiers, because of the politically-oriented
War Department. Opponents charged that to appoint civilians
made a mockery of the officer training system in military sci-
ence, and many officers resigned to accept civilian positions
rather than continue military careers. These openings, too,
were, more often than not, filled with civilian favorites of
politicians. Quartermaster General Thomas Jesup and other
military reformers were alarmed at the attrition of professional strength in the officer corps, and recommended that vacancies be filled only with qualified men and that a pension plan
be instituted to attract and hold good officers.[5]

During the 1820's, openings for professional military men
were so scarce that West Pointers graduating as second lieu-
tenants had to be assigned to field units as brevet second lieu-
tenants. Several of Arbuckle's officers held brevet rank.
Critics claimed that the situation provided the War Depart-

[4] Davenport to Hook, August 28, 1823. National Archives, War Department, Quartermaster General Letters Received File.
[5] Arbuckle to Kirby, July 2, 1821. National Archives, War Department, Adjutant General, Letters Received File.

ment an inexpensive method of rewarding officers, because brevet promotion carried no increase in pay unless the officer was in a command position that warranted use of the rank his brevet called for. Brevets were generally used to recognize gallantry in battle and to reward longevity and faithful service.[6]

Perhaps the person most detested by the officer corps during the 7th Infantry days at Fort Smith was Major Abram R. Woolley, Arbuckle's second in command. A stickler for regulations and army protocol, Woolley required staff officers to attend drills and inspections and demanded their presence and participation at most military exercises at Belle Point. Commissary Officer Lieutenant John Clark led an anti-Woolley coup among the 7th Infantry officers by complaining to the secretary of war about Woolley's harsh and unreasonable requirements. Arbuckle remained aloof; the War Department sustained Woolley, who punished Clark's rebels by increasing their extra-duty assignments. In explaining his position, Woolley gruffly declared that "the moment he exempted members of the staff from elementary instruction that moment they ceased to be Soldiers and became mere handfuls of weights and measures." Woolley thought that even "a little guard duty would not hurt" the staff officers.[7]

Factionalism appeared early in the reorganized 7th Infantry officer corps. It became quiet only after the professional and personal reputations of several officers were put on the line and examined by penetrating investigations and courts-martial. Pro- and anti-Arbuckle factions appeared soon after the regiment was reassigned from Fort Scott, Georgia, to the Southwestern frontier. Colonel Arbuckle, easygoing and generally

[6] William A. Ganoe. *The History of the United States Army*, 121–53.

[7] Woolley to Hook, April 24, 1822. National Archives, War Department, Quartermaster General Letters Received File.

effective as regimental commander, seemed to be imposed
upon by Surgeon Thomas Lawson and Lieutenant Colonel
Zachary Taylor. Lawson apparently resented Arbuckle's appropriation of the more attractive women who followed the
regiment to Fort Smith either as officers' wives or as mistresses.
Taylor's battalion at Fort Selden, Louisiana, was under Arbuckle's command, and Taylor, who seemed prodigiously
ambitious, immodestly regarded himself eminently superior
to Arbuckle as an officer. After Arbuckle had left Fort Selden,
Taylor even wrote to the War Department about Arbuckle's
lack of talent for the command position in the regiment.[8]

Lawson as regimental surgeon was, however, frequently at
Fort Smith, and thus Arbuckle had to face his not too subtle
contempt. Taylor and Lawson drew followings at both Fort
Smith and Fort Selden, and their partisans spent many hours
belittling Arbuckle and scheming ways to destroy him. Arbuckle too drew partisans, less through design on his part than
out of contempt for Taylor and Lawson. The leader of Arbuckle's faction was hot-tempered Lieutenant Richard J.
Wash, who thrashed Lawson in a bloody fist fight.[9]

The Taylor-Lawson campaign against Arbuckle produced
results in late summer, 1822. The plan was apparently to
damage Arbuckle by accusing Lieutenant Wash. In late
August, Taylor advised Arbuckle that he planned to submit
to the Western Department Command charges of conduct
unbecoming an officer which Surgeon Lawson had preferred
against Lieutenant Wash.[10]

When authority was received to hold Wash's court-martial,

[8] Gaines to Arbuckle, May 15, 1822. National Archives, War Department, Western Department, Letters Sent File.
[9] Colonel Mathew Arbuckle's Court-Martial. National Archives, War
Department, Judge Advocate General Files.
[10] Ibid. Gaines to Calhoun, December 11, 1822. National Archives,
War Department, Western Department, Letters Sent File. Nourse to
Arbuckle, August 2, 1822. National Archives, War Department, Adjutant General, Letters Sent File.

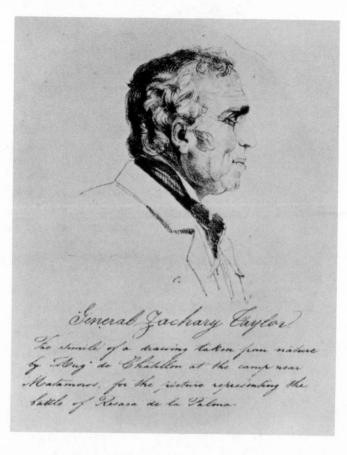

General Zachary Taylor,
from a drawing by Auguste de Chatillon.

Stephen Harriman Long.
Photograph of a painting by C. W. Peale.

General Mathew Arbuckle.

Typical of the countryside surrounding Belle Point is this landscape, "Cavaniol Mountain," from an aquatint in Thomas Nuttall's *A Journal of Travel into the Arkansas Territory During the Year 1819*, Philadelphia, 1821.

Fort Smith in 1820. Painted by Samuel Seymour, landscape painter with Major S. H. Long's expedition. (Original in the hands of a private collector)

Ring's Farm—first settlement west of Fort Smith on the California (Marcy's) Road. From a sketch by H. B. Mollhausen, 1853.

Fort Coffee, on the Arkansas River fifteen miles above Fort Smith, sketched by H. B. Mollhausen, 1853.

"Fort Smith," from an early sketch.

Arbuckle demonstrated his loyalty to friends and his talent as a splendid strategist. For Taylor and Lawson to succeed in their attempt to convict Wash, it was essential that the three witnesses to the fist fight—Lieutenant Pierce Butler, Sergeant Thompson Murrin, and Corporal John Bullard—be present and testify for the prosecution. Arbuckle suddenly found several of his companies short of personnel, and ordered Lieutenant Butler and Sergeant Murrin to Natchez to seek recruits.[11]

The third witness for Taylor and Lawson against Wash was Corporal Bullard, whom Arbuckle also disposed of, as follows. Before Wash's court-martial convened, General Edmund P. Gaines and his escort arrived at Fort Smith in the course of an inspection of Western military posts. He examined the troops, ordnance, supplies, and works at Belle Point and declared the station in a high state of readiness. Before he could continue his tour of frontier posts, several escort members were stricken with "bilious fever," and the entire party was forced to lay over at Fort Smith. During Gaines' convalescence, General Henry Atkinson arrived at Fort Smith. By the end of August, all had convalesced except one of Atkinson's waiters, who was still gravely ill in the post hospital. Gaines and Atkinson were eager to be off, and so Arbuckle accommodated them by suggesting that because Corporal Bullard had only a few months left on his enlistment he would be an ideal replacement for Atkinson's ailing servant. Gaines approved, and the inspection party moved out. Thus Arbuckle had dispatched the final witness against Lieutenant Wash. When the court-martial convened at Fort Smith, it was compelled to adjourn sine die because no one was present to sustain the prosecution.[12]

[11] Arbuckle had received permission on August 2, 1822, from the Adjutant General's office to detail men for recruiting duty. Nourse to Arbuckle, August 2, 1822. National Archives, War Department, Adjutant General Letters Sent File.

[12] Gaines to Calhoun, December 11, 1822. National Archives, War Department, Western Department, Letters Sent File.

In mid-December, 1822, when General Gaines and his party
returned to Louisville from the tour of Western forts, there
awaited him a request to investigate charges brought against
Colonel Arbuckle by Taylor and Lawson. Before considering
the court-martial that generated from the Taylor-Lawson
charges it would be well to look at another court-martial involving a former Fort Smith commanding officer which, like
Arbuckle's, grew out of a cabal of junior officers.

In 1818 Lieutenant Martin Scott sent the secretary of war
a confidential letter accusing Major William Bradford of
profiting from the labor of soldiers who had been detailed to
help with the agricultural enterprises associated with the post.
He charged that "large quantities of Cotton, Tobacco, Corn,
Cattle, Hogs, Horses, Sheep, &c. have been raised and applied"
to the Commandant's use. On June 23, 1822, General Gaines
sent out an order from his Louisville headquarters notifying
Arbuckle that a court-martial was to be held for Major Bradford, based on charges made by Lieutenant Scott. The court-
martial was to sit at Fort Smith, its sessions to begin no later
than August 10. Arbuckle was to notify Bradford, who was at
Fort Selden, and Colonel Taylor who was to accompany
Bradford and sit on the court. Lieutenant Scott and all other
witnesses were to be at Fort Smith by August 10. Bradford
was to consider himself under arrest as soon as he was handed
a copy of the charges.[13]

Lieutenant Scott, chief witness for the prosecution, failed
to appear, so the trial adjourned. Bradford was vindicated by
a statement from Hugh Glenn, former contractor at Fort
Smith. He said that probably only a hundred pounds of cotton

13 Glenn to Calhoun, April 21, 1821. National Archives, War Depart-
ment, Adjutant General, Letters Received File. Gaines to Arbuckle,
June 23, 1822. National Archives, War Department, Western Depart-
ment, Letters Sent File. Gaines to Taylor and Bradford, June 23, 1822.
National Archives, War Department, Western Department, Letters
Sent File.

had been raised at Fort Smith since it was established in 1817. Glenn added that Bradford raised only enough tobacco for his own use, and as to cattle, Bradford kept only enough to supply his wife with milk and butter. The hogs belonged to Glenn; he ran them on the public lands around the post while he served as contractor. After his trial, Bradford joined the Gaines-Atkinson inspection party on its trip to Fort Atkinson. In 1823 he resigned his commission, paid a brief visit to the Belle Point post he established in 1817, then went to Kentucky.[14]

In mid-January, 1823, Gaines ordered Arbuckle to stand a general court-martial and directed him to turn his command over to Captain William Davenport and to go to Baton Rouge, where he would report to President of the Court General Atkinson and be placed in arrest. Arbuckle could take such witnesses as he deemed necessary for his defense. Apparently, Arbuckle regarded the trial as harassment and the charges frivolous. He spent little time preparing a defense but, rather, drafted several letters to Quartermaster General Jesup concerning the need for enlarging and strengthening Fort Smith, including elaborate lists of "plank, hardware," and other construction items.[15] He chose as traveling companions and defense witnesses Captain Granville Leftwich, Lieutenant George Murdock, and Private John Williams. The general court-martial began on March 8, 1823. The specifications against Arbuckle included:

> In that he did at Fort Hawkins, Georgia, in the Month of September, 1819, traverse the character of Brevet Major General Edward P. Gaines of the United States Army, his

[14] *Arkansas Gazette*, January 23, 1823, and Gaines to Calhoun, December 11, 1822. National Archives, War Department, Western Department, Letters Sent File.

[15] Arbuckle to Jesup, January 2, 1823. National Archives, War Department, Quartermaster General Letters Received File.

immediate Commanding officer, by saying that he believed the General to be a man who would destroy any person to aggrandize himself.

In that he did at Fort Scott, Geo., in November, 1820, assign Elijah Montgomery, late Captain of the 7th Regiment of United States Infantry, to the Command of the 2d Light Company of the 7th Infantry, notwithstanding he had repeatedly promised that Captain Granville Leftwich of the 7th Infantry should be appointed to the Command of the Company.

In that he did at Fort Scott, Geo., sometime in September, 1821 violate the sanctity of a private seal, by breaking open a packet of letters, marked private, directed to Lieutenant W. W. Outlaw of the 7th Infantry.

In that he did at Fort Scott, Geo., on or about the 16th of June, 1821 not with a view to the public good, but in order to gratify his resentment towards Surgeon T. Lawson of the United States Army arrest Surgeon Lawson, at a time, when the services of Surgeon Lawson could not be dispensed with, without injury to the Command.

In that he did at Fort Scott, Geo., during a part of the Months of November & December 1820, & during the Months of January, February, March, April, & May, 1821, frequently pry into the amours of the officers & the women of the 7th Infantry, by interrogating the officers about the women, the women about the officers & the one woman about the others; yet whenever he ascertained that an improper intimacy existed between an officer & a woman did not in a manly way correct the evil by punishing the officer, but commonly persecuted, & in some instances unjustly the woman.

In that he did at Fort Scott, Geo., in the Months of November & December, 1820, & during the Months of January, February, March, & April, 1821, encourage open prostitution, within his command, by authorizing, advising, nay almost forcing married women in this Cantonment to live with other men than their husbands, particularly Mrs.

Ellen Wonderly, Ruth Ellis, alias Grey, & Elizabeth Akins.

In that he did at Fort Scott, Geo., in the Months of April, May, June & July 1821 permit Mrs. Anne Miller, a Camp woman, to keep a house of prostitution in his very Cantonment, & also to sell Whiskey, &c. to the soldiers of the 7th Infantry; a good portion of which Whiskey was gotten on prescriptions signed by himself.

In that he did, while descending the Apalachicola river, & Bay of Apalachicola, East Florida, in October 1821, publicly associate with Ruth Ellis, alias Grey, a Camp woman, by having her through the day & night, on the quarter deck of his Boat, & under the same awning with himself, & there holding social converse with her in the presence of officers & soldiers.[16]

Other specifications included the complaint that he had deliberately ordered away all witnesses for Lieutenant Wash's court-martial, thus compelling adjournment of the trial. After the specifications were presented, there followed weeks of testimony, examination, and cross-examination. On April 1, the general court-martial issued its verdict exonerating Colonel Arbuckle of the charges presented by Taylor and Lawson. Arbuckle remained in Baton Rouge with his party for a few days to celebrate his acquittal, and then visited friends in the lower South. He arrived at Fort Smith aboard the steamer *Alleghany* in late May.[17]

Colonel Arbuckle's vindication by general court-martial had the effect of calming officer discontent in his regiment, but his difficulties continued with the officer hierarchy at the command level. Among the many problems awaiting his attention at Fort Smith was attrition in the ranks due to expiration of enlistment, death, and desertion. From experience he found that to keep his regiment at full strength army recruiters

[16] Colonel Mathew Arbuckle's Court-Martial. National Archives, War Department, Office of the Judge Advocate General Files.
[17] *Arkansas Gazette*, May 5, 1823.

had to supply him between a hundred and a hundred and fifty
new men each year. Customarily, he appealed directly to the
War Department for aid in filling his manpower needs, and
usually he had as prompt results as the slow communications
system would permit. Then, in 1823, the War Department
changed the assignments of two of its senior officers. General
Edmund P. Gaines, Arbuckle's superior, was transferred to
the Eastern Military Department, and General Winfield Scott
became the commander of the Western Military Department.
About the only thing Scott retained from Gaines' administration of the Western Military Department was the Louisville
headquarters. Scott was a painful stickler for military rules
and regulations, and seemed to regard it his special mission to
reform Arbuckle by forcing him to abandon his loose if effective methods of administering Fort Smith and Fort Selden.
Thus, when he found that Arbuckle had directly written the
adjutant general in Washington for assistance in filling the
manpower needs at Fort Smith, General Scott sent Arbuckle
a blistering note which reminded him that Louisville was on
the postal route from Fort Smith to Washington and that Scott
did not believe it necessary "to deviate from the usual channel
of military communication." Scott trusted that in the future
"a rigid attention to the Army Regulation on the subject of
military correspondence" by Arbuckle would prevent a re-
currence.[18]

As matters developed, Arbuckle received authority for filling his depleted ranks, but General Scott's insistence on the
use of military channels slowed the recruitment process by at
least six months. Arbuckle relied upon local as well as Eastern
sources to replenish the Fort Smith garrison. He kept an
officer and enlisted escort on recruiting duty in the settlements
at the mouth of White River, at Natchez, New Orleans, and

[18] Scott to Arbuckle, January 15, 1824. National Archives, War Department, Western Department, Letters Sent File.

St. Louis on a more or less regular basis, but Western enlistments declined noticeably within a year after the arrival of the 7th Infantry Regiment at Fort Smith. Arbuckle accounted for this condition by pointing to the expanding opportunities on the frontier for men of military age. He added that his recruiting details found their work increasingly difficult because of the growing reputation of Fort Smith as a post where service life was rigorous. Therefore he had to rely more and more on Eastern enlistment centers, especially the Philadelphia Recruit Depot, because men of military age in that region were far removed from the frontier and, in their ignorance, could be more easily misled by recruiting officers. But even there army recruiters met a growing reluctance among the native-born to join up. The image of the army had deteriorated. It was becoming common knowledge that the rank and file, wherever assigned, could expect few rewards for the difficult and often dangerous duty they performed. Then too, the peacetime army of 1823 still contained a sprinkling of veterans of the War of 1812, who monopolized the noncommissioned grades. Discipline, built upon a hierarchy of rank, was harsh, and the only military men entitled to privileges and special consideration were those in command either as officers or as noncommissioned officers. Standards were regularly lowered in order to fill the billets, with the result that the native-born who enlisted were often illiterate, former criminals, renegades, and the insecure seeking escape from unpleasant conditions at home, who looked upon the army as a refuge where clothing, food, and a measure of security could be obtained.[19]

Critics said "a respectable character is very scarce in the U. S. Army," and ordinary recruits "consist either of scum of

[19] Arbuckle to Nourse, July, 1823. National Archives, War Department, Adjutant General, General Letters Received File. William L. Gordon-Miller. *Recollections of the United States Army*, vii–xi.

the population of the older states or of the worthless German, English, Polish or Irish immigrants." Lowered standards to fill enlistment quotas were reflected in a surgeon's survey of fifty-five recruits. Almost 90 per cent of this group had enlisted to escape difficulties with women; forty-three were drunk to some degree when they took the oath of office to faithfully serve their country; and thirteen had changed their names.[20]

Each recruit was given only the most cursory examination, probably out of fear that a penetrating look might result in his rejection. The recruiting surgeon had to certify that the candidate was not a habitual drunkard, that he was not subject to convulsions, not afflicted with piles or other infirmities, and that he had "perfect use of his limbs; that he had no tumors, ulcerated legs, rupture, nor chronic cutaneous affliction." All recruits who had not had the disease were vaccinated for smallpox.[21]

To fill vacancies at Fort Smith and other posts, Eastern recruiting officers posted handbills in public places stating that they would take all men of good character to the age of thirty-five. These announcements, pitched to appeal to the prospect's sense of security, stressed the good treatment, physical comforts, sufficient and wholesome diet, ample clothing, and excellent medical care an army enlistment provided. Occasionally, enlistment bounties were paid, and recruiters pointed to the 320 acres of free land for any soldier who gave ten consecutive years of service.[22]

Another way to fill vacancies was to persuade men whose five-year enlistments had expired to re-enlist. Less than one-

<hr />

20 *Ibid.*
21 *Ibid.*
22 Arbuckle to Nourse, October 2, 1822, and Arbuckle to Nourse, July, 1823. National Archives, War Department, Adjutant General Letters Received File. John F. Callan. *The Military Laws of the United States,* 270.

tenth of Arbuckle's men chose to continue in the service even though they would receive three months' pay as re-enlistment bounty plus a short furlough. Arbuckle explained this reluctance to continue at Fort Smith by saying that the "soldiers hadn't joined the army with the expectation of doing much hard work, and the character of Frontier service disappoints their expectations."[23]

Each infantryman assigned to Fort Smith received an issue of clothing consisting of boots, socks, cotton and wool jackets, drawers, cap and coat, cotton and wool overalls, cotton and flannel shirts, and two blankets. Dress uniform regulations required laced bootees extending four inches above the ankle and pantaloons, gray in winter and white in summer. The parade coat was blue, single-breasted, with a standing collar four inches wide bound in white braid and fronted with a row of ten buttons. Drummers and fifers were conspicuous with their scarlet cloth coats. Arbuckle's men topped their attire with the leather "tar bucket," a tall billed cap crowned with a white pompom to distinguish the infantry from other military branches. At inspection, men of the 7th Infantry Regiment were expected to present themselves with hair cropped. Whiskers were not to extend below the lower tip of the ear "in a line hence with the curve of the mouth."[24]

The Fort Smith infantryman's weapon, selected by the United States Army Chief of Ordnance, came from government arsenals at Springfield, Massachusetts, and Harpers Ferry, Virginia. Instructor's guides for firearm drill described the weapons issued to the Fort Smith garrison as model 1795, 1812, or 1816. Improvements included use of ball and cartridge, but a continuing problem at Belle Point was the scarcity

[23] Arbuckle to Nourse, November 4, 1823. National Archives, War Department, Adjutant General Letters Received File.

[24] *General Regulations for the Army*, 154–62. "2d Infantry Regiment," *Military Collector and Historian* (March, 1951), 16–17.

of cartridge paper and, in 1822, only a small amount of cask powder. Arbuckle's inspection reports disclosed that the men in two companies were armed with "worn out muskets" and that nearly the entire regiment was equipped with muskets, generally "in good order but of the old pattern and of various manufacture."[25]

An important part of each company's equipment issue at Fort Smith consisted of axes, timber saws, and other tools. The 7th Infantry Regiment was more than a fighting unit; it was also a construction and engineering organization with the collateral duty of erecting buildings, establishing bridges and ferries, and hewing roads through the wilderness.[26]

Rations for the garrison at Belle Point varied with the season. In the summer, the post gardens provided roasting ears, melons, onions, squash, potatoes, and other fresh vegetables. From time to time, hogs and cattle from the garrison herds were slaughtered; the post commissary officer occasionally purchased cattle from settlers and Cherokees.[27]

Most of the year, however, the daily ration was tiresome, usually consisting of about a pound of salted pork or bacon, eighteen ounces of hard bread, beans, occasionally coffee or tea, topped with a gill of whisky. The private's daily ration was worth about eighteen cents. An officer received as many as eight rations daily; if none was provided, he was reimbursed in cash.[28]

The rations contracted for by the commissary-general for Fort Smith in 1824 illustrate the volume and variety of sub-

[25] Inspection Returns for the 7th Infantry Regiment, Fort Smith, April 30, 1822. National Archives, War Department, Western Department, Reports Received File.

[26] Inspection Returns for the 7th Infantry Regiment, Fort Smith, December 31, 1823. National Archives, War Department, Western Department, Reports Received File.

[27] Woolley to Hook, April 12, 1822. National Archives, War Department, Quartermaster General Letters Received File.

[28] Ganoe. History of the United States Army, 106, 183.

sistence required to accommodate Arbuckle's troops. The specifications read: "470 barrels of the Flour, 2,650 gallons of good Whiskey, 240 Bushels of good sound Beans, 3,300 pounds of good hard soap, 1,100 pounds good Tallow Candles with cotton wicks, 50 bushels good clean salt [and] 300 gallons good cider Vinegar." The pork, flour, whisky, beans, salt, and vinegar were to be delivered to Belle Point in full hooped barrels. The ration list called for two hundred barrels of pork "to consist of an entire hog to the barrel, except the feet, legs and ears and snout, all of which are inadmissible. Should the hog be of less weight than 200 pounds, the deficiency is to be made up of good fat side pieces."[29]

Like the rations at Belle Point, the daily routine was also tiresome. Arbuckle's men began their day with reveille at daybreak. They assembled in front of their quarters for roll call and were then dismissed to put their quarters in order, police the parade ground, water and feed the post livestock, and perform other fatigue duties. Company commanders handed their morning reports to the assistant adjutant, and the sick call sounded. This was the signal for the first sergeant to conduct the ill to the post hospital to see the surgeon. At eight o'clock, at the signal "Molly Put the Kettle On," the men tramped to breakfast. After the morning meal, sergeants posted the guard and assigned fatigue details their tasks for the day. These activities were interspersed with company and battalion drill and inspections of quarters, grounds, scullery, kitchen, and dining area. At noon, another roll call sounded and, in response to "Peas Upon the Trencher," the men sat down to eat. At one o'clock, the drummers beat a call to fatigue duty and the companies worked about the post or drilled. The "Roast Beef" call signaled the evening meal. Twenty minutes before sunset, the companies marched onto the parade ground, where the fifers and drummers sounded

[29] *Arkansas Gazette*, August 5, 1823.

retreat. Arbuckle or his deputy reviewed the parade, received the salute, and the troops were dismissed. After retreat, the men returned to quarters, fatigue details bedded down the livestock, and the musicians assembled for tattoo. Rolls were called for the fifth and final time, and, as tattoo sounded, all lights were extinguished. Tattoo in summer was at nine o'clock; in winter, one hour earlier.[30]

As the frontier crisis abated, more men of the 7th Infantry Regiment were brought in from scattered patrol stations to the post, where they spent an increasing amount of time in company and battalion drill and garrison general duty. As members of fatigue parties, they kept the station tidy, worked on the post farm, herded garrison livestock, and cut timber to expand and repair the post. Each summer, sections of several companies went to the meadows around the post and cut hay for winter livestock forage. Occasionally, details were selected for escort, recruiting, and other special missions; enlisted men vied for these monotony-breaking assignments. Each private had to serve his turn on scullery detail and guard duty, the latter requiring special attention to instructions and learning all sentry challenges.[31]

Certain local assignments, such as serving as surgeon's assistant in the post hospital, were coveted because these exempted the men from drill, sentry, and other duties. Enlisted men were also detailed as orderlies. One private described his duties as orderly as walking after his officer at a respectable distance from sunrise until tattoo, taking his cap off whenever the officer talked to him, standing erect and placing his hands along the seams of his pantaloons, chest forward and shoulders square. Another special assignment welcomed by privates was

[30] "Systems of Martial Law, Field Service and Police." *American State Papers, Military Affairs*, VI, 208–9.

[31] Arbuckle to Jesup, August 14, 1823. National Archives, War Department, Quartermaster General Letters Received File.

as waiters in the officers' mess, where they were exempt from various company duties and where they usually ate well.[32]

The level of medical care Arbuckle's troopers received at the Fort Smith hospital was primitive but about as good as was prevalent everywhere at that time. Calomel was fed to the troops "to ward off the influence of the sickly season"; castor oil was used for the obvious purpose; from Peruvian Bark was blended a general tonic. The surgeon was trained to mix and apply mustard and linseed plasters and poultices for drawing boils and reducing muscular inflammation. Most patients could expect a round of bloodletting either surgically, by "cupping the temples," or by application of leeches.[33]

The common ailments of the Fort Smith garrison were diarrhea, dropsy, typhoid, congestive and bilious fevers, malaria, spasms, ague, inflammation of the bowels, and dysentery. Illness reports from the Fort Smith hospital frequently read "disease unknown." Diphtheria, measles, and mumps were not unknown, and pneumonia struck in winter. Summer's heat seemed always to bring the "ague and bilious fever"; in August, 1822, one-half of Company G was in quarters or in the post hospital with this malady, and other companies were hit in varying proportions. Deaths each month during the "sickly" season—July, August, and September—ranged from one to five per company. Men became suspicious of the post surgeon, and charged that no soldier who entered his hospital came out alive. They blamed their ailments on several things, including the drinking water from the post well. And they did

[32] Gaines to Calhoun, December 11, 1822. National Archives, War Department, Western Department, Letters Sent File. Inspection Returns for the 7th Infantry Regiment, Fort Smith, October 31 and December 31, 1822. National Archives, War Department, Western Departments, Reports Received File. Ganoe, *History of the United States Army*, 174–75.
[33] Arbuckle to Nourse, July, 1823. National Archives, War Department, Adjutant General, Letters Received File.

a great deal of their own doctoring, using home remedies for such ills as colds and stomach disorders. A favorite treatment was to purify their drinking water with a "liberal infusion of Old Rye."[34]

Each year the Belle Point burying ground received its human tribute exacted by the harsh frontier. In the "sickly" season, there were usually several funerals each week. The procession marched to the cemetery in cadence to muffled drums and the mournful tones of *Roslin Castle*. When an enlisted man died, his company officers arranged for burial. Soldiers with reversed arms listened to a prayer offered by a comrade; grave attendants lowered the body; volleys of musketry were fired over the grave. When an officer died, his fellow officers wore the badge of mourning for thirty days as tribute, sent a message of condolence to the family of the departed, and drank toasts to his memory.[35]

A grim phase of garrison life at Fort Smith was the system of punishment for violations of military rules and regulations. One of the first buildings constructed at Belle Point was the guardhouse, which never lacked occupants from the day of its completion. During certain seasons, especially after those rare visits by the paymaster, it was full. The guardhouse was used to incarcerate military prisoners regarded as dangerous to the peace and safety of the garrison, to hold certain types of offenders, notably deserters, for trial, and to sober up inebriated infantrymen.[36]

[34] Inspection Returns for the 7th Infantry Regiment, Fort Smith, August 31 and October 31, 1822. National Archives, War Department, Western Department, Reports Received File.

[35] Inspection Returns for the 7th Infantry Regiment, Fort Smith, August 31 and October 31, 1823. National Archives, War Department, Western Department, Reports Received File.

[36] Inspection Returns for the 7th Infantry Regiment, Fort Smith, April 30 and June 30, 1822. National Archives, War Department, Western Department, Reports Received File.

The most common offenses among the men of the 7th Infantry Regiment were sleeping on sentry duty, drunkenness on the post, striking an officer, being absent without leave, desertion, having lighted candles in the barracks after tattoo, and neglect of duty. Company commanders personally tried offenders for such minor violations as carelessness in person and failure to pass inspection; those guilty of more serious violations were 'tried by regimental courts-martial.[37]

Throughout the United States Army in the 1820's and 1830's, military punishment was calculated to humiliate and intimidate rather than to rehabilitate. Some of the more common sentences handed down by army courts-martial in both the Eastern and Western Military Departments were reducing in rank of noncommissioned officer, holding in service after expiration of enlistment to make up time lost in misconduct, and ordering hard labor in public. Enlisted men found drunk on duty or while on the sick list were usually fined and sentenced to perform at least twenty hours of special duty. Tough company commanders were known to sentence a trooper found with clothes and equipment in bad order to fifteen days in the guardhouse on bread and water. A soldier absent without leave could usually expect a five-dollar fine and the additional punishment of having to parade in public carrying a thirty-pound weight for seven days. For the same offense, some soldiers received fifty lashes on the bare back or were made to walk the post carrying a bag of shot on the shoulder.[38]

Men convicted of theft were often drummed out of the service. A deserter was forced to pay the reward offered for his capture, usually thirty dollars, to be deducted from his pay; this punishment was severe, because a private earned only thirty dollars in six months. The deserter could expect to serve

<hr>

[37] Inspection Returns for the 7th Infantry Regiment, Fort Smith, April 30, 1822. National Archives, Reports Received File.
[38] William B. Morrison. *Military Posts and Camps in Oklahoma*, 14.

a term in the guardhouse on bread and water, wear a ball and chain or iron collar on his leg or neck, have his head shaved, perform hard labor in public, sometimes receive a blistering brand, wear a straw rope around his neck, and stand on a barrel in a public place.[39]

All these punishments or some variations were used at Fort Smith. Drunkenness and desertion were the most common offenses among Arbuckle's men, and the punishments inflicted by regimental courts-martial were usually regarded by the officer corps as sufficient for the crime. Fort Smith's most sensational crime, however, baffled the staff, and the offender was finally turned over to civil authorities for trial and punishment. This was the famous McGranie case.

Private Daniel McGranie had been assigned to a log-cutting detail as a carpenter. On the morning of June 10, 1822, as his fatigue party prepared to go into the forest, McGranie handed Private Benjamin Clark a small sum of money to hold for him. McGranie had been drinking since daylight, and by the time the party entered the woods he was drunk. McGranie suddenly demanded that Clark return his money. The latter answered that he had left the money at the fort and dared not return for it because that would be a violation of orders; he promised McGranie that he could get his money that evening when they returned to Belle Point. McGranie seemed satisfied until the detail reached the place where they were to cut logs. Then he resumed his demand, repeating it several times. Clark put him off as before, and the men began their work. McGranie took a position on a log which Clark was hewing, and, biding his time, suddenly struck the unsuspecting Clark across the neck with a savage swing of a broad ax, nearly severing his head from his body. McGranie fled into the woods, but returned to Fort Smith that evening and was arrested and placed in the guardhouse. For nearly a year, post

[39] Ganoe. *History of the United States Army*, 173–75.

officers held McGranie in custody as they attempted to reach a decision on his fate. Finally, he was transferred to civil authorities at Little Rock, and in early 1823 he was brought to trial. His attorneys won his acquittal on a plea of temporary insanity, but his freedom was brief. A squad of infantrymen from Fort Smith intercepted McGranie at the courthouse door, shackled him, and returned him to the Belle Point guardhouse.[40]

The McGranie case pointed up the growing problem of intemperance among the troops at Belle Point, and even the easygoing Colonel Arbuckle became alarmed. The daily ration at Fort Smith included a gill of whisky, but most of the men were hardened, inveterate drinkers, and a quarter-pint each day was hardly enough to make them tipsy. The source for heavy drinking was the settlement which was growing up near the post and where army wives, mistresses, and laundresses were domiciled. Several crude taverns, with abundant stores of locally produced whisky selling for twenty-five cents a pint, soon appeared. Many of the men spent their off-duty hours at these dives playing cards and drinking. From the quantity of whisky confiscated at inspection of the quarters and the number of men found drunk on duty, it was apparent that whisky was being carried onto the station and nipped throughout the day. The large number on sick call for "ailments unknown" caused Arbuckle to suspect the "bad whisky" his men obtained from the taverns. He attributed several deaths in the battalion to intemperance and declared that he would "remedy the evil" if the adjutant general would give him authority to raze the emerging settlement and to deport the tavern keepers.[41]

[40] Inspection Returns for the 7th Infantry Regiment, Fort Smith, April 30 and June 30, 1822. *Arkansas Gazette*, August 26, 1823.

[41] Arbuckle to Nourse, August 2, 1823. *Territory of Arkansas*, XIX, 536.

The rise of a civilian community at Belle Point reflected the inevitable American frontier trend of advancing settlement and augured that Fort Smith's days were numbered. One purpose for the existence of this post was to protect the western margins of settlement. Squatters from Arkansas were already jumping the Osage line and establishing settlements west of Fort Smith, both in Lovely's Purchase and south of the Arkansas on the Choctaw cession. They came from Missouri along the Osage Trace and the Texas Road which flanked Grand River, and even penetrated up the Red River into the Kiamichi valley from the lower Louisiana settlements.[42]

Arkansas Territory had a proprietary attitude toward the garrison at Fort Smith and the land west of the post to the mouth of Grand River. The editor of the *Arkansas Gazette* spoke of the territory's pride at having a military station on its western border, and declared that it was essential to the defense of the nation for an enemy force approaching east along the Arkansas would "find Fort Smith a little Gibraltar."[43]

Leaders in Arkansas Territory, ambitious for statehood, wished to include as much of the land west of Fort Smith as possible within the territorial domain of their emerging state before admission to the Union. Their desires were supported in Congress by Arkansas Territorial Delegate Henry W. Conway, who proposed that his territory be permitted to annex the land west of Fort Smith on a line from the mouth of Grand River south to Red River. The need for this annexation was urgent because the federal government had already ceded land south of the Arkansas and Canadian to the Choctaws and there was talk of granting the Cherokees Lovely's Purchase. Although territorial leaders regarded the garrison at Fort

[42] Arbuckle to Secretary of War, January 12, 1822. *Territory of Arkansas*, XIX, 480.
[43] *Arkansas Gazette*, July 23, 1822.

Smith as the special protectors of Arkansas, they thought less in terms of a permanent installation at Belle Point and more in terms of Arbuckle's troops as a mobile force to be dispersed so as best to serve their western border defense needs. Because settlements had extended west of Fort Smith and because Arkansas hoped to annex the country as far west as the Grand River, Conway proposed that the Belle Point garrison be relocated at more strategic spots at the mouths of the Verdigris and the Kiamichi. Ironically, Arkansas won on one count, in that the 7th Infantry Regiment was moved from Fort Smith to new posts west of Belle Point, but lost on the other—the land west of Fort Smith was reserved for the emigrating Eastern Indians.[44]

[44] *Arkansas Gazette*, April 13, 1824. Conway to Calhoun, January 30, 1824. *Territory of Arkansas*, XIX, 602.

# CHAPTER SIX

# Fort Smith in the Interim

On April 2, 1824, Colonel Mathew Arbuckle received orders to abandon Fort Smith. He welcomed General Winfield Scott's letter containing directions to transfer his 7th Infantry force to a position west of Belle Point, and hoped that a new assignment would lift his men from their boredom and improve their spirits. Arbuckle's troops were becoming increasingly entrenched in garrison routines and, with little to do but maintain the post, drill, and guard the Belle Point works, they had become intensely bored, as was reflected in growing discipline problems, desertion, intemperance, and a swelling guardhouse population.[1]

A bit of excitement had been generated at Fort Smith in the summer of 1823 when news reached Arbuckle that an Arikara force had ambushed a fur-trading party on the upper Missouri. Western Military Department headquarters at Louisville had issued orders in July alerting commanders of posts in the department and directing them to hold troops ready for assignment to the troubled area. Arbuckle was ordered to prepare four companies and to hold them in readiness to move on a moment's notice. To the disappointment of many action-hungry soldiers at Belle Point, their preparations were for naught; Colonel Henry Leavenworth's column from Fort Atkinson moved against the Indians and forced them to an

[1] Scott to Arbuckle, March 6, 1824. National Archives, War Department, Western Department, Letters Sent File.

armistice on August 11. The momentary lift in spirits which the prospect of a new assignment produced among his men convinced Arbuckle that the solution for the mounting morale problem at Belle Point was in a change.[2]

It had become increasingly apparent to Arbuckle that Fort Smith's role had diminished as a frontier protection point. His men had pacified the Osage boundary region. Turbulence continued, but consisted mainly of isolated bandit actions occurring so far west of Fort Smith as to be outside the effective surveillance range of Arbuckle's patrols. Both Cherokee and Osage leaders disavowed responsibility for these renegade bands, but Arbuckle feared that unless they were promptly and vigorously checked they might infect the more peaceable factions in each Indian nation and cause a resumption of border strife. Arbuckle pointed out to the Western Military Department command the additional consideration that the Arkansas frontier situation was complicated by the fact that the line of settlement which Fort Smith was required to protect from Indian raids had jumped west of Belle Point and was moving up the Illinois, Grand, and Kiamichi rivers. All in all, he believed that his regiment could better serve the national interest by being stationed west of Belle Point at the mouth of the Verdigris or Grand.[3]

As early as 1822, Arbuckle had suggested to the War Department that the Fort Smith garrison be relocated at a more strategic spot on the Arkansas frontier, and his recommendations became more urgent as a frontier town grew up at Belle Point and the opportunities for trouble for his troops increased. Each time until 1824 his suggestions for reassigning the 7th Infantry to a more critical location on the frontier met

[2] Gaines to Arbuckle, July 23, 1823. National Archives, War Department, Western Department, Letters Sent File.

[3] Arbuckle to Nourse, September 30, 1822. *Territory of Arkansas, 1819–1825*, (vol. XIX of *Territorial Papers of the United States*, ed. by Clarence E. Carter), 462–63. *Arkansas Gazette*, November 28, 1822.

with a rebuff from the adjutant general, who declared that the secretary of war deemed it "inexpedient to move the Site of the Military post on the Arkansas to a position higher up the river."[4]

By 1824, however, several developments in the country west of Fort Smith brought the secretary of war and his advisers to Arbuckle's point of view. One was the political pressure of Arkansas Territory, led by Congressional Delegate Henry W. Conway, to move the western boundary of Arkansas to a line through the mouth of Grand River and south to the Red and to establish a military post on that line to protect the new Arkansas settlements in Lovely's Purchase and along the lower Kiamichi.[5]

Another development was the disturbing influence of renegade Osage and Cherokee bands raiding, killing, and burning in the country between the Poteau and the Cross Timbers. One of the most dangerous elements was Tick-e-Toke's Cherokee followers, who, distressed at the growing tendency toward peace among the Western Cherokees, had pulled away in protest. His band of about fifty warriors and their families squatted on lands in the lower Kiamichi valley, established a settlement, planted corn, and comprised a disturbing influence both north and south of Red River. This more or less permanent occupation of Osage hunting grounds invited retaliation. In March, 1823, an Osage party ambushed a Cherokee en route from his nation in Arkansas to visit his people in Tick-e-Toke's Kiamichi colony. During July, Osage raiders swept through the Cherokee settlement on the Kiamichi and ran off ten or eleven horses. They also plundered neighboring white settlers, robbing households and taking four of their

[4] Kirby to Arbuckle, December 12, 1822. *Territory of Arkansas*, XIX, 472–73.

[5] Conway to Calhoun, January 30, 1824. *Territory of Arkansas*, XIX, 602.

horses. Eleven warriors from Tick-e-Toke's town volunteered to recover the missing animals. They trailed the Osages to the Canadian, raided their camp, and made off with forty horses. This inevitably led to new incidents, retaliations, thefts, and killings. The fact that white settlers scattered through the country exposed to these raids were caught up in the Indian vendetta made the situation increasingly dangerous.[6]

Another frontier incident which influenced the War Department decision to abandon Fort Smith and move the 7th Infantry to a more strategic location was the Welburn massacre, which occurred in November, 1823. Frederick Notrebe and Antoine Barraque, French traders from Post of Arkansas, financed an expedition up the Red seeking beaver-trapping grounds. Assisted by twelve Quapaw hunters, Barraque established a camp on Blue River, north of the Red in the country recently assigned to the Choctaws. Barraque was joined at the Blue River camp by Curtis Welburn and seven trappers. Welburn was especially concerned about the possibility of Osage raids, and, at his urging, Barraque detailed Quapaws to guard the camp and watch for a lurking enemy. Daily incidents served as grim warnings of the hazards of their being in the Osage hunting grounds. Prairie fires, mysteriously started, nearly enveloped the party on one occasion and, on another, came within a fraction of destroying the camp. One straggler was later found brutally emasculated, his scalped head thrust on a pole. On November 16, Quapaw scouts sighted an Indian, identified as an Osage, watching the camp. The next day the enemy struck with bloody fury. Four trappers and a Negro slave belonging to Barraque were killed. Two wounded trappers escaped into a canebrake. On November 29, twelve days after the attack, the survivors straggled into Fort Smith. Barraque told Arbuckle that the attack was the work of

[6] Arbuckle to Nourse, September 3, 1823. *Territory of Arkansas*, XIX, 545–46.

Osages and that five of his men had been killed, four were missing, thirty-two horses had been stolen, and goods and other property worth four thousand dollars had been carried off.[7]

Arbuckle notified Western Military Department headquarters of the raid and again stressed that in order to effectively check frontier brigandage, troops had to be closer to the source. A few days after his orders to relocate Fort Smith arrived, there occurred an incident which surpassed the others in depravity and brutality. And it is likely that had not all the other causes been working for improving frontier security in the area west of Fort Smith, this incident alone would have convinced headquarters of the need. Because of his dedication, energy, and high purpose, Osage Agent Nathaniel Philbrook was unusual among officials working to advance the interests of the Indian tribes. Much of the credit for decreasing Cherokee-Osage tensions and for bringing relative peace to the troubled border belongs to him. In early April, 1824, he stopped at Fort Smith long enough to tell Colonel Arbuckle of his progress in achieving a lasting settlement of Cherokee-Osage differences. Then Philbrook set out alone for the Osage villages. Later, his horse was found near the mouth of Grand River. At first, it was thought that he had drowned. After his body had been found in the Arkansas, an autopsy disclosed that bullet wounds in the back had been the cause of death. Both Osages and Cherokees were blamed. Whoever the killers, the needless taking of Philbrook's life was a tragic and climactic demonstration of the need for a restraining force west of Fort Smith.[8]

In early 1824, the War Department authorized General Winfield Scott to reassign the Belle Point garrison. On March

---

[7] Arbuckle to Nourse, December 3, 1823. *Territory of Arkansas*, XIX, 570–71.

[8] *Arkansas Gazette*, April 20 and May 24, 1824.

6, Scott wrote Arbuckle directing him to establish a new position at or near the mouth of the Verdigris. For the time being,
Fort Smith was to be completely abandoned as a military
station, although Arbuckle was permitted to leave a detachment at Belle Point to guard any public property or military
stores not carried west as a part of the general evacuation. Besides being responsible for selecting the site for a new military
post on one of the principal tributaries of the Arkansas above
Belle Point and supervising its construction, Arbuckle had the
added duty of seeing that a companion post was erected at the
mouth of the Kiamichi. The troops from Fort Smith were to
remain with him on the Arkansas, and the garrison for the new
post on the Kiamichi near the Red was to consist of two companies to be derived from 7th Infantry detachments at Cantonment Jesup and Sulphur Fork.[9]

Scott's courier arrived at Fort Smith on April 2, 1824.
Arbuckle promptly convened his staff and worked out plans
for an orderly but speedy evacuation of the Belle Point works.
He assigned Lieutenant Joseph A. Phillips responsibility for
transporting the ordnance stores; Lieutenant Thomas Mc-
Namara, for moving commissary and quartermaster supplies.
Military gear and supplies were loaded on two keelboats at
the Fort Smith landing. After the river craft were stowed to
capacity, many of the remaining items were loaded in military
wagons. Even with the greatest care in packing the keelboats
and wagons, a substantial amount of public property remained;
so Arbuckle left Lieutenant Benjamin L. E. Bonneville and a
fourteen-man detachment at Fort Smith as a guard force.[10]

Arbuckle hoped to be off by April 6, but his officers and
men were not ready on that date; it was not until April 9 that

[9] Scott to Arbuckle, March 6, 1824. National Archives, War Department, Western Department, Letters Sent File.

[10] Inspection Returns for 7th Infantry Regiment, Fort Smith, April
30, 1824. National Archives, War Department, Western Department,
Reports Received File.

the 7th Infantry departed Fort Smith. Most of the troops and the wagons moved overland along the well-marked trace that skirted the north bank of the Arkansas.

On April 20, Arbuckle selected a site for the new post on the east bank of the Grand River about three miles above the Arkansas. His troops pitched their tents and went to work cutting timber. In a few weeks the 7th Infantry had erected log huts to shelter the companies and supplies pending construction of permanent barracks surrounded by a stockade. At first the new station was called Grand River, Arkansas; Arbuckle named it Fort Gibson; when it was discovered that the name did not conform to the nomenclature required by departmental orders, it was redesignated Cantonment Gibson.[11]

The *Arkansas Gazette* incorrectly informed the citizens of the territory:

> The place selected for the future site of the garrison, is at the junction of the Verdigris with the Arkansas; about 80 miles above Fort Smith, and 50 below the Osage Village, and is a few miles west of the proposed boundary of this Territory. It is said to be a fine, commanding, and healthy situation, and, if a competent force should be kept there, will be admirably calculated to give security to our western frontier.[12]

Throughout most of 1824, the post on Belle Point was occupied by Lieutenant Bonneville's detachment to guard the military stores left there when the 7th Infantry moved to the Grand River. When Arbuckle could spare men from work on Cantonment Gibson, he sent wagons and a party down to Fort Smith to load some of the remaining equipment and supplies; by autumn, the old post was cleared of supplies and men. Sur-

---

[11] *Arkansas Gazette*, April 13, 1824.
[12] *Ibid.*

prisingly soon, the elements of destruction and ruin set to work. Major Stephen H. Long's elaborate moat and battlement system crumbled and filled. Picket logs in the fortress walls began to rot. Even though Fort Smith remained a United States military reservation, settlers from the emerging town near the post helped themselves to windows, doors, planks, and anything else of value they could carry off to improve their own crude dwellings.[13]

In spite of its steadily deteriorating condition, old Fort Smith for several years continued to play a conspicuous and significant role in frontier affairs. During 1825 and 1826, the Belle Point station served as headquarters for the Choctaw Boundary Commission. In 1820, by the Treaty of Doak's Stand, the United States granted a vast domain south of the Arkansas and Canadian to the Choctaw Nation of Mississippi as a future home. It was expected that most of the Choctaws would soon be moving west, but by 1825 less than a thousand had migrated to the tribe's new home. A howl went up in Arkansas Territory when federal commissioners negotiated the Treaty of Doak's Stand, which conveyed to the Choctaws a grant containing an estimated 8,900,000 acres, its southeastern quarter overlying southwestern Arkansas Territory, which already contained settlements and organized counties. Added to this was the fact that settlements from Arkansas had extended well into the Choctaw cession west to the Kiamichi, where Arkansas citizens had organized Miller County.[14]

In 1824, Arkansas Territory made a big play in Congress to have the western boundary of the territory set on a line extending through the mouth of the Grand River south to include the Kiamichi valley to the Red River. The people of

[13] McClellan to Barbour, February 16, 1827. *Territory of Arkansas, 1825–1829* (vol. XX of *Territorial Papers of the United States*, ed. by Clarence E. Carter), 393–94.

[14] Charles J. Kappler (comp.). *Indian Affairs: Laws and Treaties*, II, 191–95.

Arkansas had every reason to be confident that their demands
would be granted. All along the frontier, from the Atlantic
to the Mississippi River, settlers were voters—Indians having
no franchise—and always had their way at the expense of
tribal interests. The certainty that Arkansas would have its
western boundary moved to the Grand River was one of the
principal reasons for moving the Fort Smith garrison to its
new post.[15]

A complicating factor was the curious conflict between the
interests of Arkansas Territory and those of the Southern
states. The states, being older and better organized were in a
stronger position than territories to have their interests satisfied. Southern Congressmen and senators were urging the
federal government to remove the Choctaws and other tribes
and to open up new lands in their states and provide more opportunities for their constituents. The federal government was
caught in the dilemma of attempting to placate states as well
as territories, but an overriding consideration was to protect
the interests of the emigrating tribes and carefully to fulfill
all removal-treaty obligations so that the Indians would have
no excuse for not moving west. Thus a measure of Arkansas'
interest had to be sacrificed.

To demonstrate the good faith of the United States in nego-
tiating the Treaty of Doak's Stand, federal commissioners
met with Choctaw representatives in Washington on January
20, 1825, and negotiated the Choctaw Boundary Treaty. By
its terms, the Choctaw eastern boundary—Arkansas' western
boundary—was set on a line beginning on the Arkansas River
one hundred paces east of Fort Smith and running due south
to Red River. The United States government pledged to remove all settlers west of that line, and Choctaw leaders agreed

15 Conway to Calhoun, January 30, 1824. *Territory of Arkansas*,
XIX, 602. Senate Committee Report Re Western Boundary, 18 Cong.,
1 Sess. *Territory of Arkansas*, XIX, 628–29.

to relocate their people who had already moved to the new country and were then living in villages east of the boundary. To make the treaty more palatable to the Choctaws, the United States agreed to pay the tribe six thousand dollars annually forever and an additional six thousand dollars for sixteen years and to accept responsibility for paying certain Choctaws several thousand dollars to satisfy various claims for damages caused by settlers.[16]

The *Arkansas Gazette* denounced the Choctaw Boundary Treaty of 1825, charging that it cut off from Arkansas Territory all of Miller County, a large part of Crawford County, and three thousand citizens who would have to move east of the line, abandoning cleared farms, homes, towns, roads, and other improvements. The Arkansas Territorial Assembly vigorously and violently protested the treaty, and expressed public sentiment in several memorials to Congress begging for a new treaty more favorable to Arkansas. Settlers wrote letters to President John Quincy Adams pleading for a suspension of the treaty. The Choctaws remained adamant, their leaders declaring they "would accept no other boundary" than the one set in the 1825 treaty. Secretary of War James Barbour regarded it a fair compromise, because, by the 1820 treaty, Arkansas would have lost to the Choctaws much of the territory's southwestern quadrant, and which had now been recovered for the citizens of Arkansas. He pointed out that the Choctaws gave up about one-fourth of their nearly nine million acres when they signed the Choctaw Boundary Treaty.[17]

Despite nearly a year of delay by Arkansas Territory in attempts to thwart the treaty, plans went forward to enforce it. On November 12, 1825, the Choctaw Boundary Commis-

[16] Kappler. *Indian Affairs: Laws and Treaties*, II, 211–14. *Arkansas Gazette*, March 29 and April 5, 1825.
[17] McKenney to Barbour, January 4, 1827. *Territory of Arkansas*, XX, 352–55. *Arkansas Gazette*, March 29, 1825.

sion met at Fort Smith and established headquarters at the old post for the purpose of establishing the Arkansas–Choctaw Nation boundary. Commission members included James S. Conway and the Choctaws John Pitchlynn and Tom Wall. The survey party and commissioners went to work from the Fort Smith base almost at once, and completed their task on January 7, 1826.[18]

Fort Smith performed additional service in settling frontier problems in 1825 when it was designated headquarters for the Western Choctaw Agency. Territorial Governor George Izard, as superintendent of Indian affairs for the region, was determined to achieve a prompt and thorough evacuation of Choctaws from southwestern Arkansas. Even while the boundary commission was preparing to establish the line, Izard sent Choctaw Agent William McClellan to the Mississippi River settlements to purchase corn, meat, and other subsistence items. McClellan was to ship the stores to Fort Smith, which was to serve as a depot for Choctaws moving from Arkansas as well as for those expected from Mississippi. He was at Fort Smith in late October, 1825, to make arrangements for storing Choctaw subsistence supplies.[19]

McClellan became involved in relocating the Choctaw communities in southeastern Arkansas west of the new boundary. The tribesmen in that area simply moved along Red River and did not travel north to clear through his supply depot at Belle Point, with the result that he was unable to return to Fort Smith until February 16, 1827. He noted that the post had deteriorated considerably since his earlier visit. The barracks'

18 Conway to Izard, November 2, 1825. National Archives, Office of Indian Affairs, Letters Received File. *Missouri Intelligencer*, January 18, 1826.

19 Izard to McClellan, October 10, 1825. *Territory of Arkansas*, XX, 122. Izard had been named by President Adams in March, 1825, to replace Miller as governor of Arkansas Territory.

"floors, doors, & windows" had been carried off, and the structures were a "perfect Rack." Only the quartermaster building was intact; he used it for storing the Choctaw emigration supplies. McClellan renovated a barracks building for quarters for himself and his staff—a blacksmith and interpreter.[20] He was surprised to find the north blockhouse occupied by Colonel John Nicks and Captain John Rogers. Nicks explained that he was an old friend of Colonel Arbuckle, having served in the 7th Infantry Regiment, and that for a time he held the appointment of post sutler at Fort Smith. According to Nicks, Arbuckle had placed Rogers and him in charge of the Belle Point works for the government flatboat, which they used as a ferry.

McClellan immediately had trouble over the ferry. Peter Folsom, an enterprising Choctaw mixed-blood, applied to McClellan for a franchise to operate his own boat as a ferry at Belle Point. Because the area as defined by the recent boundary treaty was in the Choctaw Nation, McClellan granted Folsom's request and ruled that thereafter Nicks and Rogers could carry only military traffic while Folsom would have a monopoly of the civilian traffic across the Arkansas.[21]

Nicks and Rogers complained to Arbuckle at Cantonment Gibson, and the 7th Infantry Regiment commander wrote McClellan that Fort Smith was "yet in the Charge of the Military, to be again occupied by Troops, or otherwise disposed of as the Government may instruct." He explained to the Choctaw agent that Colonel Nicks and Captain Rogers had been placed "in possession of the buildings & a public Flat, and are held responsible for their preservation & to ferry the Military." He believed that "no one, without authority from

[20] McClellan to Barbour, February 16, 1827. *Territory of Arkansas*, XX, 393–94.
[21] McClellan to Arbuckle, February 2, 1827. *Territory of Arkansas*, XX, 395.

the General Government, would have interfered with this arrangement."[22]

Arbuckle's rebuke irritated McClellan, who resented the favored treatment Arbuckle's friend Colonel Nicks received at the expense of what McClellan regarded to be the public interest, especially since Nicks and Rogers had been singularly derelict in protecting and preserving government property at Belle Point. McClellan reflected this resentment in the complaint he submitted to the secretary of war. He said that he did not regard the franchise granted to Folsom an unwarranted favor because the area covered by the privilege was within the Choctaw Nation. Then too, he was distressed that private citizens, operating under a verbal license granted by a personal friend who was also the chief military officer in the region, were privileged to turn public property to their personal benefit. He disclosed that Nicks and Rogers operated a cotton gin in the north blockhouse, and charged also that they had set up a store and tavern in another post building. Since his return to Fort Smith, he had been distressed to observe "a great many Indians, with bottles of spirits, & intoxicated." When questioned as to the source of the strong drink, the tribesmen said that they had obtained it from Nicks' and Rogers' store at Fort Smith. McClellan said that it was startling to learn that the firm of Nicks and Rogers held a federal license to trade with the Indians at Fort Smith. McClellan closed his letter to the secretary of war with a request for a ruling on whether Fort Smith was Choctaw land and under the control of the agent or whether Nicks and Rogers were in charge.[23]

When Arbuckle learned that McClellan had written the secretary of war concerning the state of affairs at Fort Smith,

[22] Arbuckle to McClellan, February 9, 1827. *Territory of Arkansas*, XX, 394.

[23] McClellan to Barbour, February 16, 1827. *Territory of Arkansas*, XX, 393-94.

he wrote Quartermaster General Thomas S. Jesup an explanation of what he claimed was the true situation at Belle Point. Because of the heavy work load placed on his men in hewing the wilderness and constructing Cantonment Gibson, Arbuckle could spare no troops to guard Fort Smith. Consequently, he had placed the post in "care of Nicks & Rogers, who were bound to take charge of the public buildings, & were furnished with a public Ferry-boat, on the condition of their passing the Military free of expense." Then McClellan had been permitted to occupy such of the Fort Smith buildings as the public service and his own convenience required. McClellan had promptly placed "a half breed Choctaw" in possession of Belle Point ferry, and had issued orders prohibiting Nicks and Rogers from handling any traffic except military. Arbuckle assured Jesup that because McClellan's complaints reflected on him he would in a few days order Lieutenant James L. Dawson to Fort Smith "to regulate" the matter of the ferry, and to "make further arrangements for the preservation of the buildings." The fort, Arbuckle argued, would prove "of much importance" if the government were successful in its efforts to prevail on the Indians living in the East to emigrate to the West. If they did, the federal government would be compelled to provide the emigrants with "provisions for some time; & the Storehouses at Fort Smith will be found very conveniently situated for the reception of their supplies."[24]

Nicks and Rogers had friends in high places, as was evidenced by the openness with which they flouted their operations at Fort Smith. The influence of these friends was evidenced, too, by action taken by the War Department. A letter of March 30, 1827, from Commissioner of Indian Affairs Thomas L. McKenney ruled against McClellan as to who

[24] Arbuckle to Jesup, February 26, 1827. *Territory of Arkansas*, XX, 402–403.

had jurisdiction over the ferry at Belle Point. The landing was upon "grounds necessary for military purposes." McClellan would have to yield control of the ferry to Colonel Arbuckle —in this instance to his agents Colonel Nicks and Captain Rogers.[25]

McClellan could not match the power of Arbuckle's friends at Fort Smith. He was concerned over the ease with which Indians could obtain whisky at Belle Point, and so he decided to move the Choctaw agency to Pebble Springs, eighteen miles west of Fort Smith. Even though the administrative center for Choctaw affairs in the West was at Pebble Springs, Fort Smith continued as his supply depot for emigrating Choctaws because of its storage facilities. Corn and other rations, guns, kettles, and traps were stored there. McClellan's blacksmith, who was also a gunsmith, remained at Fort Smith to watch over the weapons and other metal goods and keep them free from rust.[26]

Fort Smith, after its evacuation by the 7th Infantry, served also as headquarters for military survey and roadbuilding crews during the 1820's. It is significant that military planners recognized its strategic location on Belle Point. All primary roads radiated from it, and points of reference for the Southwest were usually stated in such terms as "west of Fort Smith," "south of Fort Smith," "east of Fort Smith."

By means of a series of bills which were enacted between 1825 and 1827, Congress authorized the construction of a system of military roads on the Arkansas frontier, all focusing on Fort Smith. One ran east from Fort Smith to Little Rock; another extended west from Fort Smith to Cantonment Gibson; and a third was to be constructed from Fort Smith to Cantonment Towson. War Department planners

25 McKenney to McClellan, March 30, 1827. *Territory of Arkansas*, XX, 439.
26 McClellan to Porter, September 28, 1828. *Territory of Arkansas*, XX, 753-54.

observed that this federal highway system would improve
United States defenses on the Southwestern frontier, facilitate
communications in that region, encourage settlement and development in western Arkansas, and assist the federal government in relocating Eastern tribes in the Indian country west
of Fort Smith.[27]

Lieutenant James L. Dawson, an experienced military engineer who had served on the Arkansas frontier since 1822,
was selected by Quartermaster General Jesup to supervise
construction of this military road network. Dawson spent
some time in Washington discussing his assignment with General Jesup, and returned to Cantonment Gibson on November
6, 1826. Colonel Arbuckle announced that the Cantonment
Gibson fortifications were in an "advanced state" and that in
a few weeks he could spare Dawson sufficient men to begin
work on the road. Dawson immediately began a survey to set
as direct a route as possible for the Fort Smith–Cantonment
Gibson road. Arbuckle ordered scrapers, shovels, bars, and
other tools, set a detail to making wagons, and collected horse
and ox teams. Congress appropriated seven thousand dollars
to cover the expense of opening the roads from Fort Smith to
Cantonment Gibson and from Fort Smith to Little Rock.
Dawson hoped to use 7th Infantry work details exclusively
on the road from Fort Smith to Cantonment Gibson, thus
entailing only a small outlay from the appropriation to pay
the troops for extra duty. This would save most of the seven
thousand dollars to be used on the Fort Smith–Little Rock
road, most of which would be constructed by civilian contractors. Arbuckle and Dawson planned also to use 7th Infantry work details on some of the road construction immediately east of Belle Point.[28]

[27] Dawson to Jesup, November 16, 1826. *Territory of Arkansas*, XX,
303–305.
[28] Arbuckle to Jones, April 23, 1827. *Territory of Arkansas*, XX,
414, 416, 451–52.

The wagons were ready and the tools delivered in early spring, 1827. Captain Pierce Butler was placed in charge of the 7th Infantry road-building detail, which included Lieutenant John Archer and fifty-five enlisted men; Lieutenant Dawson was chief engineer on the road. During September, Butler's crew completed the road from Fort Smith to Cantonment Gibson. Arbuckle decided to relieve these men—they were exhausted, and "their clothing was worn out"—and select another detachment to work on the road east of Fort Smith.[29]

Lieutenant Dawson advertised in the *Arkansas Gazette* for bids for the road from Fort Smith to Little Rock; these were approved in late 1827. He surveyed the route and supervised construction. He divided the road into divisions of five miles each. Workmen from the 7th Infantry opened only about twenty miles of the road east of Fort Smith, most of the remainder being completed by civilian workers under contract. Some counties on the route took the initiative in order to hasten completion of the road to Little Rock. Crawford County decided not to wait for government assistance, but pushed ahead with the construction of fifteen miles of the road within its jurisdiction.[30]

During late autumn, 1827, Lieutenant Dawson ran his survey from Fort Smith to Cantonment Towson for the military road southwest of Belle Point, and troops from Towson worked from the Red River northeast toward Belle Point through the rough Kiamichi highland country. Dawson used Fort Smith as headquarters for his survey parties and construction groups, as a storage place for tools and equipment, and as a center from which to inspect the various roads radiating from Belle Point.[31]

[29] Jones to Arbuckle, March 6, 1827. Jesup to Dawson, March 8, 1827. Arbuckle to Jones, September 4, 1827. *Territory of Arkansas*, XX, 528.
[30] Dawson to Jesup, August 28, 1827. *Territory of Arkansas*, XX, 519–22.

With the completion of the road system, it appeared unlikely that additional uses would be found for Fort Smith in opening the Southwestern frontier. Indian Agent McClellan preferred to manage Choctaw affairs from the Pebble Springs agency; because of the growth of the settlement at Belle Point, he believed it best to move the Indian emigration supplies closer to his own headquarters.

Fort Smith's rotting palisade walls and deteriorating interior were regarded by certain officials as a menace to the settlement at Belle Point. Several advocated demolishing the works before some drunken settler or Indian set fire to the place. Fort Smith came close to being totally destroyed in 1828, and was spared only because McClellan defied a direct order and wrote the secretary of war for clarification.

Reports reached Governor Izard in April, 1828, that the "Public Buildings at Fort Smith" were "in part so ruinous as to be incapable of being applied to any useful purpose; & that their remaining there is considered as injurious to the health of the neighbouring Inhabitants." Izard wrote McClellan on April 24, directing him to select such parts of the fort "as are yet Inhabitable, or applicable to the Public Services as Stores or Ware Houses, and cause the rest to be demolished." The governor believed that material salvaged from the razed buildings could be sold to cover the cost of demolition.[32]

McClellan hesitated to carry out the governor's order. He was not particularly a defender of the old post or in favor of its preservation. As headquarters for the Nicks-Rogers trading enterprise and tavern, Fort Smith had caused him much inconvenience, especially in extricating drunken Choctaws fired up with Belle Point whisky. Yet the role of destroyer, in which Izard's order placed him, was more than he could accept with-

[31] Cummings to Jones, November 1, 1827. *Territory of Arkansas*, XX, 550.
[32] Izard to McClellan, April 24, 1828. *Territory of Arkansas*, XX, 730.

out additional verification. First, he again inspected the quarters formerly occupied by the garrison, and found the lower logs "nearly all rotten, & . . . in a dry ruinous situation." He agreed with Izard that if the quarters were allowed to remain in their present state, they would be harmful "to the health of the neighbouring Inhabitants."

Then, on August 14, McClellan wrote the secretary of war for clarification of instructions. He made it clear that he was not advocating preserving the post at Belle Point. If additional troops were to be detailed to guard the frontier in the area, the "most Eligible" site would be near the Choctaw agency, eighteen miles west of Fort Smith. He claimed that soldiers "posted at Fort Smith would be isolated and no benefit to the agency or frontier," and recommended that a company of infantry be posted within two or three miles of Pebble Springs to "keep peace between the whites & Indians."[33]

Secretary of War Peter B. Porter studied the question of razing Fort Smith and finally came to agree with Governor Izard. Commissioner of Indian Affairs McKenney wrote that, besides being governor of Arkansas Territory, Izard was also superintendent of Indian affairs for the region and that McClellan was responsible to him. A letter was written directing McClellan to comply with Governor Izard's order to demolish the works at Belle Point.[34]

Slow mail service saved Fort Smith. A chain of circumstances removed McClellan from Governor Izard's supervision and therefore from the obligation to carry out his order to destroy Fort Smith. In 1828, the federal government removed the Choctaw agency from the Arkansas governor's jurisdiction. Temporarily, Choctaw affairs were to be administered

33 McClellan to Porter, August 14, 1828. *Territory of Arkansas*, XX, 729–30.
34 McKenney to McClellan, October 28, 1828. *Territory of Arkansas*, XX, 759.

by the Cherokee agent who had recently moved west of Fort Smith into Lovely's Purchase and who was busily relocating the Western Cherokees from their home in northwestern Arkansas to their new domain. Thus McClellan had to ask for new instructions on the demolition of Fort Smith because the source of his order to destroy had been removed. This took additional time, and meanwhile new uses developed for Fort Smith.

The Western Cherokee Treaty of 1828, providing for the transfer of this branch of the tribe from northwestern Arkansas to the Indian country west of the old Osage boundary, was followed in 1830 by the Treaty of Dancing Rabbit Creek with the Choctaws of Mississippi. By this agreement, the Choctaws ceded their lands in the east and pledged to move to the tribe's Western domain established by the 1820 Treaty of Doak's Stand. There appeared a growing certainty in the War Department, in the face of increased Indian population on Arkansas' western border, that the strategic location of Fort Smith would make it increasingly useful to the federal government. Rather than ordering the destruction of the old fort, the War Department planned to use it as a supply depot for the emigrating Choctaws.

An additional use for Fort Smith developed from a growing problem on the Arkansas frontier—that of the contraband trade, especially in whisky. This trade had been a problem from the earliest times, but it increased drastically after 1828. Cephas Washburn, missionary and teacher among the Western Cherokees, was distressed at this stepped-up "vending of ardent spirits" among the Indians, and undertook to call it to the attention of high government officials. He admitted that it was difficult "to prevent whitemen, who are devoid of principle, from bringing this destructive article into the Indian country & of diffusing it extensively." He had hoped that, with the migration of the Cherokees to their new home in the Indian country, the sale of whisky would be curtailed if not stopped entirely. He noted, however, that the move did not accomplish this result—whisky was more plentiful than before. The Choctaw agent was concerned also as more of his charges became debauched by the steadily increasing supply of liquor sold by Arkansas citizens on the western border.

In 1830, Washburn reported to Superintendent of Indian Affairs McKenney that the traffic seemed to increase each month. Boats constantly ascended the Arkansas River into the Indian country to sell "this pernicious article in great quanties, & merchants established near the line engage in this contraband traffic to a great extent." Washburn knew of five Indians whose deaths within a ten-day period were the result of "intemperate use of whiskey." Sedate Dwight Mission was kept in a constant uproar "by the revels & noise of drunken Indians," one of whom had fallen and broken his leg. To put a stop to this "revelry & noise," Washburn said, he had purchased and poured on the ground all the whisky he could find in the mission community. On one of the barrels, which he held for evidence, was the brand of a merchant from Belle Point.

To control the liquor situation, Washburn had several suggestions. First, there should be "some modification" and strengthening of the laws regulating trade with the Indians. Second, there should be stationed at Fort Smith "an approved & faithful man with the authority of a Boarding Officer, whose duty it should be to board all boats & other vehicles going into the Indian country & to remove from them every gallon of intoxicating liquors, or else [he] should be authorized to prevent their proceeding into the Indian country."

Steps would have to be taken, Washburn continued, to prevent Indians from crossing into Arkansas to purchase whisky. Indian testimony under oath should be considered valid by the courts to convict any white man "vending spirits" to the tribesmen. Washburn urged that no person be issued a license to trade with the Indians "who is not put upon oath that he will neither sell nor give to an Indian a single glass of spirits; & in addition, a most scrutinizing search ought to be made of his Boat, Waggon, or other vehicle, that there could remain no possibility of his introducing the article among Indians."[35]

Secretary of War John H. Eaton made note of Washburn's appeal in a letter to Colonel Arbuckle. He reminded the 7th Infantry commander that, by an act of Congress of May 6, 1822, "entitled an act to regulate trade and intercourse with the Indian Tribes and to preserve peace on the frontier," he was diligently to search all goods entering the Indian country by way of Cantonment Gibson.[36]

Arbuckle responded that Cantonment Gibson's location made it impossible to enforce the law "regulating trade and intercourse with the Indian tribes." This post on the Grand River, he pointed out, was well situated to protect the Western frontier but poorly situated to watch over border traffic, because few boats laden with "Ardent Spirits" penetrated that far up the Arkansas. "The evil cannot be remedied, as respects the Cherokees and other Tribes on the Arkansas River, unless Fort Smith is again occupied by a Military force, and the Officer there in Command has full power to restrain the Indians, and those living with them, as well as our Citizens, from introducing liquor into the Indian Country." He added that it was almost impossible for him to enforce the orders he had received "to cause the laws of the United States, regulating trade and intercourse with Indian Tribes" to be made effective on the Arkansas River unless a military force was sent to Fort Smith. Reports reached him at Cantonment Gibson from

[35] Washburn to McKenney, February 2, 1830. *Territory of Arkansas, 1829–1836* (vol. XXI of *Territorial Papers of the United States*, ed. by Clarence E. Carter), 182–85.

[36] Eaton to Arbuckle, May 17, 1830. National Archives, Office of Indian Affairs, Letters Sent File (Western Cherokees).

Fort Smith that "whiskey is kept and sold to Indians . . . by the
barrel." Moreover, Arbuckle had reason to believe that the
Cherokees and Choctaws were "furnished with whiskey by
almost every Steam-Boat or Boat of any description which
passes up the Arkansas, about Fort Smith."[37]

In 1831, preparations were undertaken to facilitate removal
of the Choctaws from Mississippi to their new home. Commissary General George Gibson ordered Captain John B. Clark
of the 3d United States Infantry to Fort Smith. Clark was to
see that the buildings at the post were repaired, so that Belle
Point could be used as a depot for the provisions the government was obligated to issue the emigrating Indians. He reached
Fort Smith on April 13, and was distressed at what he saw.
"The buildings of the old Fort [are] in a much worse condition than I had anticipated, the floors, doors, and windows, are
destroyed, and logs torn out of the body's of most of the
[barracks], the sills and bottom logs in all are decaying rapidly, and the [buildings] sinking to the ground, the roofs are
falling in on many, and much decayed on all." Clark proposed
to repair some of the buildings, for which Arbuckle was to
furnish a work detail from the 7th Infantry at Cantonment
Gibson. Clark planned to obtain materials to renovate the
buildings by razing the "others that are too much decayed"
to be of further service. The 7th Infantry detachment commanded by Lieutenant Gabriel Rains, reached Fort Smith
from Cantonment Gibson on April 26, 1831. Once again, the
Gibraltar of the Arkansas had a garrison.[38]

[37] Arbuckle to Headquarters, Western Department, May 4, 1830.
Arbuckle to Eaton, June 26, 1830. *Territory of Arkansas*, XXI, 242–43.
[38] Clark to Gibson, April 13, 1831. *Territory of Arkansas*, XXI, 336.

# CHAPTER SEVEN

# The White Lightnin' War

Lieutenant Gabriel Rains' 7th Infantry detachment arrived at Fort Smith on April 26, 1831, and reoccupied the old post on Belle Point. Soldiers went to work at once razing barracks and salvaging logs and planks to repair buildings required to house Choctaw emigration supplies. By the time the first contingent of Indians arrived from Mississippi, Rains hoped to have ready facilities to hold fifteen hundred bushels of corn and meat and salt stores.[1]

Meanwhile, Captain John B. Clark scoured the country for provisions to subsist the emigrating Choctaws. Cattle for slaughter and issue as fresh meat were scarce because the unusually severe winter of 1830–31 had taken heavy toll of Arkansas herds. Clark also found corn scarce on the Arkansas below Fort Smith, but he hoped to secure several thousand bushels from Cherokee farmers. Besides collecting subsistence stores for the major Choctaw emigration depot at Fort Smith, Clark had also the duty of establishing and stocking intermediate supply points at Post of Arkansas and Camp Pope, three miles below Little Rock. Because provisions were slow in reaching Fort Smith, Clark requested that Arbuckle rush a hundred barrels of pork from Cantonment Gibson to Fort Smith as a temporary solution to the ration scarcity.[2]

[1] Rains to Gibson, August 4, 1831. National Archives, Office of Indian Affairs, Letters Received File.
[2] Rains to Gibson, June 5, 1831. National Archives, Office of Indian Affairs, Letters Received File.

Choctaw leaders had assured the federal government that the emigration would begin in the autumn of 1831. In the third week in October, Choctaw emigrants began to assemble for the movement across the Mississippi. Word reached Fort Smith that about seven thousand Indians planned to move at once. More than five hundred would rely on their own resources and accept "commutation of $10 per head, offered by the Government, on their arrival at their new homes"; the others preferred to move under government agents. Some Choctaws crossed the Mississippi at the Helena ferry, but most members of the 1831 migration gathered at Vicksburg, where the government had chartered steamers to carry them to the Post of Arkansas. By the end of the first week of December, two thousand Choctaws had landed at Post of Arkansas. The agent in charge contracted with the master of the rugged river steamer *Reindeer* to transport the Indians on to Little Rock. Low water, however, kept the steamer at its berth, and most members of the first contingent came overland on horseback, in wagons, and afoot to Little Rock by the road across Grand Prairie. Camp Pope received the migrants and provided an interim resting place on their journey to the Indian country.[3]

From Camp Pope the Choctaw emigration trail branched. One fork went southwest to their lands on Red River; the other continued up the Arkansas to Fort Smith. Heavy rains in January brought a rise on the river, and the *Reindeer* set out from Post of Arkansas with a keelboat in tow and transported 1,100 Indians to Camp Pope. It returned at once to shuttle another group upstream. In late January, 1832, the *Reindeer* returned to Camp Pope and then continued upriver toward Fort Smith. Low water at Dardanelle halted the steamer; the Choctaw passengers took keelboats on to Belle Point, arriving there on February 10.[4]

[3] *Arkansas Gazette*, October 19, November 16, and December 14, 21, and 28, 1831.

President Andrew Jackson appointed Major Francis Armstrong "Superintendent of Indian Affairs for the Choctaw Nation West of the Mississippi." Armstrong reached Fort Smith in early February, just ahead of the first Choctaw contingent. He inspected the depot prepared by Lieutenant Rains' detachment, and then pushed on into the Indian country to make "himself acquainted with the situation of the Indians whose interests he had been sent to guard and protect" before he returned to Mississippi by way of Washington to supervise the organization of additional Choctaw emigration parties. During November, Choctaws aboard steamers out of Vicksburg were stricken with cholera. News of the epidemic preceded the emigrants and caused great fear in the settlements along the Arkansas. The citizens at Little Rock were panic-stricken. Hundreds of Choctaws were violently ill for several weeks at a quarantine camp near Rock Roe; of a thousand exposed to the disease, sixteen died. After the epidemic passed, Armstrong organized the Choctaws into traveling bands of about six hundred each and proceeded up the Arkansas.[5]

Armstrong was startled and shocked at the reception the Choctaws received at Belle Point. Many Indians had cash from the sale of improvements on their Mississippi lands or from the commutation payment. Traders met them at the landing and plied them with blankets, baubles, and trinkets, and tavern keepers solicited their patronage with rounds of free drinks. Lieutenant Rains' troops moved the Indians a safe distance from the vendors; but Armstrong knew this was a temporary and futile action, for it was only a matter of time until many of the Indians would be at the mercy of the traders and tavern keepers. Most of the Choctaws drew their supplies and equipment at Fort Smith and moved on west along the Arkansas and Canadian to open the wilderness and establish

[4] Ibid., January 4, 11, 18, 25 and February 1, 1832.
[5] Ibid., March 21, November 14 and 21, 1832.

settlements. But several hundred remained near Belle Point, and became the object of sustained exploitation by the local population. Wishing for a permanent solution, not only to protect the Indians remaining near Belle Point but also because several thousand additional Choctaws were expected soon to clear the Fort Smith emigration depot, Armstrong reported the situation to the secretary of war. He pointed to the 10th Article of the Treaty of Dancing Rabbit Creek, which prohibited introduction of spirits into the Choctaw Nation. Armstrong revealed that citizens of the growing Belle Point community had erected taverns within a hundred yards of the Choctaw line and within two hundred yards of the Fort Smith landing; that they sold spirits directly on the line to the Indians; and that they were opposed to any regulations which restricted "their opperations in the Smallest degree."[6]

While waiting for clarification of his authority in handling the problem of the illicit trade, Armstrong called on Lieutenant Rains for help in protecting the Choctaws from the designing Belle Point traders. Rains was cooperative and energetic, and put his troops on the Choctaw line just east of the old post. The troops turned back Indians attempting to cross into the Belle Point settlement, and restrained traders from going into the Choctaw camps. But Rains had less than a company, the task was too great for so few men, and thirsty Choctaws managed to obtain whisky. When Rains found that his limited manpower could not control the traffic, he decided to attempt to close the Belle Point taverns through court action. He "employed a Choctaw Indian, assisted by two of his soldiers dressed in squaw's or Indian disguise, to approach at night, the store-house of Du Val & Carnes—the disguised

6 Armstrong to Cass, May 1, 1832. *Territory of Arkansas, 1829–1836* (vol. XXI of *Territorial Papers of the United States*, ed. by Clarence E. Carter), 504–505.

soldiers remaining out-side of the store, to listen to the trans-action." Entering the store, the Choctaw said that he needed "some whiskey for a sick Indian, a good man, not addicted to intemperance." The clerk at first refused, but changed his mind and sold the Choctaw a bottle.[7]

Rains swore out a warrant for the clerk's arrest, "alleging that whiskey had been sold" to the Indian, which was testified to by the two soldiers. Crawford County Justice of the Peace Matthew Moore threw the case out of court because evidence was introduced to show that Rains had promised the two soldiers ten dollars "whether he failed in the prosecution or not."[8]

Moore's dismissal did not close the matter. Rains discovered that not all the settlers at Belle Point were frontier renegades. Several of the law-abiding citizens agreed to testify before a federal grand jury convened in July, 1832, at Little Rock to investigate violation of United States laws.

Nearly all the witnesses concurred in stating that "intemperance does exist to an unfortunate extent, among all the Indians that have recently been removed to the west of Arkansas." Citizens living at and near Fort Smith swore that the Indians found means of purchasing large quantities of whisky, and several testified that they knew of one instance when as much as sixty barrels of whisky had been taken into the Indian country. Drunkenness had led to bloodshed. Law-abiding citizens living in the Fort Smith neighborhood were alarmed for their safety. The public buildings at Fort Smith were said to be "in great danger of destruction, by fire, from the number of drunken Indians constantly at that place." The public buildings had been set afire three times, and only the exertions of Lieutenant Rains and his troops had saved them from being reduced to ashes. According to witnesses, there were at Fort

[7] *Arkansas Gazette*, October 10, 1832
[8] *Ibid.*

Smith "six-mercantile establishments, all of which are located within a few paces" of the Choctaw line, and all but one stocked whisky in large quantities. Although searching questions were asked, the members of the grand jury declared that they were unable to obtain sufficient evidence to indict anyone for selling whisky to Indians in the Fort Smith area.[9]

The grand jury did admit that illicit trade existed there, and observed that it was apparent the tavern keepers were well aware of the existence of laws against the illegal trade and employed "every precaution" to avoid detection. Sales and delivery of whisky to Indians were effected in the absence of witnesses, and persons engaged in this business could not "be coerced to give evidence to criminate themselves."[10]

Upon reviewing legislation forbidding the sale of "spirituous liquors" to Indians, the grand jury found that it provided for action by the president, through his officers and agents, only against transactions that took place in Indian Territory and not within the organized jurisdiction of any state or territory. When they examined the laws of Arkansas Territory, the jurors found a statute that read, "If any person within the Territory, except by permission of the Superintendent of Indian Affairs, shall sell, exchange, furnish or give, to any Indian, any spirituous, vinous, or other strong liquor, and shall be convicted thereof, he or she shall forfeit and pay a sum of not less than $30 not more than $100, or shall be imprisoned."[11]

Because of the large number of Indians living west of Arkansas and the fact that more would be moving west, the jurors expressed alarm at the whisky traffic at Belle Point, declaring that it was clearly an evil that should be opposed by the entire community and one that called loudly for reform.

[9] Grand Jury Presentment, July 12, 1832. *Territory of Arkansas*, XXI, 517–19.
[10] *Ibid.*
[11] *Ibid.*

But the jurors were satisfied that there were "two insuperable obstacles to their arresting this great and growing evil." First, there was the difficulty of securing necessary testimony to insure a conviction. Second, a federal grand jury's jurisdiction was limited by acts of Congress to coping with "vending or distributing spirituous liquors among the Indian tribes within the Indian country." Because most of the sales in the Fort Smith area were taking place within Arkansas Territory, it was the responsibility of a grand jury empaneled by the circuit court of Crawford County to investigate these offenses.[12]

The Belle Point tavern keepers were apparently stung by the federal grand jury report, but they were determined to have the last word. For this purpose, they purchased space for an answer in the *Arkansas Gazette*. They branded the grand jury report a gross misrepresentation. Rains was castigated as a meddler, and his investigations and those of other federal officers were called an "inquisition into the conduct of the citizens of this Territory . . . against whom there is not the shadow of a charge."[13]

The Little Rock grand jury investigation and the complaints and protests from Superintendent Armstrong and Indian leaders, who charged that unscrupulous traders and tavern keepers were debasing Choctaws and desecrating tribal honor, received surprisingly prompt attention in Washington. The president and Congress were not particularly concerned with Indian welfare. They were anxious that the Choctaws and other tribes in Mississippi, Alabama, Georgia, and Florida move to their new domains in Indian Territory as quickly as possible. Any circumstance, such as the reports of debauchery at Belle Point, which threatened to discourage removal, was a matter of general concern to the government. In the summer of 1832, Congress adopted legislation aimed at controlling

[12] *Ibid.*
[13] *Arkansas Gazette*, October 10, 1832.

both commercial intercourse and illicit traffic in the Indian country.[14]

Armed with new authority, the War Department directed agents in Indian Territory to "seize the prohibited article, whenever and wherever found" within their agencies. If there was a military post in the area, the agent was to deliver the confiscated liquor to the commanding officer; otherwise, he was to place it beyond the reach of Indians. Agents were to explain to the Indians that this "measure is dictated equally by the regard the Government is bound to pay its own Character and Obligations, and by the interest it feels in the physical and moral welfare of the Red Men; to whom it Sustains a parental relation."[15]

General Order Number 7, drafted by the War Department to assist in the enforcement of the ban on introducing spirituous liquors into the Indian country, directed Colonel Arbuckle to detach a company from the Fort Gibson garrison (Cantonment Gibson had been redesignated Fort Gibson in 1832) and send it to Belle Point to reoccupy Fort Smith. This force, in cooperation with the Indian agents, was to expel intruders from the Indian country and to enforce "the laws prohibiting the introduction of Ardent Spirits among the Indians."[16]

Arbuckle selected Captain John Stuart to command the Fort Smith garrison. Stuart's men reached Belle Point on March 29, 1833, and went to work attempting to check the contraband trade along the Arkansas. After a month of patrolling the approaches to the Choctaw and Cherokee nations, Stuart reported to Secretary of War Lewis Cass that his men had

[14] *United States Statutes at Large*, IV, 564.

[15] Robb to Vashon, August 16, 1832. *Territory of Arkansas*, XXI, 908–909.

[16] Jones to Arbuckle, January 30, 1833. *Territory of Arkansas*, XXI. 909.

been successful in thwarting illicit trade along the river but that whisky runners were introducing their product in "Waggons, Pack horses, &c., along the numerous by roads and Paths which cross the Line into the Indian Country." The land traffic was almost impossible to control, Stuart said, because people living on the western border of Arkansas were "either adventurers from different Parts of the world, whose Purpose it is to make money in any way they can, without regard to Laws or they are such as have been all their Lives moving along in Advance of Civilization and good order." Such persons lacked all regard for the "Law or honesty," and would sell liquor to Indians "whenever and wherever they can find Purchasers."[17]

Stuart observed to the Secretary of War that he had no knowledge of local laws providing for the punishment of contraband runners who vended to Indians within Arkansas Territory. If there were legislation, he doubted that it could be enforced. He said that it was impossible "to get a Legal Decision made against an offender, when Neighbourhood Interests, are involved." For example, there was an Arkansas statute which prohibited the "Sale of Whiskey to Soldiers." Stuart reported that he took advantage of this law and brought charges in five cases against merchants selling spirits to his troops. He was unable to get the local courts to act. He accounted for this by the fact that "the Magistrates are all Elected by the Tag, rag, and bobtail population of the country, and they are for the most part, Ignorant men and feel them selves bound to comply in all cases with the will of the Majority whether that be Law or not."[18]

Stuart said it especially distressed him that saloonkeepers, in full view and within a hundred yards of his quarters, sold whisky to Indians. If he sought to disperse the Choctaws who

[17] Stuart to Cass, May 1, 1833. *Territory of Arkansas*, XXI, 710–12.
[18] *Ibid.*

crossed the line, or if he tried to seize their whisky, the merchants would claim that the Indians worked for them. At the same time, they threatened to sue Stuart "for damages in interfering with the rights and Privileges of the *free* Democratic ... citizens, of the *Sovereign* Territory of Arkansas." Therefore Stuart had made no arrests inside the territorial limits. After the Indians had purchased their whisky, they were in the habit of strapping the kegs to their backs and breaking "into the thick brush and underwood, and cross the Line wherever it may suit their convenience." An "attempt to catch them with the means" he had available would be futile.[19]

The Fort Smith commander pointed out to War Department officials that several Cherokee and Choctaw settlements were near the Arkansas border. The Indians and whites, according to his observation, spoke the same tongue and possessed the same sympathies, and could not be kept separated. Even if he had sufficient men to post a sentinel at hundred-yard intervals from the Missouri line to the Red River, it would still not stop the illicit traffic in liquor.[20]

Stuart considered the Cherokees further advanced in civilization than any other tribe in Indian Territory. Indeed, the captain found them "very little behind the people of Arkansas Territory in that respect" and "Infinately a better and more orderly people" than whites living along the border. At the same time, the Cherokees were almost "as clamorous about their Cival rights, and Indian Privileges," as the South Carolina nullifiers were about the rights of their sovereign state. Many Cherokees had declared in Stuart's presence that it was "their right to have whiskey in their country if they Please."[21]

In June, Stuart's men, ranging from their base at Fort Smith, seized two barrels of whisky. One barrel was taken from John

[19] *Ibid.*
[20] *Ibid.*
[21] *Ibid.*

Davenport, a trader who had attempted to smuggle the spirits upstream aboard a steamboat in a cask marked "cider." Davenport escaped from the boat before Stuart was able to determine that he was the owner. The second barrel was discovered in the Cherokee Nation opposite Fort Smith, lodged in a drift in the Arkansas. Stuart sold the whisky at public auction and turned the proceeds over to the finder.[22]

During the summer of 1833, the Fort Smith commander launched a determined campaign to put a "speedy and full stop to the circulation of Whiskey in the Indian Country." His men seized every drop they found in the Indian nations except that dispensed in the bars aboard river steamers. Amounts taken from individuals ranged from one pint to five gallons. Stuart found the public auctions a nuisance, and believed that it would be best to pour the liquor on the ground as soon as it was seized.[23]

Although Stuart's vigorous actions drastically cut the sale of whisky to Indians in the Fort Smith area, "and the place" had been "restored to something like order," the sale of whisky to soldiers increased. The latter problem had actually become the greater one at Belle Point, and the post was in "a constant state of disorder." While Stuart's company was at Fort Gibson, where whisky was more difficult to obtain, the unit had been rated one of the most orderly at the post, but two months at Fort Smith had made it "about one of the Worst in the Army." Stuart reported to officials in Washington that he had little hope for the men's reformation as long as the post was convenient to the Fort Smith taverns.[24]

On the night of August 27, there was trouble between four of Stuart's soldiers and Jonas Bigelow, a Fort Smith tavern keeper. Bigelow, a friend of John Rogers, kept a combination

[22] Stuart to Cass, June 30, 1833. *Territory of Arkansas*, XXI, 744–45.
[23] *Ibid.*
[24] *Ibid.*

general store and tavern just across the Choctaw line from
Belle Point. He sold liquor to both Indians and soldiers. Stuart's
men had grumbled that Bigelow took advantage of them, and
had warned that they were watching for an opportunity to
obtain redress. That night, Bigelow, his brother, and J. C.
Carter (an employee), retired about nine to the second story
of the tavern. Carter and Bigelow slept on pallets; the brother,
in a hammock. About three in the morning they were "awak-
ened by a tremendous explosion." Scrambling to his feet,
Bigelow saw that a hole had been torn in one of the walls of
the room. He raced to the opening, and "saw four soldiers,
belonging to Capt. Stuart's Company, with the six-pounder,
within ten steps of the door." After an excited conversation,
during which time Bigelow was able to recognize two of the
men, the soldiers wheeled the cannon back to its station at the
post. When Bigelow and Carter examined the building in the
morning, they found "a six pound ball, and between fifteen
and twenty pieces of iron. The ball had entered above the
door, and struck the joist" upon which the merchant slept,
nearly cutting it in two. It then struck a second joist,
glanced, and cleared a shelf, demolishing everything in its
passage. After spending its force, the projectile fell to the
floor, where it had been picked up by Bigelow. He protested
to Captain Stuart, and swore out warrants against the can-
noneers. Stuart gave him little satisfaction, pointing out that
the bad whisky he sold the soldiers had caused them to act as
they had.[25]

In September, 1833, Stuart wrote Secretary of War Cass
that in order to assure stricter enforcement of the nonintercourse laws another company of the 7th should be assigned to
contraband patrol. This unit should be posted in either the

[25] Stuart to Adjutant General, September 5, 1833. National Archives,
War Department, Adjutant General Letters Received File. *Arkansas
Gazette*, September 11, 1833.

Cherokee or the Choctaw nation, several miles west of the Arkansas line. In addition, his command should have at least twenty-five horses, to enable his soldiers to pursue suspected smugglers, and carbines, which would be more useful than muskets in the woods.[26]

Stuart observed that the bootleggers were becoming wiser and that his troops were encountering considerable difficulty in carrying out their duties. The river was simply too wide for his sentinels. Smugglers were in the habit of holding their boats below Belle Point, waiting for a dark, rainy night to slip by. Because of his limited manpower, Stuart found it impossible to post men on the north bank of the Arkansas. Other bootleggers, using wagons, were operating out of Van Buren. They would camp within a short distance of the border and, as soon as the patrols relaxed their vigilance, would slip into the Cherokee Nation, and, by traveling day and night, would outdistance the soldiers.[27]

During the summer, Lieutenant John P. Davis and a detachment of foot soldiers had pursued several smugglers for twenty-five miles on the military road to Fort Gibson but had been unable to overtake them. Stuart told Cass that his spies reported a party of bootleggers with several barrels of whisky was camped on the Arkansas a short distance below Belle Point awaiting an opportunity to slip by the guards.[28]

Stuart also reported that on September 19 the troublesome Bigelow had attempted to smuggle nine or ten barrels of whisky up the river. Finding that he was being watched by a military patrol, Bigelow dropped downstream. Stuart believed that Bigelow, frustrated in his efforts to use the river, would carry his whisky in wagons into the Indian country. He would

[26] Stuart to Cass, September 20, 1833. *Territory of Arkansas*, XXI, 797–98.
[27] *Ibid.*
[28] *Ibid.*

undoubtedly succeed, Stuart explained, "as it is impossible owing to the extremely sickly conditions of the Company to persue and watch him." The Fort Smith commander charged that for several years Bigelow had been

. . . one of the most notorious whiskey smugglers on the frontier. Lieut. Davis has since the last of August lain concealed six or eight nights on the other side of the river with a [detail] in hopes to catch some of these abandoned Villians, but Bigelow is supposed to be connected with nearly all of them, and by his living so near the Garrison (150 yards) and having formed a connection with some of the most abandoned . . . Soldiers, receiving information of every movement that is made.[29]

After almost a year of intensive campaigning against the whisky runners, Stuart and Arbuckle pointed both to successes and to new problems. First of all, since the reoccupation of Fort Smith by Stuart's company, there had been a marked decrease in the whisky trade, which had brought wealth and prosperity to the Belle Point community. The garrison's surveillance on the Arkansas had stopped most of the river traffic carrying liquor to the Creeks, who were settled west of the Cherokees and north of the Choctaws. The Creeks still obtained whisky, but it came to them by circuitous trails flanking the wide-ranging patrols from Fort Smith and Fort Gibson. Arbuckle confirmed that Stuart's vigorous action had nearly stopped the whisky trade by way of the Arkansas and Belle Point, but that the runners had simply changed their methods. He advised the adjutant general that the long border extending from the Missouri to the Red could not possibly be patrolled completely, and that runners found dim trails and slipped across into Indian Territory. Reports reaching Arbuckle indicated that not less than fifty barrels of

[29] *Ibid.*

whisky were within three miles of Fort Gibson, and that it was "productive of great disorder among the Soldiers and frequent quarrels and fights between them and the Indians."[30]

Stuart and Arbuckle said that Van Buren had replaced Belle Point as the frontier contraband center. The whisky runners from Van Buren used Indians in their illicit commerce; the runners became merely the suppliers, and the Indians served as carriers and vendors. Stuart's patrols reported that Cherokees were doing more of their trading at Van Buren. The Indians were better acquainted with the border country, its secret trails, and were more difficult to watch and apprehend than the white traders.[31]

Besides gaining an advantage by changing their import methods, the contraband runners also had law and distance on their side. About all that Arbuckle's officers could do was to harass the traders by watching their movements and by seizing and selling their whisky at public auction. At worst, the traders were inconvenienced, because they often retrieved their goods through agents bidding for them at the auction at the cost of what amounted to only a small fine. Even if contraband runners were captured and their goods seized, it was difficult to prosecute violations of the Indian Territory commercial-intercourse law because of the distance from a competent court and the cost to the United States of instituting suit. Then too, there was the problem of getting witnesses to travel great distances to testify. Partly to remedy the situation, Arbuckle suggested that the secretary of war modify the rules concerning contraband to allow his officers to make seizures and immediately empty the whisky on the ground. The 7th Infantry commander was satisfied that this was the only way

[30] Arbuckle to Jones, January 26, 1834. *Territory of Arkansas*, XXI, 890–91.

[31] Arbuckle to Jones, October 29, 1833. *Territory of Arkansas*, XXI, 811–13.

to relieve the Fort Gibson garrison "from the serious evil attending, the great quanity of Whiskey kept continually on hand by the Cherokees & Indian Countrymen residing in the vicinity."[32]

Another problem Stuart pointed to as responsible for increasing the difficulty of enforcing the Indian Territory commercial-intercourse law was a group of frontier lawyers who were "Continually prowling" the border communities and military posts "for the purpose of producing difficulties between the Civil and Military, and the officers, and the soldiers." As the captain recalled, this problem of interfering frontier lawyers existed long before his contraband campaign. According to his recollections, in 1827 and 1828, while Fort Gibson was within the limits of Arkansas Territory, an officer "could not give a Soldier a Corrective tap with the side of his sword, or any thing else without lying himself subject to prosecution for an Assault and battery." Enlisted men were therefore known to have "grossly insulted Officers" to provoke them to retaliate so that they could bring suit. Stuart said that he knew of instances of lawyers' having paid enlisted men "a considerable sum" to instigate suits in which the lawyers represented the soldiers in court.[33]

Border attorneys increased the enforcement problem by advising traders and river boatmen of their rights. On advice of counsel, masters of steamboats engaged in transporting merchandise into the Indian Territory contended that the laws of the United States guaranteed their privilege to navigate all rivers in the area, and that the military's right to examine goods was limited to those belonging to licensed traders. Recently, a steamer had tied up at Belle Point landing with goods con-

[32] Arbuckle to Jones, January 26, 1834. *Territory of Arkansas*, XXI, 890–91.
[33] Stuart to Jones, September 19, 1833. *Territory of Arkansas*, XXI, 794–96.

signed to a trader in the Cherokee Nation. Information reaching Stuart led him to suspect that whisky was hidden among the stores in one of the holds. To inspect the craft would have required the master to unload part of his cargo; as expected, he objected to any delay, and "spoke of his ability to recover damages" for unwarranted interference. Because the boat's destination was near the Cherokee agency, Stuart sent an armed party aboard. When the vessel was unloaded, his men found no contraband. Stuart was relieved; if he had compelled the boat to lay up and submit to an inspection, he would have been sued. Fearful of damage suits growing out of his enforcement of the nonintercourse laws, he transferred title of his property to a relative, and stood "Stripped, but Strongly nerved between my duty and the Populace."[34]

The growing influence of Arkansas citizens over border affairs also distressed Stuart and interfered with his enforcement campaign at Fort Smith. Through the work of the territorial delegate to Congress, policies were shaped, laws were passed, and rules handed down which ramified to the benefit of border citizens and to the detriment of the military at Fort Smith and of the interests of the Indian nations Stuart was obligated to protect. He said that local people were forever sending petitions and memorials to the Arkansas Territorial Assembly, to the Congress, and to the War Department asking for something. Stuart said that Belle Point citizens wanted him replaced, ostensibly because of his arrogance but really because of his devotion to duty and his interference with their prosperous if illicit traffic. When he read the resolutions listed in the *Arkansas Gazette* for October 23, 1833, as forwarded by the territorial assembly to Congress, Stuart was aghast to find a memorial asking for an appropriation of twenty-five thousand dollars to open a road in western Arkansas paralleling the

[34] Stuart to Case, February 7, 1834. *Territory of Arkansas*, XXI, 896-99.

border. He described this as "so pregnant with fraud and deception . . . that I cannot help but express my astonishment," and said that the road would facilitate the operations of "a Parcel of Whiskey Smugglers, Maurauders, and horse thieves common to the Country." Stuart argued that the road previously opened by the 7th Infantry from Fort Smith through the Choctaw Nation to the vicinity of Fort Towson was "Sufficient for all the necessary traveling in that direction for years to come." The major objection voiced against that road was that troops examined all wagons suspected of transporting whisky.[35]

Stuart was disturbed also by another set of petitions and memorials emanating from the border communities and concerning a proposition to expand the military works at Fort Smith. Stuart claimed that John Rogers, the Belle Point trader and tavern keeper, was having petitions circulated to persuade the War Department to expand the garrison at Fort Smith to six companies or to remove Stuart's company. Stuart's informants said that Rogers had employed three men to obtain petition signatures and paid them a set fee for each signature they obtained, including those of children and of persons no longer living. The purported grounds for calling in additional troops was that Indians were "committing depredations upon the Property of the Whites." Stuart characterized this charge as false.[36] He said:

> The Indians of this Country are . . . Perfectly quiet, and are on the most perfect terms of friendship with the whites, and have never manifested the least appearance of having any feelings to the Contrary, and according to my opinion the

[35] Stuart to Cass, November 10, 1833. *Territory of Arkansas*, XXI, 845–46. *Arkansas Gazette*, October 23, 1833. Cantonment Towson had been relocated and designated a fort by the War Department in 1831.
[36] Stuart to Cass, October 21, 1833. *Territory of Arkansas*, XXI, 803–805. Stuart to Adjutant General, October 10, 1833. In *ibid.*, 799–80.

Cherokees are a more orderly and respectable people, than three fourths of their White neighbours of the Arkansas Territory, and if Troops are ever Stationed in this Territory, for the avowed purpose of giving protection of the White inhabitants against the neighbouring Indians, difficulties and contentions will at once arrise between the two parties. The depraved portion of the Whites, feeling themselves Protected by the Military will commence their Lawless outrages on the Indians, by Killing and Stealing their property and often molesting their person.[37]

Stuart believed that the best way to preserve peace on the frontier was to maintain the status quo. Each party was to be made to understand that "their future quietude, and happiness, will alone depend upon their . . . conduct towards each other, and that both will be alike, protected by the Military."[38] He charged that the entire scheme had been launched "by a parcel of Stump Speakers, who have Seized upon that as a Hobby to forward their Electioneering Interest." The real reason for the call for troops was that the "money paid to them ought to be expended among the people of the Territory in place of among the damned Indians." The truth was, Stuart claimed,

Pecuniary interest, and not fear of Indians, is the Sole Cause of Wanting a large body of Troops at this place; Captain Rogers wishes to Sell his land; and others wish to Sell Corn &c., and I think that when individuals will go so far as to use Legislative Means, to defraud the Government, that, it is full time for every Officer of the Government knowing to the fact, or having good reasons to believe such a state of things to exist, to lose no time in imparting the Same to the Proper authority.[39]

It was natural, Stuart said, for Rogers to be the prime mover

[37] *Ibid.*
[38] *Ibid.*
[39] *Ibid.*

in this scheme to expand Fort Smith. His 640 acres adjacent to the post had a price tag of thirty thousand dollars. Stuart was satisfied that Rogers' land was not worth more than two dollars an acre. He described Rogers' tract as "generally poor and unfit for Cultivation," while "the most valuable Timber has been cut off it, for the erection and use of Fort Smith, during its first Occupancy by the Troops, and the Subsequent use of Several Mercantile Establishments on the point." If the government actually needed Rogers' land for military purposes, Stuart could excuse his machinations, but the captain hoped that the government would "never find it necessary to Purchase his land at any price." To reinforce his view, Stuart observed that there were other sites in the "neighbourhood that can be occupied free of cost, which bid fair to be more healthy, and which are Infinitely better Calculated for Military purposes, than this is." He said that the latest reports indicated that Rogers had obtained and forwarded to the Arkansas Territorial Assembly petitions with the signatures of five hundred persons.[40]

Stuart had another reason to be suspicious of the move to have Fort Smith expanded. On July 14, 1832, Congress had authorized the appointment of three commissioners to adjust difficulties among the emigrating Indians. President Jackson named former Governor Montfort Stokes of North Carolina, Reverend J. F. Schermerhorn of New York, and Judge Henry Ellsworth of Connecticut as members of this group, known as the Stokes Commission. The commissioners spent many months on the frontier. Among their recommendations was one proposing Fort Smith as the proper location for the principal military post on the Arkansas. Their view was that the 7th Infantry should return to Belle Point and that Fort Gibson should be abandoned or at best be garrisoned by one company. In February, 1834, Governor Stokes told Arbuckle confiden-

[40] *Ibid.*

tially that this was contrary to his opinion but that the other members had pushed it. Later, in Arbuckle's presence, Ellsworth confirmed this and said that during his recent trip to Washington he had recommended to the War Department that Fort Gibson be abandoned and Fort Smith be expanded.[41]

Even more significant was news that Ellsworth had purchased a site near Fort Smith, where he was having a sawmill and gristmill erected. It was rumored also that Schermerhorn was interested in the mill. Arbuckle was informed that Ellsworth had purchased additional land on the Arkansas River twenty miles below Fort Smith, and it was expected that this property would increase in value by the return of the 7th Infantry to Belle Point.[42]

Arbuckle suspected that business interests had swayed Ellsworth's and Schermerhorn's better judgment in causing them to suggest the removal of the Fort Gibson garrison to Belle Point. Moreover, other reports detrimental to the character of Ellsworth and Schermerhorn reached him, charging that they were engaged in speculation and had misapplied public funds. Arbuckle called on Stokes and Colonel Samuel C. Stambaugh, commission secretary, to determine if these reports were "well or ill founded." They corroborated all that the colonel had heard, and added some additional information and urged that the public interest required that the commission as organized be disbanded as soon as the period expired for which the commissioners were appointed.[43]

Arbuckle was opposed to moving from Fort Gibson. He reported his findings on Ellsworth's and Schermerhorn's frontier investment activities to the secretary of war. Captain Stuart continued his campaign to thwart Rogers' scheme to expand Fort Smith. His regular letters to the War Depart-

[41] Arbuckle to Jones, February 10, 1834. *Territory of Arkansas*, XXI, 901–904.
[42] *Ibid.*                              [43] *Ibid.*

ment pointed out that if a permanent work were established
at Fort Smith or within the geographic limits of Arkansas, it
would be impossible for a military command to exist unless
the territorial jurisdiction could be removed for a distance of
two or three miles from the post. The only other recourse
would be to confine the soldiers to their base; if this were
done, half of them would die during the summer. He favored
a remote location in Indian Territory, where the soldiers
would be separated from the "Whiskey dealers" who exer-
cised so much influence in Crawford County.[44]

While the contest raged locally and in Washington over
whether to abandon Fort Gibson and move the 7th Infantry
to Fort Smith and expand the post into a permanent installation, Stuart continued to agitate for authority to move his
contraband-control detachment to a better location. He
claimed that the problem of suppressing the whisky trade
among the Indians had actually increased. Experience gained
during the previous year had given "additional facility to the
Whiskey Smugglers in forwarding their lawless & clandestine
purpose."[45]

The unit's being stationed on the border at Belle Point
merely afforded "additional security to the Smuggler," as it
allowed them to keep tab on the troops' movements. Stuart
observed that whenever a patrol moved out, the bootleggers
held back; as soon as the soldiers returned, they sallied forth.
If the post were removed a short distance into the Choctaw or
Cherokee nations, his scouts could be dispatched "without the
Knowledge of the Smugglers." Roadblocks could be established to intercept them, and within a short time the whisky
trade would be so hazardous that the smugglers would search
for other ways to make a living.

[44] Stuart to Cass, June 30, 1833. *Territory of Arkansas*, XXI, 744–45.
[45] Stuart to Cass, February 7, 1834. *Territory of Arkansas*, XXI,
896–99.

Then too, the health of Stuart's men was bad. Since reoc-cupation of the post at Belle Point, eight privates and the assistant surgeon had died. The captain believed that there were two sites on the Arkansas within ten miles of Fort Smith which would be better locations for a contraband-control post. Swallow Rock, ten miles above Belle Point on the Choc-taw side of the river, where "the land back from it is high and dry with a proper proportion of Timber, and Prairie, and has every appearance of being healthy," was his first choice. Swal-low Rock was "just as much a key to the passage of the River" as Fort Smith, and was located where "the troops would be out of the reach of the Corrupt Whites and would be every way as well calculated to prevent or stop the use of ardent spirits in the different Indian Nations." Another strategic check point was on the Cherokee side of the river two miles below Swallow Rock near the mouth of Skin Creek.[46]

Major Armstrong, the Choctaw agent, seconded Stuart's recommendation of moving the troops to Swallow Rock, for he wanted a force closer to the Choctaw settlements. He be-lieved that patrols from this location could better protect the Choctaw towns from threatened raids by the plains tribes, and that a station here would more effectively curtail the whisky trade being carried on from Belle Point and other Arkansas communities. Armstrong pointed out that bootleggers caught deep in the Choctaw Nation would be "definitely under the control of the military," and could be dealt with in summary fashion not possible at Fort Smith because of the interference of local citizens.[47]

Colonel Arbuckle, not impressed by the Swallow Rock site, opposed moving Stuart's contraband-control detachment

[46] *Ibid.* Stuart to Jones, September 19, 1833. In *ibid.*, 794–96.
[47] Armstrong to Commissioner of Indian Affairs, October 16, 1833. National Archives Western Department, Headquarters of the Army Letters Received File.

there, saying that it was "inaccessible to our Citizens: as the Poteau River would have to be crossed, which is swimming for several months of each year. . . ." Moreover, he believed that a military station at Swallow Rock "could not prevent the sale of liquor at Fort Smith to the Indians in *large* quantities, or its introduction by Land into the Choctaw or Cherokee Nations."[48]

On May 10, 1834, despite Arbuckle's objections, the adjutant general wrote Captain Stuart that it had been "determined to remove the troops from Fort Smith" and to use them to establish a post at Swallow Rock. As soon as practicable, Stuart was to select a suitable site, transfer his effective force there, and begin erecting quarters. The new post was to be designated Fort Coffee in honor of the late General John Coffee. Adjutant General Jones said, "It is not contemplated to make any thing more than . . . a Comfortable Covering for the Officers and men, to be attended with as little expense as possible in the Construction." Stuart evacuated Fort Smith in June and marched his troops to Swallow Rock, where they began building the new post. He followed his instructions— "build with as little expense as practicable consisting with the object intended, the health & comfort of his command, and to give a neat and Military Appearance. The logs should be sided, and the whole whitewashed when completed."[49]

The struggle continued over the question of whether to abandon Fort Gibson and expand the Belle Point works into a permanent military station. For four years the old post moldered unattended after Stuart's men marched through the sagging palisade gate. Then, in 1838, the Rogers campaign bore fruit.

[48] Arbuckle to Jones, October 29, 1833. *Territory of Arkansas*, XXI, 811–12.

[49] Stuart to Jones, June 7, 1836. *Territory of Arkansas*, XXI, 1227–28. *Arkansas Gazette*, July 1, 1834. Jones to Stuart, May 10, 1834. *Territory of Arkansas*, Vol. XXI, 937–39.

# CHAPTER EIGHT

## The Belle Point Phoenix

Fᴏʀᴛ Sᴍɪᴛʜ was like the legendary phoenix—with one essential difference. The phoenix accomplished its fabled regeneration through its own efforts; Fort Smith had some help from John Rogers, Arkansas politicians, and the Congress. Rogers gained control of a substantial amount of public land abutting the old post on Belle Point, and regularly pointed to the need for protection from the Indian menace and petitioned for the reactivation of Fort Smith. Arkansas Territory leaders took up the cause. At first, their campaign seemed ambivalent—in the early 1820's, they had urged moving the Belle Point garrison to a new post on the Grand or Verdigris. The important point was that Arkansas desired a military post on its western border, which, in 1824, was expected to be established at the mouth of the Grand. A year later, the Choctaw boundary treaty changed the situation, and the military post—Cantonment Gibson—intended as a bastion on the Arkansas border, was eighty miles west in the heart of what had become the Cherokee Nation. Arkansas leaders wanted the post returned to the territory's western border as established by the 1825 treaty. After a sustained campaign in Congress and the War Department, this was finally accomplished in 1838.

The genesis of Arkansas' campaign for the restoration of the Belle Point post, which dated back to 1825, took on a formal and calculated aspect in 1834. Sparked by Rogers' petition drive, the Territorial Assembly prepared a memorial on the subject of western border defenses, which Territorial Delegate Ambrose H. Sevier introduced into Congress on January 13, 1834. The request that the 7th Infantry be moved from Fort Gibson to Fort Smith was referred to the House Committee on Military Affairs. The committee report observed that a garrison at Fort Gibson, in the midst of an Indian country eighty miles west of the nearest Arkansas settlements, could offer no protection for Arkansas. The members, agreeing that it was "bad policy to have an armed force stationed so remote from the frontier, and in the midst of an Indian country," recommended moving the Fort Gibson garrison to the western border of Arkansas, where it would assure the citizens more effective protection and "bring troops nearer to the point from which [they] draw their subsistence and support." Congressman Robert D. Johnson of Missouri introduced a bill "to provide more effectually for the defense of the Arkansas frontier." The bill was promptly tabled.[1]

The Fort Smith advocates had a strong champion in Colonel Arbuckle. For some curious reason, possibly his friendship for Rogers, Arbuckle favored reoccupying Fort Smith. Seven years after establishing Fort Gibson, he advised the War Department that it would be wise to throw up "a strong work at Fort Smith or in that vicinity" as a depot to store arms and ammunition, to be distributed to the Arkansas militia if warfare should break out on the border. Arbuckle stressed that the Belle Point site was preferable to all others in the region. He said that whether an enlarged post was erected on Choctaw land or on property owned by Captain Rogers, two additional sections of public land east or southeast of the boundary should be reserved from sale by the General Land

[1] *House Journal*, 23 Cong., 1 Sess., 197. Report of the House Committee on Military Affairs re Frontier Posts, 23 Cong., 1 Sess., February 10, 1834. *Territory of Arkansas, 1829–1836* (vol. XXI of *Territorial Papers of the United States*, ed. by Clarence E. Carter), 899–900. *Arkansas Gazette*, March 18, 1834.

Office to provide the garrison with firewood and timber. He urged that a *"strong work"* at Fort Smith would "give security to the Frontier of Arkansas Territory," but continued that his long experience in the region had convinced him that Fort Gibson should also be maintained because it was the best site from which to restrain the tribes from acts of hostility against one another or from launching attacks on the United States. But, Arbuckle warned, if the tribes resolved their differences and directed their energies to a war against the settlers, a "strong work" at Belle Point, with its magazines well stocked with arms and ammunition, would add to the security of Arkansas Territory.[2]

For several years Captain John Stuart had been a lone voice of protest against the campaign to restore Fort Smith. With obsessive dedication, he had sought to discredit Rogers and to thwart his Belle Point development scheme. As commander of the contraband detail, Stuart had personally observed the callousness of certain merchants and tavern keepers in the growing Belle Point community. He had pointed to the deadly effect of their traffic on his troops and the Indians and had urged the government to authorize him to relocate the Indians and his troops sufficiently west of Fort Smith to remove them from the contaminating influence of border traders until the War Department allowed him to move the contraband-control company ten miles up the Arkansas to Swallow Rock, where he established Fort Coffee.[3]

Stuart searchingly questioned War Department officials on the issue of restoring and enlarging Fort Smith. He asked why the government should pay Rogers forty dollars an acre for poor, denuded land, expose troops to taverns and loose women, and contribute to the moral deterioration of his men when the

[2] Arbuckle to Adjutant General, July 29, 1832. Arbuckle to Macomb, June 30, 1833. *Territory of Arkansas*, XXI, 523–25, 737.
[3] Stuart to Jones, June 7, 1834. *Territory of Arkansas*, XXI, 1227–28.

War Department could find much better military sites farther west which could be occupied "free of cost" in a better environment for troops. He charged that "pecuniary interest, and not fear of Indians, is the Sole Cause of Wanting a large body of Troops" at Belle Point.[4]

Stuart submitted detailed reports to the War Department on the Belle Point environment and its effect on the health and well-being of the troops. In searching through the early Fort Smith records, he found that in 1823 about fifty men of the 7th Infantry had died. During the first months of reoccupation of the Belle Point works by his own company, eight enlisted men and the assistant surgeon had died. In the same period, thirteen citizens in the adjoining community had also died. He argued that Fort Smith should not be occupied because Belle Point was an unhealthful spot. Stuart blamed the Poteau for most of the illness and death at Fort Smith, explaining that high water in the Arkansas backed up this tributary for twenty miles. When this occurred in the summer, the water became stagnant and was covered with "a Green or Yellow Scum, and emits at times a very offensive Effluvia." He warned that if, in view of the facts, the 7th Infantry Regiment were returned to Fort Smith, "extreme Sickness and destruction of the Troops by death, will inevitably follow."[5]

Stuart's evaluation of Belle Point was confirmed by Charles B. Welch, an assistant surgeon who came out from Washington to prepare for Surgeon General Joseph Lovell a study of the "Medical topography . . . climate, the prevailing complaints, their probable causes, and all other facts" pertaining to Fort Smith. Welch's report described the terrain and flora, and focused on the Poteau. He wrote that the river was a

[4] Stuart to Cass, October 21, 1833. *Territory of Arkansas*, XXI, 803–805.
[5] Stuart to Cass, February 7, 1834. *Territory of Arkansas*, XXI, 896–99.

still, sluggish stream, meandering through a level and swampy valley, abounding in sleeping lakes and stagnant bayous; the current is scarcely ever preceptible ... in consequence of the floods in the Arkansas—the water is completely stagnant—covered with a singular kind of aquatic vegetable, giving the appearance of a floating island to the whole river—and from which there arises a most noisom effluvium.

He said that across the Arkansas from the fort was an alluvial bottom, sloping northward to a distance of five miles and paralleling the river for eight or ten miles. At certain seasons this bottom was inundated; when the river fell, it left "stagnant waters that are only carried off by evaporation"—another source of illness. The weather at Belle Point also came in for study. Welch noted that the cold winters and hot summers, with an atmosphere containing a "surcharge with humidity," were damaging to health. In general, the climate was "extremely fickle and variable." From his study of the Fort Smith records, Welch found that the most frequent complaints among the troops had been "bilious remittent and intermittent fevers of every grade and type," along with the "whole class of cachectic complaints: pneumonia, pleurites, and the other phlegmasia of the respiratory organs. Diarrhea, chronic enteritis, and the rest of the phlegmasia of the alimentary canal and its accessory organs felled many troops." Welch was certain that the Surgeon General, after studying his description of the Fort Smith area, would agree that the region was "unfavorable to health." In conclusion, Welch wrote that after careful investigation, he believed that Fort Smith was "intrinsically unhealthy and will continue to be . . . and the interests of the Government would be enhanced by abandoning plans to reoccupy it."[6]

[6] Welch to Lovell, February 28, 1834. *Territory of Arkansas*, XXI, 916–18.

While Rogers' partisans, on the one hand, and Stuart's, on the other, struggled to promote or defeat Fort Smith's reactivation and expansion, the issue was caught up in a broad plan of frontier defense. In December, 1834, John Dougherty, Indian agent at Fort Leavenworth, presented to the War Department a scheme to provide greater security for the border settlements, including a line of military stations extending from the Missouri to the Red. Independent of Dougherty's plan but eventually incorporated into it was a recommendation offered the next month by Colonel Henry Dodge, commander of the First Dragoons, that the War Department authorize construction of a military road connecting Forts Leavenworth and Gibson to facilitate the movement of Dodge's regiment. Missouri citizens found Dougherty's plan attractive because it would provide that level of military defense required on their western frontier, and they called it to the attention of the United States Senate in the form of a memorial.[7]

In February, 1836, Missouri Senator Thomas Hart Benton acknowledged the prospects of the Dougherty plan and asked Secretary of War Lewis Cass to use it as a basis for preparing a comprehensive scheme for protecting the Western frontier settlements against Indian raids and other security threats. Cass submitted his recommendations to the Senate Committee on Military Affairs on February 19, saying that the time had "arrived when a systematic plan for the protection of our frontiers, ought to be devised and adopted." Heretofore, he noted, posts had been "established upon our extensive inland boundary" as circumstances required without regard to a master plan. Until this time, it had been impossible to draw a line dividing the land belonging to the Indians from that open to settlement by whites. Cass continued that posts had been selected with reference to their geographical advantages and

[7] *American State Papers*, V, *Military Affairs*, 730.

"to the moral effect they were calculated to have upon the Indians." Changes in policy had caused the military frontier in the West to advance and then recede. He said that the abandonment of a post excited the Indians, and had occasionally been followed by serious difficulties. The Indians could not comprehend the motives behind abandonment, and attributed such measures "to a sense of our weakness or to a fear of them." Cass urged that a post established in Indian country should never be abandoned except in extraordinary circumstances. If moved at all, a fort should be pushed westward.

Since the removal program began, 31,348 Indians had been moved from east of the Mississippi River. Another 62,181 could be expected to emigrate to the area between the Mississippi and the Rockies, thus increasing the Indian population there to more than 244,000. Cass said that although many of these Indians lived a long distance beyond the frontier, "all of them are roaming in their habits, and the nature of the country, as well as the general possession of horses, enables them to extend their war excursions to great distances."

The Secretary of War reminded the Senate that the government had promised the emigrant tribes protection in their new Western homes. The War Department would be unable to honor this guarantee unless it adopted "vigorous measures" and established a "system of defence adequate to any exigency that may arise." Cass warned that when the Indian removal project was completed, there would be an "immense body of Indians . . . placed upon the borders of our settlements." As the population of Indian Territory increased, friction would develop, both among the tribes and between the Indians and the white settlers. To counteract this discord, Cass strongly advocated the "distribution along the frontier of a sufficient military force," with such arrangements for its employment as circumstances warranted.

Cass' purpose was to establish a line of posts along the Indian frontier. The garrisons would be able to intercept war parties attempting to slip across the line and raid settlements and also to protect Indian communities from unscrupulous frontier whites. Roads would link these forts and afford a means of effecting "a speedy concentration of troops" at danger points. The Secretary suggested that the military road should begin on the Red River near Fort Towson, pass west of the Arkansas and Missouri borders, and reach the Mississippi somewhere between the mouths of the Des Moines and the St. Peters rivers. Fortified posts should be established at strategic points along the military road. Such an undertaking would afford a high degree of protection to the frontier at a moderate cost to the taxpayer. According to the latest estimates prepared by army engineers, the military road would be "upwards of 800 miles" long. After the route had been surveyed, it would be necessary to fell trees in timbered areas to give the road its proper width; in marshy places, the road would be "cause-way'd." Smaller streams were to be bridged where there were no fords. Preliminary reports indicated to the Secretary that "a great deal of the Country, over which the road will pass, [is] so favorable, that scarcely any work will be done upon it. It will be seen from this description that such a mode of construction is contemplated as will be economical and at the same time sufficient for the object."

The projected military posts were to be "similar in their character" to stockaded forts already on the frontier. A strong striking force of dragoons would be stationed at the forts at the ends of the roads and at the immediate post. The rest of the posts would be occupied by infantry.

Cass informed the Senate that until a thorough reconnaissance was made, the War Department had no way of "determining the number of posts" which ought to be occupied between the Mississippi and the Red rivers. If Forts Snelling, Leavenworth, and Towson were kept, not more than four or five others would be necessary. The department's object would be to establish the new posts "at proper geographical points where the supplies may be most easily furnished, and sufficiently near to the Indian settlements, to produce a proper effect upon them, and also at such distances from one another that the necessary communications may be preserved with facility."

After the forts had been laid out, experience might demonstrate that it would be advisable for the government to erect blockhouses at intermediate points, such as supply depots and ferries. These temporary works could be constructed by the troops. If the War Department's plan were to succeed, the infantry units stationed at the forts would have to be highly mobile and ready to take the field on a moment's notice. Part of the work contemplated could be carried out by the troops, the extent depending upon their health and their other duties.

According to estimates prepared by Quartermaster General Thomas S. Jesup, the entire project, "including the construction of the road, and the establishment of the posts," might be completed for $100,000. The figure was "very uncertain, because there is little precise information on the subject" in the hands of the War Department. Colonel Dodge had stated that the military road could be constructed "at a very little expense." Even if the cost of the project should exceed $100,000, Cass believed that it was sufficiently important to justify its adoption. The Secretary was "satisfied that no other plan can be devised, which will afford adequate protection to the frontiers, and not involve far greater expenditures than this."[8]

Bills making provision for Cass' frontier defense plan were introduced into both the House and Senate in March. Members of both houses reported that they had received memorials from the Arkansas Territorial Assembly asking that Fort

[8] Cass to Benton, February 19, 1836. National Archives, Records of the General Land Office, Fort Smith, AMR File.

Gibson be abandoned and a new garrison post erected on Arkansas soil.[9] On May 14, an appropriation of $332,000 was made to the account of the Quartermaster's Department, part of the sum being earmarked for the removal of Fort Gibson to an eligible site near the western boundary of Arkansas.[10] Events moved swiftly. On July 2, Congress enacted a bill providing for the surveying and opening of a military road, as Cass had recommended, to begin on the west bank of the Mississippi at some point between the mouths of the St. Peters and the Des Moines rivers, pass west of Arkansas and Missouri, and terminate on Red River. All military posts west of the projected road were to be removed to it. The sum of $100,000 was made available for the survey and construction of this communication link.[11]

On July 16, 1836, Secretary of War Cass named Colonel Stephen W. Kearny and Captains Thomas F. Smith and Nathan Boone as commissioners to survey the road and select the sites for the posts. In November, the commissioners went to work, with the special instructions that the new posts were to be located on navigable streams and that Fort Gibson was to be relocated on the Arkansas River near the western boundary of Arkansas.[12]

A month later, Kearny's commission was on the Arkansas, visiting Fort Gibson, Fort Coffee, and old Fort Smith among other places. The commission filed its report from Columbus, Arkansas, on December 11. In it Kearny and his army colleagues concluded that Fort Gibson was too important to be abandoned, and said that it was "*the key to the country around it.*" Moreover, the government, in removing the Indians from the East, had pledged "its faith to protect them from each

[9] *American State Papers*, VI, *Military Affairs*, 366–67.
[10] *United States Statutes at Large*, V, 30.
[11] *Ibid.*, 67.
[12] *House Document No. 278*, 25 Cong., 2 Sess., 9.

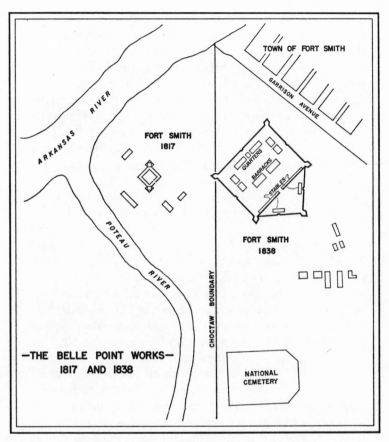

THE BELLE POINT WORKS, 1817 AND 1838.

other, and from the wild Indians of the Prairies." The commissioners recommended that new barracks be erected near
the site of Fort Gibson. It was their opinion that "the presence
of a military force near Fort Gibson is indispensable . . . [for]
the preservation of peace amongst the Indians themselves."
The report concluded with the statement: "We are of the
opinion . . . that [Fort Coffee] combines, more advantages for
a Mily. Post, than any other points we have seen or heard of,"
and that therefore it, rather than Fort Smith, should be made
the permanent military post near the Arkansas border.[13]

The Kearny report aroused protest in Arkansas. In June,
1836, Arkansas was admitted to the Union. As a state, its influence and power substantially increased over what it could
muster as a territory. The people of the new state still resented
the thwarting of their scheme of 1824, to extend their western
boundary to a line from the mouth of the Grand River due
south to the Red. This prize was snatched from them in 1825
when the Choctaw Boundary Treaty set the western limits of
Arkansas at a point a hundred paces east of Fort Smith. Arkansas expected reparations, and the *sine qua non* was an income-
producing federal establishment on its western border.

While the Kearny commission continued its military survey, Arkansas politicians labored to prevent a War Department decision on the Arkansas River post location and to build
a strong case for Belle Point. Petitions bearing the signatures
of border residents and urging reactivation of Fort Smith
reached Congress with increasing regularity. Delegations from
western Arkansas traveled to Washington to appeal to those
persons who would have a role in the decision. When it became apparent that Fort Smith had a bad name in Washington,
owing to Captain John Stuart's scathing reports on debauch-

[13] Commissioners to Secretary of War, December 11, 1836, *ibid.*, viii.
National Archives, Records of the General Land Office, Fort Smith,
AMR File.

ery and degradation in the Belle Point community, Arkansas promoters sought to clean up the Fort Smith image. Congressmen and War Department officials were informed that at one time Belle Point had been an evil place. Arkansas spokesmen admitted that Captain Stuart's charges of community depravity were justified, but said that the situation had improved. Fort Smith advocates pointed out that no less authority on Western defense needs than Colonel Mathew Arbuckle was of the opinion that Fort Smith "must again be occupied by a considerable force."[14]

John Rogers carried on an aggressive private campaign to promote selection of Fort Smith by the War Department as the principal post on the Arkansas. During 1837, he advertised in the *Arkansas Gazette* and in several Eastern newspapers plans to convert 160 acres of his Belle Point holdings into town lots. The first sale was to take place in May, 1838. He wrote letters to Kearny commission members, Congressmen, and War Department officials expressing his gratification that Fort Smith had been "spoken of among many others as a suitable site for the erection of the Contemplated New Garrison." Rogers revealed that he would be willing to sell any of his land in the area in question to the government at a fair and reasonable price, and would welcome "the proposals of any authorized Agent appointed to make a purchase." Although he planned to plat a "town immediately at this point," he wished to give the government first call on the available land as a site for the fort. He was willing to hold in abeyance his plan to divide his land into lots if the government would give him some indication of interest. If War Department officials believed his price too high, he would submit to an impartial appraisal.[15]

[14] Rogers to Fulton, October 13, 1837. National Archives, Records of the General Land Office, Fort Smith, AMR File.

[15] Rogers to Commissioners, September, 1837. National Archives, War Department, Quartermaster General, Letters Received File.

One of Rogers' letters to Arkansas Senator William S. Fulton, posted on October 13, 1837, apparently set in motion those events which culminated in the War Department's selecting Belle Point for its Arkansas River post. Senator Fulton confronted Secretary of War Joel Poinsett with Rogers' letter. Poinsett agreed that if the frontier survey commissioners would recommend the reoccupation of Fort Smith, Rogers' proposal would be "duly considered."[16] This marked the first break in the War Department's resolve to exclude Fort Smith from consideration. The Arkansas congressional delegation stepped up its pressure on Poinsett. Letters from Arkansas constituents, memorials, and personal calls on Poinsett by Arkansas Representative Archibald Yell and Senators Ambrose H. Sevier and Fulton amounted to calculated harassment. The harried Secretary of War admitted that he had followed the Kearny commission recommendation and had directed that the permanent post be erected at Swallow Rock on the Fort Coffee location, but that, in view of the overpowering Arkansas remonstrance, he had suspended the order. Further, to placate Arkansas interests, he had directed "an examination to be made of a site within the State of Arkansas in order to place the fort in a situation which would be agreeable to the people of that country and conformable to the implied intention of Congress."[17]

On February 7, 1838, the Senate was induced by Senators Fulton and Sevier to adopt a resolution calling on Secretary Poinsett "to report whether a site for a new fort had been selected on the western border of Arkansas and the land contracted for and if not, why not." This resolution was adopted against the advice of leading military thinkers. Expressing

[16] Poinsett to Fulton, December 19, 1837. National Archives, Records of the General Land Office, Fort Smith, AMR File.

[17] Poinsett to Yell, October 16, 1837. National Archives, War Department. Adjutant General's Office, Letters Sent File.

Fort Smith during the Indian Council of 1865.

Whipple expedition in the field—typical equipment and livestock provided by
the Fort Smith Quartermaster. From a sketch by H. B. Mollhausen, 1853.

*From the Whipple Collection*
*Courtesy of the Oklahoma Historical Society*

Whipple expedition in the field—indicating equipment and livestock provided by the Fort Smith Quartermaster. From a sketch by H. B. Mollhausen, 1853.

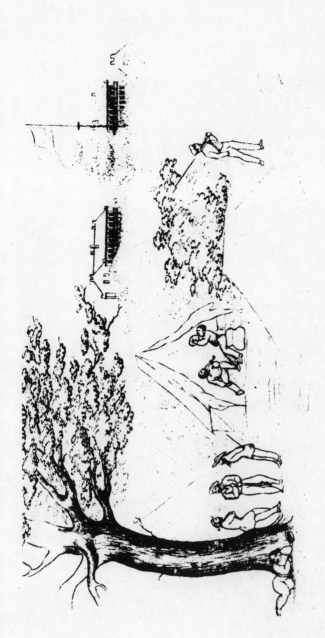

"Camp Wilson with glimpse of Fort Smith in background," from an original drawing by H. B. Mollhausen, July, 1853.

Courtesy of the University of Oklahoma Library

City and garrison of Fort Smith, Arkansas, in 1871.

Officers' Quarters A, Fort Smith, Arkansas, 1865–70.

*Courtesy of the University of Oklahoma Library*

Artist's conception of Fort Smith on the eve of the Civil War.

Pen drawing of old commissary building, Fort Smith, 1917. From a drawing by R. H. Mohler.

their opposition, army officers "contended that there was not the slightest military reason for a fort in or near Arkansas."[18]

Army officers familiar with the purposes and problems of frontier garrisons argued that the post should be at least twenty miles west of the Arkansas border. There it would be well beyond the "reach of the vendors of whisky who were among those urging the location of garrisons in the states."[19]

The Arkansas delegation, however, knew what they wanted, and continued to press for the prompt establishment of a permanent fort on the Arkansas. On April 4, Congress passed a joint resolution authorizing "the Secretary of War to purchase a site for a fort at or near the western boundary of Arkansas." This was in direct contradiction to the established military policy of constantly pushing the army posts west with the advancing frontier.[20]

In light of this development, Secretary Poinsett called on Major Trueman Cross, acting quartermaster general, to report on the sites under consideration on the Arkansas. Cross submitted his findings on April 9. He observed that military principles dictated that, because of its advanced position, Fort Gibson should be retained. Fort Coffee had been designed for the "more immediate protection of the border settlements of Arkansas." Cross believed that Fort Coffee, because it was only ten miles west of the Choctaw-Arkansas line, fulfilled this purpose. But, he cautioned, the people of Arkansas who lived along the border did not share the opinion of the military, and were anxious to have the new post erected nearer than Fort Coffee. Cross accordingly recommended the "site of Old Fort Smith . . . as the most eligible position." Fort

[18] *American State Papers*, VII, *Military Affairs*, 905. Henry P. Beers. *The Western Military Frontier, 1815–1846*, 128.

[19] Grant Foreman. *Advancing the Frontier*, 52.

[20] Joint Resolution of April 4, 1838. National Archives, Records of the General Land Office, Fort Smith, AMR File.

Coffee should be abandoned and its garrison given a new assignment.[21]

Rogers, keeping abreast of developments in the capital, appeared in Washington at the opportune time. Poinsett authorized Cross to negotiate with Rogers for the purchase of land required for a military reservation at Fort Smith. Cross and Rogers reached an agreement on April 12. For fifteen thousand dollars, Rogers agreed to convey to the United States "clear of all liens or encumbrances 296 acres of land adjoining the public reservation at Fort Smith."[22]

When engineers surveyed the land which Rogers had agreed to convey to the government, they found that the tract contained 306 acres. By June 17, the survey had been completed, the title searched, and a bill of sale drawn. Two weeks later, the United States attorney for the District of Arkansas examined the documents, found them in order, and certified his approval of the transaction.[23]

Major Cross named Captain Charles W. Thomas, on duty at Buffalo, New York, in the assistant quartermaster's office, to head the Fort Smith project. His decision was influenced by the fact that Thomas had spent several years at Fort Gibson and could be expected to be familiar with the area and its people. On April 10, 1838, Cross directed Thomas to prepare himself for frontier duty at Belle Point "for the purpose of erecting barracks." Before starting west, Thomas was to submit "an Estimate of the probable expense of the work." In preparing the estimate, he was to take into account War De-

[21] Cross to Poinsett, April 9, 1838. National Archives, Records of the General Land Office, Fort Smith, AMR File.

[22] Deed, Rogers to United States, April 12, 1838. National Archives, Records of General Land Office, Fort Smith, AMR File. Rogers to Cross, April 14, 1838. National Archives, War Department, Quartermaster General, Letters Received File.

[23] Deed of Trust, Rogers to United States, June 17, 1838. National Archives, Records of the General Land Office, Fort Smith, AMR File.

partment plans to abandon Fort Coffee. The Swallow Rock garrison could be expected to "afford *important aid* in the construction of the new work." Cross ventured that stone could be obtained "at a convenient distance" and that, unless the cost of quarrying was too great, the new fort should be constructed of stone instead of brick.[24]

Thomas expressed to Cross his regret that pressure groups had dictated the choice of Fort Smith for the permanent post on the Arkansas. It was his recollection that when old Fort Smith had been manned by the army, large numbers of men were stricken during the annual "sickly season." But "possibly with good, roomy, & well ventilated quarters, it may prove a better site . . . [than] it is now thought to be by the military."[25]

In discussing his assignment, Thomas advised Cross that until he reached Belle Point and studied its resources he would be unable to decide whether brick or stone would be the most economical building material for the new post. He noted that the cost of quarrying and hauling stone would have to be taken into consideration. Thomas was doubtful that he would find much good building timber on the "school section" near the post site; his experience on the frontier had demonstrated that settlers considered "timber common property" and cut it wherever it was "most convenient." He thought that construction lumber could be obtained from pine forests along the Poteau or from mills on the Arkansas. Moreover, he hoped that the sum allocated for constructing the new post would include funds for purchase of a steam mill, which, in his opinion, would soon pay for itself.[26]

In Washington on May 24, Cross handed Thomas his orders. He was to erect

[24] Cross to Thomas, April 10, 1838. National Archives, War Department, Quartermaster General, Letters Sent File.
[25] Thomas to Cross, April 20, 1838. National Archives, War Department, Quartermaster General, Letters Received File.
[26] *Ibid.*

works of defence [to] consist of a stone wall about twelve feet high, and from two to three feet thick enclosing an area of six hundred feet by four hundred feet, with a block house bastion, two stories high at each angle. The Barracks & quarters will not for the present exceed the extent required for the accommodation of four companies, two of which will probably be Dragoons, requiring stabling for their horses. It is desirable, that the work should be commenced as early as practicable & prosecuted with energy. Your arrangements will therefore be made accordingly. *Important aid in the way of labour may be relied upon from the Troops*, should the army be increased at the present session. Otherwise it would hardly be practicable to obtain *more than* the company now stationed at Fort Coffee.[27]

Thomas was authorized to employ

Mechanics . . . at fixed rates of wages, with a ration to be adjusted by you, and inasmuch as the public will incur considerable expense in transporting them to the West, they should be bound in a reasonable penalty to serve for at least one year, after they arrive, at the rate of wages agreed upon. The right of discharging them at any time being reserved by the United States.

In addition, for the sake of economy, he was directed to purchase from Eastern suppliers a steam saw mill, hardware, and building materials; prices were substantially higher at New Orleans, the customary supply source for Southwestern posts.[28]

Thomas attempted to recruit workers in New York and Boston, but tradesmen refused to sign up unless they were promised what the captain considered to be excessive wages.

[27] Cross to Thomas, May 24, 1830. National Archives, War Department, Quartermaster General, Letters Sent File.
[28] *Ibid.*

He pushed on to Bangor, Maine, where he believed that he "could get good mechanics" at a moderate wage. At Bangor, he found thirty-nine tradesmen and sixteen laborers willing to accompany him to the Arkansas. Skilled mechanics contracted to work for $1.50 a day; laborers, for fifteen dollars a month.[29]

On the way west with his Maine workmen, Thomas received the construction plans for the new post. Lieutenant Colonel Joseph G. Totten and Sylvanus Thayer had designed the new Fort Smith. The construction plans called for a five-sided defensive wall, with a stone blockhouse at each intersection point.

Thomas made stops at various cities to purchase equipment and material. At Pittsburgh, he ordered from McClung and Wade a steam engine to power the sawmill; at Cincinnati, he purchased tools, materials, and provisions for the workmen. Thomas' party took passage out of Pittsburgh on the steamer *Dayton*. Low water on the Arkansas halted the boat at Lewisburg, and the men walked the remaining hundred miles to Belle Point, arriving there in late July, 1838.[30]

Part of the land Rogers sold the government had been occupied by the Belle Point settlement. Tavern keepers, traders, and other citizens had abandoned their log buildings and were already erecting a new settlement on the rim of the military reservation. Thomas found the old Belle Point settlement area "covered with filth and rubbish of years"; the buildings, except for one house, matched, in ruin and desolation, the dilapidated structures of old Fort Smith looming to the west. Thomas put his men to work clearing the grounds and repairing the buildings, both at the Belle Point settlement and at old Fort Smith. He planned to use the settlement buildings for

[29] Thomas' Report of Operations at Fort Smith, 1838 to October, 1840. National Archives, War Department, Quartermaster General, Letters Received File.
[30] *Ibid.*

housing his workers, and the old military structures for storing supplies, equipment, and building materials.[31]

Once shelter and storage had been provided, Thomas sent his men in crews on various assignments—surveying the perimeter of the post and staking sites for barracks and other buildings in the interior. Nearby, his master brickmaker found clay suitable for firing into brick; after some experimenting, he hit upon a mix for a strong construction brick. A crew went to work setting up a brickyard. They erected a shed capable of holding two hundred thousand bricks, made brick molds, and dug two wells to provide water for mixing. During the winter, six men cut and stacked a supply of wood to fire the kiln.

Thomas sent a crew to open a quarry on Belle Point. The workmen exposed the rock layers and cut pieces of building stone for foundations and walls. The masons needed lime for mortar, the closest known supply of which was near Fort Gibson. Colonel Cross directed Lieutenant John P. Davis, stationed at Fort Gibson, to supply Thomas with five hundred barrels of lime, the first shipment of which arrived at Belle Point via keelboat in January, 1839.[32]

The basic materials for the new post were to be stone, brick, and lumber. Thomas had found a means of supplying stone and brick. Lumber was the problem. The timber near the post had been either cut by Major William Bradford's Rifle Regiment company in constructing the original Fort Smith or poached by squatters. Because Fort Coffee was to be abandoned, Thomas suggested to Colonel Cross that the buildings be razed and the materials rafted down the Arkansas to Fort Smith. This would be a relatively easy task, he explained, because most of the timber was cottonwood. The heavy oak beams could either be mixed with the cottonwood on rafts or be sent down the Arkansas in boats. The War Department

[31] *Ibid.*    [32] *Ibid.* Cross had been promoted to colonel on July 7, 1838.

failed to provide a prompt answer, and so Thomas had to look elsewhere for construction lumber. In November, he sent a foreman and twelve men up the Poteau to the pine woods, where they found saw logs in good supply and of high quality. Lumberjacks felled the trees, and ox teams snaked the logs to the river. The Poteau's shifting bottom, ubiquitous sand bars, and the rapid rise and fall of the river level—all made it difficult to move logs. One timber raft the woodcutters sent to Belle Point contained eight hundred saw logs. Near the mouth of the Poteau, carpenters built a boom to swing into the river, trap the log rafts, and draw the logs to the mill ramp. In November, 1838, the Arkansas was navigable and the keelboat *United States* reached Fort Smith with the steam engine and sawmill machinery. By March, 1839, the mill was producing timbers and planks.[33]

While his workmen gathered materials, Thomas collected work animals. To supplement the four horses that Captain William G. Belknap of Fort Coffee had transferred to him, Thomas purchased enough additional horses from local traders to make up ten teams. He also obtained twelve "fine unbroke mules," which he hoped would soon be made gentle and ready for work. For heavy hauling, Thomas preferred oxen, of which the Fort Coffee garrison gave him four poor specimens and of which he purchased twenty more from settlers. The workmen constructed a horse barn with a loft for storing hay, threw up sheds for oxen, built a corral, and cleaned out an old well for watering the stock. With winter approaching, Thomas purchased two hundred tons of prairie hay from John Rogers for $2,400.[34]

[33] Thomas to Stanton, May 5, 1839. Thomas to Jones, November 8, 1838. National Archives, War Department, Quartermaster General, Letters Received File.

[34] Thomas' Report of Operations at Fort Smith, 1838 to October, 1840, National Archives, War Department, Quartermaster General, Letters Received File.

During the winter of 1838–39, the men from Bangor missed few days in making preparations to begin construction in the spring. Besides making brick, quarrying stone, and cutting and sawing logs into construction lumber, they repaired wagons which Thomas had borrowed from Fort Gibson, built a blacksmith and carpenter shop, and made stone carts, tools, and harness. Thomas had high praise for his crew of hardy, versatile New England workmen. He reported to Cross that when he informed them that they must make all preparations, including the production of basic building material, before they could demonstrate their crafts and skills, they went to their tasks with a will: "saw logs procured—charcoal burned—stone coal dug" and material of every description collected,

> before the mechanics could be employed at their respective trades. At all this work soldiers could have been employed, equally well, if not to more advantage than the men . . . [he] had hired. Fortunately . . . [his] mechanics were all good men, from the north, where during the winter they are generally employed at various kinds of labour different from their trades . . . and . . . [he] found them useful at almost any kind of work.[35]

Spring came early to Belle Point in 1839, and Thomas' men launched construction of the new Fort Smith in late February. Crews with teams and drags graded for the foundation wall and outlined the perimeter of the fort. Masons laid the first stones in the foundation for bastion number one, and by May 5 they had completed six hundred feet of wall to a height of four feet. On the same date, walls for bastion number one were six feet off the ground, and bastion number two had risen to four feet.[36]

[35] *Ibid.*

[36] Thomas to Stanton, May 5, 1839. National Archives, War Department, Quartermaster General, Letters Received File.

The New England tradesmen were hard-working, capable, and thoroughly reliable, and Thomas dreaded the approach of July 1, when their contracts were due to expire. Most of them planned to return to their homes, and so Thomas would have to rely upon local labor. This made the future of construction at Belle Point highly uncertain. Throughout the winter, he had attempted, through advertisements in Arkansas papers, to add to his labor force by hiring locally, but no applicants had come forward. After talking with settlers, Thomas was convinced that local men would not *"engage to work,* unless at extravagant wages," and then only on a short-term basis. He claimed that they would leave whenever another employer offered a few cents more per day or when they believed that they were being worked too hard, and that he could obtain satisfactory additional labor only by recruiting east of the Mississippi, which he was reluctant to do because of the expense in transporting the workers to Belle Point. Therefore, the most immediate need was to get the most from the Bangor men and have the post well on the way to completion before their contracts expired on July 1. To save them for skilled work, he was eager to have troops detailed for such labor as grading, cutting stone in the quarry, working at the brick plant and sawmill, and carrying materials to the craftsmen.[37]

Thomas' original orders had authorized him to draw on military commanders in the region for troops to assist in constructing the new Fort Smith, and he had been assured the services of the Fort Coffee garrison because the Swallow Rock post was to be abandoned. His extended efforts to obtain troops as construction workers to expedite building of the new Fort Smith reflected shame on the officer corps, exposed the pettiness and deception of certain junior officers, and demonstrated a complete disregard of orders from the

[37] Thomas to Stanton, April 18, 1839. National Archives, War Department, Quartermaster General, Letters Received File.

secretary of war. Of more direct importance, Thomas' attempt to obtain workers from the military units actually slowed construction on the new post, inasmuch as it became a contest for rank and privilege, sapping his energy and patience and wasting precious time.

Soon after Thomas and the New England workers reached Belle Point, troops arrived to garrison old Fort Smith. Captain Benjamin L. E. Bonneville's Company F of the 7th Infantry, ordered there by Colonel Mathew Arbuckle at Fort Gibson, was to prepare storage at old Fort Smith to receive government property removed from Fort Coffee by Captain Stuart's company.[38]

Rather than helping Thomas, these troops added to his problems. Bonneville, Surgeon William Hammond, and Lieutenant Forbes Britton demanded quarters "befitting their rank." Thomas declared that the buildings purchased from Rogers were for "exclusive use of the workmen" and that he did not intend to turn out any of his men for the "purpose of furnishing quarters for the company of Infantry now at this Post." As an inducement to attract the Maine workmen to this wild frontier, he had promised them comfortable shelter and he would not evict a single worker for any officer.[39]

Britton and Bonneville cited paragraph 44 of Quartermaster's Regulations and demanded that Thomas "distribute 'the public quarters' according to Regulations." When Thomas again refused, both Bonneville and Britton complained to officials in the War Department. Britton charged that his men were "in Tents & Major Thomas' laborers are in comfortable houses," and that he had taken two rooms with a settler several miles from the post. "This is most inconvenient but the

[38] Arbuckle to Adjutant General, July 24, 1838. National Archives, War Department, Second Military Department, Western Division, Order Book.

[39] Thomas to Britton, October 11, 1838. National Archives, War Department, Quartermaster General, Letters Received File.

weather precluded his family living in tents." Britton believed
that if anyone had to go into tents, it should be the workmen
—not the military, to whom army regulations assured quarters.
He charged that skilled mechanics were getting from $1.50
to five dollars per day whereas enlisted men received from
seven dollars to fifteen dollars a month.[40]

Surgeon Hammond, unhappy with the building Thomas
had assigned him, complained to the surgeon general that his
post hospital consisted of "two very indifferent apartments,
one as a Dispensary, the other as kitchen and Ward Room
cojointly with one door and one window"—with neither sash
nor glass in the latter. He charged that Thomas had ignored
his request for chairs, table, and other furnishings. While he
was in this humble state, "the common day labourer is both
comfortably fixed in quarters and other accomodations."
Hammond claimed that his quarters were even worse: an "old
dilapidated building, in half falling condition—with five windows, with neither glass, sash or shutters, and from present
appearances there is no prospect of having its condition improved before the cold and rainy season sits in." He had no
kitchen, but was compelled to prepare his meals, rain or shine,
on "an old stack of a chimney without covering." According
to Hammond, Thomas ignored his plea for better accommodations and treated him with "neglect and indifference." Worse,
Thomas seemed to be doing everything in his power "to
render the day labourer Comfortable." Hammond reported
that the other officers fared worse than he—they had to live
in tents. He was especially annoyed by the fact that Thomas
was quartered in a building "with five or six comfortable
rooms, with a good Kitchen and other out Buildings," and had
a family which had no claim on the army staying with him.
Hammond closed his denunciation with the charge that

[40] Britton to Cross, October 11, 1838. National Archives, War Department, Quartermaster General, Letters Received File.

neither he nor the hospital had been furnished firewood in accordance with army regulations—on several occasions, a few chips and "immense logs, twenty and thirty feet long" had been dragged to the door.[41]

When Thomas asked Bonneville for a detail of troops to push construction on the new post, Bonneville retaliated for Thomas' refusal of quarters by flatly rejecting the request. He declared that he did not believe that he or his men were "to assist in the erection of the New Works," and that their only construction duty was to prepare storage at old Fort Smith to receive the military goods coming by keelboats from Fort Coffee. Thereupon, Thomas offered to lend some of his workmen to rush the storage repair, so that Company F men would be available sooner to help Thomas on the new post; Bonneville rejected Thomas' offer.

Thomas then went to Fort Coffee to confer with Captain William G. Belknap, who commanded Companies B and H of the 3d Infantry, which had just returned from constructing a military road to the Red River. Thomas handed Belknap a copy of Cross' order directing local commanders to detail men to work on the new fort. Like Bonneville, Belknap refused to comply because, he claimed, he was transferring his command to old Fort Smith, where his men would be occupied erecting cabins for their own use; subsequently, he planned to put his two companies back on road-building duty.[42]

Thomas informed Cross of Bonneville's and Belknap's refusal to comply with the order to detail troops for construction work on the new post. Cross notified the adjutant general

41 Hammond to Lawson, October 2, 1838. National Archives, War Department, Quartermaster General, Letters Received File.

42 Thomas to Cross, August 2, 1838. Thomas' Report of Operations at Fort Smith, 1838 to October, 1840. National Archives, War Department, Quartermaster General, Letters Received File.

of the impasse. On September 11, the adjutant general sent an order to Bonneville directing him to see that work on the new post was expedited and to assign to Thomas all soldiers who could be spared from their military duties.[43]

Bonneville's company, along with the other companies of the 7th Infantry, was soon assigned to Florida for duty against the Seminoles. Belknap's two companies became the garrison for old Fort Smith, where they arrived on October 24, 1838, after marching from Fort Coffee. Bonneville's company was preparing to move but still occupied the old station, and so Belknap put his men to work erecting cabins half a mile southeast of the new post site. The 3d Infantry camp was named Cantonment Belknap. Thomas showed Belknap a copy of the recent order concerning assignment of troops to the new works, and asked for between forty and a hundred men as soon as the cabins were completed.[44]

On three different occasions Belknap refused to assign Thomas troops for construction duty. Each time Thomas informed the War Department. Officials in Washington were apparently puzzled by the reluctance of company commanders to obey direct orders. Various excuses were found by the War Department staff. In early April, 1838, the adjutant general noted that Belknap's two companies had only sixty-four men and needed 113 recruits to bring the units to full strength. The adjutant general was satisfied that the personnel shortage explained Belknap's failure to detail men to work on the new post. Eighty recruits were known to be at New York awaiting transportation to Belle Point via New Orleans. The adjutant general was sure that as soon as the new men arrived, Belknap

[43] Jones to Bonneville, September 11, 1838. National Archives, War Department Quartermaster General, Letters Sent File.
[44] Thomas' Report of Operations at Fort Smith, 1838 to October, 1840. Thomas to Stanton, January 11, 1839. Belknap to Adjutant General, November 4, 1838. National Archives, War Department, Quartermaster General, Letters Received File.

would "apply a considerable portion of his force upon the new work as directed."[45]

The adjutant general notified Belknap that the Quartermaster's Department was upset by his failure to cooperate. To avoid future misunderstandings on this point, Belknap must realize that the work at Fort Smith had high priority and was of considerable interest to the secretary of war. The adjutant general expected that as soon as the recruits reached Cantonment Belknap, Belknap would have "nearly all the old soldiers" report to Major Thomas. "Nor is it doubted [that] you and your command will essentially assist the Quarter Master's Department in building up the fort."[46]

Even after the recruits arrived, Belknap refused to cooperate with Thomas but sent both the recruits and older troops off on road-building assignments. Thomas appealed to Arbuckle at Fort Gibson for assistance in forcing Belknap to observe the adjutant general's order. Arbuckle told Thomas that he presumed Belknap, on his return to Fort Smith, would comply with the War Department's directive. But, he added, Belknap's soldiers were entitled to a brief rest to recuperate from their arduous duty on the military road. If in the future Belknap declined to honor Thomas' call for fatigue parties, Thomas was immediately to notify Arbuckle.[47]

Added to Thomas' problem of recruiting an adequate labor force was the uncertainty of his own status. It was rumored about Belle Point that Belknap was actively engaged in a cabal to discredit Thomas and to bring about his removal as superintendent of construction at Fort Smith. Thomas confronted

45 Adjutant General to Stanton, April 11, 1839. National Archives, War Department, Quartermaster General, Letters Sent File.
46 Adjutant General to Belknap, April 11, 1839. National Archives, War Department, Quartermaster General, Letters Sent File.
47 Thomas' Report of Operations at Fort Smith, 1838 to October, 1840. National Archives, War Department, Quartermaster General, Letters Received File.

Belknap, who admitted that he was weary of Thomas' requests for troops to work on the new post. Belknap regarded these incessant demands as harassment, and had written the War Department that he considered Thomas incompetent and that he should be replaced as head of the Fort Smith project.[48]

On July 1, 1839, most of the Bangor workmen drew their pay and boarded the first steamer bound downriver. Only the masons and the brickmaker signed for another year. Although Thomas was certain that much additional work could have been accomplished if he had been assigned troops for common labor, the first year's construction on the new post was impressive. The foundation for the entire outer wall had been completed; the wall had been raised to a height of four feet; foundations for four of the five bastions had been laid and raised to a level with the walls. The quarry, brickyard, and sawmill were in good working order and turning out materials as required by the builders. Thomas believed that with a crew of artisans similar to the Bangor men, backed up by a company of troops for common labor, the post could be completed very soon. Ironically, soon after the New England workmen left, Belknap sent Thomas a party of twenty men to labor on the new works at Fort Smith.[49]

[48] Belknap to Stanton, June 17, 1839. National Archives, War Department, Quartermaster General, Letters Received File.

[49] Thomas' Report of Operations at Fort Smith, 1838 to October, 1840. National Archives, War Department, Quartermaster General, Letters Received File.

# CHAPTER NINE

# The Citizens' War at Fort Smith

Belle Point was the busiest place on the Southwestern frontier during the late 1830's. Besides being the site for construction of one of the most elaborate military installations in the United States, it had a new town named Fort Smith, platted by John Rogers in 1838, growing up on the eastern edge of the military reservation. The new town's antecedent had existed as a crude log settlement on the eastern edge of the Choctaw line. Abandoned when Rogers sold the land they occupied to the United States for the construction of a new post on the Arkansas, the old log buildings were the ones restored and used to house the construction crew Major Charles W. Thomas brought out from Bangor, Maine, in the summer of 1838.

Easily overlooked in the hustle and push of developing a new town and constructing permanent military works on the Arkansas was the fact that old Fort Smith was reoccupied in 1838 to satisfy the demands of the border settlements. The first Belle Point garrison was Captain Benjamin L. E. Bonneville's 7th Infantry company, soon ordered to Florida for duty against the Seminoles. Captain William G. Belknap and two companies of the 3d Infantry had relieved Bonneville at old Fort Smith. Near Belle Point, Belknap's men built a new log post which was called Cantonment Belknap. The troops carried out those routine post duties familiar to earlier Fort Smith garrisons, including patrolling the frontier, watching for contraband entering the Indian country, enforcing commercial-intercourse laws, building roads, escorting reconnaissance expeditions, and belatedly laboring on the new works at Belle Point.

The new Fort Smith also played an important role in frontier affairs long before it was completed. Its principal function was to serve as the supply depot for Southwestern posts. At regular intervals, a temporary log storehouse erected near the Arkansas River landing and the storehouse at old Fort Smith received from river steamers barrels, baskets, and boxes of flour, pork, beans, salt, candles, and other subsistence items, as well as tents, blankets, tools, and weapons and ammunition. Long before the new Fort Smith was completed, its function as a supply depot had been well established. Besides furnishing rations, equipment, and supplies to Fort Gibson, Fort Wayne, Fort Towson, Camp Washita, Camp Holmes, Camp Mason, and Cantonment Belknap, the post provisioned and equipped military units on their way to Western duty.

Actual construction on the new Fort Smith began in the spring of 1839. Thomas' New England workmen arrived at Belle Point in July of the preceding year, but it required several months to lay out the new installation, collect tools and equipment, install the sawmill, open the quarry and brickyard, and gather materials to get the large construction project under way. The new post was finally ready for occupancy in 1846. Its cost amounted to nearly $300,000. The slow construction and relatively high cost of the post were due to several things.

A principal cause was antipathy in the War Department, from the general staff down to junior officers in the field. The officer corps had, from the beginning, opposed selection of Fort Smith as the site for a permanent post. The choice had been made over the protests of several military commissions sent into the field to select the most strategic and effective sites for the new Western defense system developed by Lewis Cass. Military men regarded selection of the Belle Point site as a sacrifice of public interest and sound military judgment to placate selfish local interests who desired an income-producing federal installation in their midst to offset a generally poor economic region. Officers resented the power of the Arkansas congressional delegation to force the secretary of war to bow to its will. All this accounts in part for the apathy of company commanders toward providing work details to hasten completion of the post, and perhaps explains how Belknap, Bonneville, and others could defy, with apparent impunity, direct orders from the secretary of war to provide troops to work on the new installation.

Illustrative of scorn for the Fort Smith installation among military officers was Colonel Zachary Taylor's viewpoint. In May, 1841, he was ordered from Baton Rouge to Fort Gibson to take command of the Second Military Department, which included all the territory south of 37 degrees from the Mississippi River to the Mexico and Texas frontiers.[1] Taylor replaced Colonel Mathew Arbuckle, who was sent to Baton Rouge. Because there was a lack of comfortable quarters for his family at Fort Gibson, Taylor established his headquarters at Cantonment Belknap. He was there for three years, and was thus close to the Fort Smith situation and could observe it at first hand. Taylor informed Colonel Ethan A. Hitchcock that he was shocked at what he regarded useless expenditure of public funds at Fort Smith. The new station was being constructed on such a grand scale that when finished it would "serve as a lasting monument to the folly of those who planned [it], as well as him who executed [it]." He advised Hitchcock: "The plan . . . is highly objectionable. . . . A more use-

[1] Adjutant General to Taylor, May 1, 1841. National Archives, War Department, Adjutant General's Office, Letters Sent File.

less expenditure of money & labor was never made by this or any other people. . . . The sooner it is arrested the better."[2]

Major Thomas, the military engineer in charge of construction at Fort Smith with the title of project superintendent, shared the view that Belle Point was a poor choice for so extensive an installation. But he respected his orders and worked at his task with energy and surprising dedication. And he found causes other than the opposition and apathy of the officers corps for the slowness in completing the new works. A chief source of difficulty for him and a contributing cause of slow progress was the uncertainty of congressional appropriations. Apparently, there were men in Congress who shared the officers' viewpoint concerning the folly of constructing an elaborate stone-and-brick establishment at Fort Smith, with the result that it was difficult to obtain appropriations to carry it forward.

Through the years, a rather typical pattern developed. With each session, Congress passed the army appropriation bill containing no funds for Fort Smith. The quartermaster general carefully watched this bill. When it appeared that no money would be appropriated for continuing the work at Belle Point, he would direct the project superintendent to discharge artisans and other workmen and close the project. The workmen scattered to their homes. Because of the shortage of skilled labor on the frontier, many were put under contract and brought out from Cincinnati, Louisville, and other cities east of the Mississippi to Fort Smith on chartered steamers. The superintendent was embarrassed by having to liquidate contracts, discharge men, and prepare to shut down the project. Then, in the last days of the congressional session, the Arkansas delegation would put on an intensive drive and, in some

[2] Taylor to Hitchcock, November 3, 1841. Taylor Papers, Library of Congress.

years, obtain an amendment to the army appropriation bill providing for additional funds to continue the work at Fort Smith. Belatedly directed by the quartermaster general to resume work, the superintendent would scurry about to collect another labor force. This undulating process not only delayed completion but also was wasteful and added to the total cost.

Another problem that absorbed much of the superintendent's time and slowed construction was that of placating the workers. Only the first work crew imported to Belle Point— the Bangor, Maine, workmen—endured the inconvenience and hardship of frontier living without protest. Later crews from Cincinnati and other Eastern cities were chronic complainers. Eastern workers were generally accustomed to better conditions and greater comfort than they received on this frontier. They complained about the shelter, food, and the length of the working day. In most instances, the labor contracts negotiated by army recruiters provided for the "ten hour day system." Superintendent Thomas and his successor believed that the workmen should make up for time lost during the winter months, when they could work only about eight and a half hours a day, and so during the longer days of spring and summer he often worked the men for eleven and a half hours. Many of the men objected to this practice, walked off the job, and returned to their homes in protest. The food provided by the army was also a source of complaint. At first, Thomas fed his men on the job, the meals being prepared by crew cooks, but complaints became so widespread that, on January 1, 1840, he contracted with a family in the new town of Fort Smith to board the men for thirty cents a day.[3]

In addition to the shortage of labor, especially of craftsmen, there was great competition on the frontier for artisans be-

[3] Thomas to Jesup, January 12, 1840. National Archives, War Department, Quartermaster General, Letters Received File.

cause several government projects were under way in the area. A principal competitor of Fort Smith in the labor market was the new United States arsenal being constructed at Little Rock, which drew on both local workers and outside artisans and further inflated labor costs at Belle Point.[4]

Thomas blamed the greed and interference of local people as an additional cause of slow progress on the new works at Fort Smith. Everyone seemed to be in the market to profit from the construction. Thomas had to buy hay and grain from local suppliers to feed the large number of horse, mule, and ox teams used on the project. He also bought wood to fire the kilns and steam engine, stone coal for the blacksmith's shop forge, certain construction materials, and fresh meat, eggs, and vegetables for the workmen's mess. Thomas was excruciatingly conscientious in spending public funds, and negotiated very exacting contracts. Thus he became highly unpopular with Belle Point citizens in, as he put it, frustrating efforts of "speculators and peculators" to turn a fast profit. Thomas said that hucksters besieged him on all sides, asking exorbitant prices for their goods and services; he had to submit to either extortion or delay, and he preferred the latter. He gave as an example of attempted profiteering the actions of woodcutters. The customary price for wood suitable for burning bricks and firing the steam engine at the sawmill was about $2.50 a cord for cottonwood and about $3 for ash. When Thomas advertised for bids, he received none under $5.[5]

Once contracts were made, often they were not fulfilled. To save his workers for construction duty at the station, Thomas contracted with the Browne and Smith Lumber Company to cut pine logs up the Poteau and raft them to the

[4] Lee to Bomford, April 23, 1841. Yell to Secretary of War, June 5, 1841. National Archives, War Department, Quartermaster General, Letters Received File.

[5] Thomas to Stanton, July 15 and July 20, 1839. National Archives, War Department, Quartermaster General, Letters Received File.

mill. Browne and Smith failed to deliver a single log, and left the country. Thomas had depended on them to keep the saw-mill in operation, and now he had to close the mill. He assigned carpenters, who had been waiting for lumber, to common labor in the quarry. The lumber company's guarantors, who pledged to see the contract fulfilled, were John Rogers and Abel Warren of Fort Smith. Browne and Smith had clearly forfeited their bond. When Thomas went to collect it, he failed to get satisfaction. Warren had left for the Indian country to establish a trading post on the Red River; Rogers refused to honor his obligation—and he was too powerful locally and in Washington for Thomas to expect any action against him. In desperation, Thomas had his men cut ash, cottonwood, and oak logs, which were milled into construction lumber.[6]

Frontier bankers were eager to handle government drafts calling for large sums sent from Washington to pay for construction costs at Fort Smith. But when Thomas presented to local bankers War Department drafts for settling quarterly accounts, he often had to wait from one to three months—and sometimes longer—before they could honor them. Thus he did most of his business with the Citizens' Bank of New Orleans and the Planters' Bank at Natchez. His ignoring local bankers added to his unpopularity and increased the number of his enemies.[7]

Thomas' troubles were compounded by the Choctaws, whose national boundary began a hundred paces east of old Fort Smith and ran due south to the Red River. Two disputes with the Indians and their agent on two scores added to the slowdown of construction on the new post. In surveying the perimeter for the new post and staking the outer wall, Thomas

[6] Thomas to Jesup, March 13, 1840. National Archives, War Department, Quartermaster General, Letters Received File.

[7] Thomas to Stanton, August 17, 1839. Thomas' Report of Operations at Fort Smith, 1838 to October, 1840. National Archives, War Department, Quartermaster General, Letters Received File.

had inadvertently placed a wall section, including a corner where bastion number two was to be erected, forty feet across the Choctaw line. The disputed section had been graded, the foundation excavated and set, and the wall raised four feet before the Choctaws protested. The second dispute with the Choctaws grew out of building materials. The best lumber in the area was along the Poteau; Thomas' men had already cut and rafted to the sawmill more than one thousand saw logs from Choctaw forests. The quarry was also on Choctaw land; several hundred perch of stone had been removed, and a large quantity was being cut and dressed for hauling to the project.[8]

John McKenney, Choctaw chief of the Mushulatubbee District, which bounded the post on the west, filed a protest with Choctaw Agent William Armstrong, warning that the appropriation of building materials from Choctaw land was an "unauthorized encroachment" to which his people would not "submit tamely." Armstrong investigated and found that the charges were true, and was alarmed by the strong feelings aroused among the Choctaws of the Mushulatubbee District. He said he had never "known any thing to create such excitement with the Choctaws"—some of the young men were ready to take their guns, rush to Belle Point, and drive out the white men. Armstrong calmed the warriors and went to Fort Smith to talk with Thomas. They agreed to ask the commissioner of Indian affairs, the attorney general, and the secretary of war for a ruling on the rights of the army in Indian Territory.[9]

The ruling from Washington was that it was impossible for the government to waive its rights to occupy parts of Indian Territory for military purposes. The government had a right also to occupy and use part of the territory, according to the Treaty of Dancing Rabbit Creek. Nonetheless, the

[8] McKenney to Armstrong, May 27, 1839. Armstrong to Crawford, June 11, 1839. National Archives, War Department, Quartermaster General, Letters Received File.
[9] *Ibid.*

government should not exercise this right to avoid paying for
building materials taken from Choctaw land and used in constructing Fort Smith. Thus the quartermaster general was
directed to pay the Choctaws of the Mushulatubbee District
a reasonable price for wood and stone taken from the Choctaw
Nation.[10]

Another source of trouble for Thomas was the growing
Belle Point community, by now called the town of Fort
Smith, situated on the eastern edge of the military reservation.
Thomas said that the town was of the "worst kind & description," and was "inhabited by persons of every kind and character." Most of its business establishments were "grog shops,"
where the shiftless congregated. Many of the men Thomas
fired for misconduct had settled in the town, "some as whiskey
venders, others mere loafers." It was very difficult, Thomas
said, "to get along with these people," and he avoided them
except for business. He doubted that he had been off the
reservation more than half a dozen times since his arrival. His
trouble with the Fort Smith citizens grew out of their use of
the government landing. This difficulty involved him in a
controversy with John Rogers and eventually brought about
his removal as construction superintendent at the new post.[11]

In February, 1840, Thomas authorized Thomas Earhart to
establish a ferry across the Arkansas at Fort Smith. For the
grant and privilege of docking and securing his boats at the
government landing, Earhart promised to transport all troops
and their baggage across the river free of charge. This arrangement appeared to work to the advantage of the government, and so Thomas, after obtaining approval of Colonel
Arbuckle as commandant of the Second Military District,

10 Crawford to Poinsett, July 10, 1839. National Archives, War Department, Quartermaster General, Letters Received File.
11 Thomas to Jesup, March 13, 1840. National Archives, War Department, Quartermaster General, Letters Received File.

granted Earhart the ferry franchise. Earhart immediately went to work as Fort Smith ferryman. He planned to use two flat-boats—one capable of carrying a heavily loaded wagon and team, the other for horses or light carriages—and a skiff for pedestrians.[12]

John Rogers protested the Earhart grant, claiming that he held an exclusive franchise for operating the Fort Smith ferry. He complained that neither Thomas nor the United States had the right "to grant such a privilege or establish a ferry on the reservation." Thomas wrote Quartermaster General Thomas Jesup in Washington and explained that he understood Rogers was threatening to use political pressure to have Thomas removed as project superintendent unless the agreement with Earhart was annulled. Thomas said that since his arrival at Belle Point there had never been "an efficient & well run ferry" at Fort Smith. He said the people had been in the habit of using the government landing for all purposes. On several occasions, this had been adverse to the public interest. Moreover, during the nineteen months Thomas had been in the area, the people had spent neither money nor labor to improve the town landing, which was potentially superior to the government dock. Now, Thomas said, "they claim as a *right* what has been granted them as an *accommodation* and deny the exclusive right of the United States" to its landing property. Thomas explained that he did not plan to deprive the citizens of the use of the government landing unless they pushed him too hard or interfered with government business. General Jesup agreed with Thomas, and told him to grant Earhart the franchise.[13]

Rogers and his Fort Smith friends Elias Rector and A. Harris wrote Senators Ambrose H. Sevier and William S. Ful-

[12] Thomas to Jesup, February 28, 1840. National Archives, War Department, Quartermaster General, Letters Received File.
[13] *Ibid.*

ton complaining about Thomas' grant to Earhart and attempting to discredit Thomas by charging that the new fort should
now be nearly completed. "Either from mismanagement or a
wilful desire to procrastinate" on Thomas' part, they charged,
the outer wall "is hardly seen above ground and not a stone is
laid for a single building." They believed that if Secretary of
War Poinsett named a new superintendent, the change would
work wonders. In their opinion, Major Thomas was "the most
unfortunate selection that could have been made to construct"
the new post. They said that his temperament was such as
"to make himself so obnoxious to the citizens generally as to
operate seriously against the interest of the government." To
solve the problem, they urged that Captain Belknap, whom
they described as one of the "most active and energetic officers
in the army," be immediately placed in charge of the work.
The men were satisfied that under Belknap's supervision the
fort would be completed "in half the time and with half the
expense the present superintendent will require."[14] The senators carried the complaint against Thomas to General Jesup,
who took no action. But incidents continued to mount at Belle
Point.

On March 13, 1840, a loud dispute erupted between Earhart
and M. Hemby, who operated Rogers' ferry. A traveler en
route to the Choctaw agency had engaged Hemby to ferry
him and his horse across the Poteau. When Hemby's boat tied
up at the landing on the west side of the Poteau opposite Belle
Point, Earhart was hauling wood in his flatboat across the
stream for Major Thomas. While Hemby was landing his
passenger, the men assigned to load the wood had to stop
work. Before casting off, Hemby was hailed by A. Harris'
Negro slave, who was returning with a team of horses to Fort
Smith from the Choctaw agency. After taking the Negro and

14 Rogers to Sevier and Fulton, February 10, 1840. National Archives,
Records of the General Land Office, Fort Smith, AMR File.

horses aboard, Hemby recrossed the Poteau. Men with carts waiting at the landing to take the wood which Earhart was ferrying to the sawmill had to stand aside while Hemby's boat tied up. Earhart told Hemby that he could not interrupt his work, and added that Hemby had no right to land at the fort. Hemby retorted that "he would ferry as much as he pleased there." Earhart declared that he would report the matter to Major Thomas. Hemby shouted that "he did not care for Maj. Thomas that Capt. Armstrong had told him that he could ferry as many people through the Fort as he saw fit, and by God . . . [Earhart] nor all the United States should not stop him."[15] When Thomas arrived, Hemby had moved his ferry to the government landing. Thomas asked him to move his boat below the reservation line and to fasten it "at the junction of the Military road and the Arkansas River." Hemby refused, cursing Thomas, threatening his life, and swearing that he would occupy any United States land he wished. Thomas called for a squad of soldiers and ordered them to remove Hemby and his boat from government property. Except for violent words, Hemby offered no resistance as the troops moved his craft below the reservation and secured the tow rope to a tree. Hemby warned Thomas that "he had better look out" because if he did not get him, Captain Rogers would.[16]

Thomas wrote a letter to Rogers complaining of his employee's conduct and reminding him of Thomas' attempts to avoid trouble. For example, he had allowed Rogers to live in his house on the military reservation far beyond the time at which he was supposed to have vacated all property he had sold the government. Moreover, Rogers had failed to prevent his

[15] Earhart to Thomas, March 14, 1840. Rogers to Harris, March 20, 1840. National Archives, Records of the General Land Office, Fort Smith, AMR File.
[16] *Ibid.*

friend Harris from removing a building from the land purchased by the United States and which Rogers had failed to report in his inventory of property included in the sales contract. Until recently, Rogers had been permitted to use the government landing, often at great inconvenience to the military. Thomas warned Rogers that neither he nor any other private citizen had "any *right* to occupy the U. S. Landing." When "abuse was bestowed, instead of thanks," Thomas said, "forebearance ceases to be a virtue."

Thomas informed Rogers that he had good reason to believe that he was aware of Hemby's "riotous, abusive, and almost brutal conduct," and requested that Rogers make certain that Hemby refrained from mooring boats of any description "at the Shore belonging to the United States." If Hemby persisted, as he had threatened, Thomas deemed it his duty to have the boat cast loose. In closing, Thomas told Rogers: "His [Hemby's] conduct, I disregard, as well as his threats. I look higher—to [you] his employer."[17]

Rogers did not acknowledge Thomas' note, but reported the matter to Captain Belknap, commandant at Cantonment Belknap. Declining to write Thomas directly, Belknap had Lieutenant William S. Henry draft and sign the letter. Thomas was informed that Belknap was annoyed that he had used troops detailed to work on the fort to remove Hemby's boat. Further, Belknap had given Rogers written permission to operate a ferry, and wanted it understood that in the future Thomas would not employ the soldiers assigned to him "in any conflict with the citizens."[18]

Thomas expressed surprise that Belknap should side with

[17] Thomas to Rogers, March 13, 1840. National Archives, Records of the General Land Office, Fort Smith, AMR File.
[18] Henry to Thomas, March 14, 1840. National Archives, Records of the General Land Office, Fort Smith, AMR File.

Rogers without investigating what had happened. But, since Belknap had taken up the cause of the "Fort Smithites," Thomas would like to know why they had not built a landing for themselves in front of the town. Thomas believed that with little trouble the townspeople could have as good a landing as the one in front of the fort—indeed, at some stages of the river, it would be better. Such action "would *quietly and effectually prevent any interference with the progress of the work at the Fort.*" It would be better for all if there were two landings, Thomas argued, and he pointed to several incidents in 1839. Steamboats arriving with large shipments of government stores had found the landing crowded with property being received or shipped by private individuals. Occasionally, public property had remained on the landing exposed to the elements through the night; if there had been free access to the landing during the day, this would not have occurred. With the Arkansas again navigable to steamboats, Thomas was daily expecting the arrival of "large *quantities of stores.*" When the vessels tied up, he would "want *all the U. S. Landing* without interference from any one." Belknap was asked to use his influence to persuade the citizens to construct a landing for their own use. Distressed by Belknap's willingness to support Rogers, Thomas noted that he had never interfered with the commandant's duties. Accordingly, he would appreciate Belknap's not trespassing on his.[19]

Unable to gain satisfaction from Belknap, Thomas wrote General Jesup of his clash with Rogers and of Belknap's failure to sustain him. He pointed out that the landing had been built by the United States, and that in his opinion the people of Fort Smith could construct one equally good in front of the town.[20]

[19] Thomas to Belknap, March 14, 1840. National Archives, Records of the General Land Office, Fort Smith, AMR File.
[20] Thomas to Jesup, March 22, 1840. National Archives, Records of the General Land Office, Fort Smith, AMR File.

In a conciliatory move, Thomas also notified Rogers that his ferry could resume use of the landing, but that the privilege would be withdrawn if it interfered in any way with the public interest.[21]

Rogers wrote instructions for A. Harris to carry to Washington. Harris was to call on the secretary of war and inform him of an alleged agreement between Rogers and Thomas concerning the landing. According to Rogers, he had given the United States a strip of land two feet deep along the Arkansas "for the express purpose of making a mutual landing for the benefit of the town as well as the fort." Rogers wanted Harris to assure Poinsett that there was ample room on the landing for both military and civilians. Surely, he pointed out, the mooring of a small ferry would not cause the government any inconvenience. Also Rogers wanted Thomas transferred. "I do most sincerely hope," he wrote, "that this man will not be permitted to remain here to annoy us in this way, he seems to be continually getting into difficulty" with the townspeople.[22]

Harris showed Rogers' letter to members of the Arkansas congressional delegation, who drafted a letter to Poinsett to accompany Rogers' message. The congressional delegation pointed out that use of the landing was "highly important to the citizens," and hoped that the War Department would not back Thomas on his decision to restrict the landing to the military. They added that their constituents were constantly urging them to have Major Thomas transferred. In view of the latest difficulties, they were "compelled to beg that a change be made as speedily as possible."[23]

21 Thomas to Rogers, March 14, 1840. National Archives, Records of the General Land Office, Fort Smith, AMR File.
22 Rogers to Harris, March 20, 1840. National Archives, Records of the General Land Office, Fort Smith, AMR File.
23 Fulton, Sevier and Cross to Poinsett, April 13, 1840. National Archives, Records of the General Land Office, Fort Smith, AMR File.

Poinsett discussed the matter with Jesup and directed him to write Thomas requesting a full report on the landing controversy. As Thomas' dispute with Rogers intensified, Thomas requested authority to erect a fence beginning at the river, along the eastern edge of the reservation, to separate the station from the town of Fort Smith and thus to control access to the landing. He planned to allow public use of the landing only when the area was clear of steamboats and other vessels engaged in government business. In this way he hoped to force the citizens to construct a town landing. General Jesup gave his permission to erect the fence.[24]

Thomas informed Rogers of his plan to fence the boundary. Rogers became abusive and, before a large crowd, shouted that he had not sold the government any part of the Arkansas shore, that the military tract did not front on the Arkansas, and that if the landing were fenced off, the government would be trespassing on his property.[25]

Thomas prepared to construct a strong fence along the eastern boundary of the reservation from the river back to section 16. In surveying the line for the fence, he found that his line did not conform with the one Rogers' survey had established; his ran east, or downriver, from Rogers' line, extending through a corner of the town and forming a triangle of developed property platted by Rogers in 1838. The pie-shaped area had been divided into lots, on which several buildings had been erected. Thomas' survey line cut through the middle of a brick building that Rogers had recently constructed. Thomas jogged his fence line back of this development and enclosed the reservation to the river's edge. Then he checked county courthouse records, and found that Roger's

<hr/>

[24] Thomas to Jesup, March 13, 1840. National Archives, War Department, Quartermaster General, Letters Received File.

[25] Thomas to Jesup, June 3, 1840. National Archives, Records of the General Land Office, Fort Smith, AMR File.

recorded plat showed that the town limits included a band of
land fronting the river along the entire military reservation
and, in effect, cutting it off from the river. Thomas reported
both the anomaly his survey revealed and the town plat description to the War Department. Officials in Washington
checked the purchase agreement, and found that Rogers had
conveyed to the government a front of a hundred yards on the
river "applicable for military purposes." Clearly, Rogers had
crossed the reservation line near the river when he platted
the town. War Department officials were able to force Rogers
to compromise by allowing him to retain the developed triangle. He, in turn, acknowledged the government's title to a
hundred yards of river frontage and submitted to controlled
use of the government landing.[26]

Although Thomas bested Rogers in the landing controversy, Rogers had the last word regarding Thomas' future.
Thomas had irritated a powerful border clique. Besides Rogers, Harris, Bigelow, and other Fort Smith citizens who found
Thomas oppressive and obstructive to the realization of their
personal interests and ambitions, there was United States
Marshal Elias Rector. Rector and Thomas had brushed on
several occasions, but Thomas claimed that their most serious
disagreement grew out of his refusal to permit Rector the use
of wheelbarrows and other military equipment to build his
racetrack near Fort Smith.[27]

The War Department was embarrassed by Thomas' uncompromising attitude toward frontier promoters and by the
regular demands that he be reassigned, and watched for an
opportunity to remove him gracefully. Thomas received a

[26] Cross to Jesup, May 15, 1841. National Archives, War Depart-
ment, Quartermaster General, Letters Received File. Thomas to Rogers,
May 20 and 21, 1840. National Archives, Records of the General Land
Office, Fort Smith, AMR File.

[27] Thomas to Jesup, September 2, 1840. National Archives, War Department Quartermaster General, Letters Received File.

letter from the War Department advising him that he was to be relieved by Captain Samuel McRee. Thomas had begun settling his affairs at Belle Point when he was informed that the secretary of war had cancelled the transfer order. One of Thomas' few defenders in the area was Colonel Arbuckle, who reported to the War Department that Thomas was constructing the new post "in a very handsome and durable manner." And it was his considered opinion that the major had "with energy, skill and propriety discharged his duty at Fort Smith and . . . will do much credit to himself and benefit to the country if he receives the necessary support from the Government to enable him to complete the . . . Post."[28]

The War Department finally succumbed to the demands of prominent Belle Point citizens by ordering Thomas' transfer. On September 6, 1840, Quartermaster General Jesup directed Thomas to stop construction, pay off the workers, close the Fort Smith project, and report for duty in Florida. Thomas needed forty thousand dollars to liquidate all government obligations at Fort Smith. General Jesup had ordered him to close the project, but had failed to send the funds to carry it out. With loans from George and Charlie Birnie, Thomas raised about ten thousand dollars.[29]

Thomas then turned to Colonel Arbuckle for assistance. Arbuckle asked Choctaw Agent Armstrong to advance from his funds the amount required by Thomas, pointing out that if Thomas received no help, the public credit would suffer, and loyal employees who had worked long hours on the fort would be discharged without their hard-earned wages. (Thomas had ninety workers whose pay was nine months in arrears.) Armstrong came through, and Thomas signed an

[28] Arbuckle to Jesup, August 24, 1840. National Archives, War Department, Quartermaster General, Letters Received File.

[29] Thomas to Jesup, July 22, 1840. Monthly Summary Statement for June, 1840. National Archives, Quartermaster General, Letters Received File.

agreement to repay him the thirty thousand dollars out of the funds expected from the quartermaster general at any moment.[30]

Thomas' final report revealed that when construction ceased on Fort Smith on September 6, the garrison walls had been raised seven feet above the foundations, the five bastions were nearly walled, and basements for barracks and officers quarters had been excavated. Masons had walled and floored the basements, and all was ready to begin framing the first floor. The kitchens and messrooms were to be in the roomy basements.[31]

Major Thomas' successor at Fort Smith, Captain Edmund Alexander, arrived from Fort Towson on September 30, 1840. He found only three men on the premises—a forage master and two hostlers to care for the horses, mules, and oxen used as work animals on the project. Before leaving, Thomas had sharpened the tools and packed them away from the elements, covered the sawmill, painted and greased the wagons, and had all in readiness to resume construction.[32]

About the time Alexander replaced Thomas, there was a change in the Belle Point garrison billeted at Cantonment Belknap. Captain Belknap and his 3d Infantry battalion were ordered to Tampa Bay, Florida, and Captain William Lear and his Company E of the 4th Infantry became the garrison force. Lear's men guarded the new works, including the piles of lumber and building material, tools, sawmill, and other

[30] Arbuckle to Armstrong, September 19, 1840, and Thomas to Jesup, October 16, 1840. National Archives, War Department, Quartermaster General, Letters Received File, and Receipt for $30,000 signed by Thomas, September 19, 1840. National Archives, War Department, Quartermaster General, Letters Received File.

[31] Thomas to Jesup, October 26, 1840. National Archives, War Department, Quartermaster General, Letters Received File.

[32] *Ibid.* Alexander's Report of Operations at Fort Smith from October, 1841 to August 31, 1842. National Archives, War Department, Quartermaster General, Letters Received File.

equipment. The new Fort Smith, though unfinished, continued as the supply depot for Southwestern posts; so Company E troops also unloaded steamers at the landing, stored goods in the government warehouses, and issued supplies and equipment to commissary officers in from the surrounding posts.[33]

Fort Smith took on a new function in the spring of 1841. Just before Arbuckle was transferred to Baton Rouge, he came to Fort Smith with a plan of moving Arkansas militia arms stored at Fayetteville. At Arbuckle's request, Lieutenant John F. Lee of the Ordnance Department visited Fort Smith, approved the plan, and suggested that Alexander "erect a proper . . . building, as an ordnance Store House." General Jesup provided funds and directed Alexander to select a site within the new post wall and construct the ordnance storehouse.[34]

The delight of border citizens at Thomas' removal was matched by their resentment at the work stoppage on the new station. General Jesup's order to suspend construction drastically reduced the amount of federal money spent along the Arkansas, and a mild depression set in around Belle Point. As of old, local citizens drafted and circulated petitions and, through the Arkansas legislature, congressional delegation, and governor, urged the federal government to do their will. Governor Archibald Yell wrote the secretary of war that citizens in the frontier settlements had become alarmed because construction on Fort Smith had stopped. He declared

[33] Returns for 3d Infantry, August-September, 1840. National Archives, War Department, Reports Received File. Alexander's Report of Operations at Fort Smith from October, 1841, to October 31, 1842. National Archives, War Department, Quartermaster General, Letters Received File.

[34] Lee to Bomford, April 23, 1841. National Archives, War Department, Quartermaster General, Letters Received File. Arbuckle to Alexander, April 17, 1841. National Archives, War Department, Western Division, Second Department, Order Book.

that its completion was "essential to the Security and peace of
the Citizens of Ark." Yell believed that if the secretary of war
would consider the exposed condition of the western border
of Arkansas, he would "forward its Completion as rapidly as
your limited means will allow."[35]

Pressure from Yell, the congressional delegation, and groups
of citizens caused the War Department to release fifty thousand dollars in 1841 to resume construction at Belle Point.
During August, Quartermaster General Jesup directed Lieutenant James R. Irwin to recruit workers at Cincinnati and
Louisville. Irwin was to charter a steamer to transport the
men to Fort Smith, and pay was to begin when they left the
port of embarkation.[36]

Irwin hired a crew of ninety-four men. His contracts provided that master workmen were to receive ninety dollars a
month and two rations, journeymen fifty-five dollars and one
ration, bricklayers forty-five dollars and one ration, and laborers twenty-five dollars and one ration. Irwin chartered the
steamer *Rialto* to carry his crew to Belle Point. The vessel
went aground sixty miles below Fort Smith, and the men
walked in, arriving on October 6.[37]

Construction on the new Fort Smith resumed under Alexander's supervision on October 11, 1841. The men started on
the barracks to protect basements and foundations Thomas
had begun. Colonel Zachary Taylor, who had replaced Arbuckle as commander of the Second Military District, wanted
the building walls constructed of stone, rather than of brick,
because, in his view, stone was easier to obtain and cheaper.

[35] Yell to Secretary of War, June 5, 1841. National Archives, War
Department, Quartermaster General, Letters Received File.
[36] Jesup to Irwin, August 21, 1841. National Archives, War Depart-
ment, Quartermaster General, Letters Sent File.
[37] Irwin to Jesup, September 8 and October 31, 1841. National
Archives, War Department, Quartermaster General, Letters Received
File. Alexander to Jesup, October 8 and 14, 1841. National Archives,
War Department, Quartermaster General, Letters Received File.

Alexander sent a log detail to the first rapids of the Poteau, twenty miles above the mill, where the woodcutters found oak, ash, and elm plentiful along the banks. Soon the sawmill was going full blast cutting logs into framing material, joists, and flooring.[38]

On July 28, 1842, because Congress had refused to provide additional funds, Jesup told Alexander to prepare to shut down the project.[39] On August 31, he discharged sixty men, including all stonemasons and quarry laborers, retaining a small force of carpenters, bricklayers, and helpers to work on a barracks and officers' quarters which were nearing completion. Then, on August 23, Congress appropriated ten thousand dollars to continue the work at Fort Smith, and, in March of the next year, appropriated twenty thousand dollars with the proviso that it was "*for the completion* of the works at Fort Smith." Jesup instructed Alexander to keep only a master builder and to rely on troops from Cantonment Belknap for labor, inasmuch as the 1843 appropriation probably would be the final one for the post. The officers at Cantonment Belknap cooperated, and Alexander had a large if generally unskilled labor force available. During the year, he was able to raise the outer wall to twelve feet, which military engineers considered "ample for any purpose of defense." To reduce expenses for forage and grain, Alexander began disposing of the horse and ox teams at public auction.[40]

[38] Alexander to Jesup, October 14, 1841. Alexander's Report of Operations at Fort Smith from October 11, 1841, to August 31, 1842. National Archives, War Department, Quartermaster General, Letters Received File.

[39] Jesup to Alexander, July 28, 1842. National Archives, War Department, Quartermaster General, Letters Sent File.

[40] Alexander to Jesup, August 31, 1842. National Archives, War Department, Quartermaster General, Letters Received File. Jesup to Alexander, October 3, 1842, and Jesup to Alexander, March 10, 1843. National Archives, War Department, Quartermaster General, Letters Sent File.

General Winfield Scott, who became commanding general
of the army when General Alexander Macomb died in 1841,
reluctantly encouraged the War Department to see the Belle
Point project through to completion. He believed that expenditure of public funds at Fort Smith far exceeded "the
military value of the position," but because so much money
had been spent there, the army could not abandon it. Therefore, he thought it wise to reduce the scale of the work and
that the only funds allocated to Fort Smith in the future should
be those to "preserve & to render of some little use what has
already been done." Thus, in 1844, Congress, with Scott's
recommendation to "render of some little use" the Belle Point
project, and with enthusiastic assistance and support from the
Arkansas delegation, appropriated funds for Fort Smith. In
October, Jesup wrote Alexander to resume construction and
to concentrate on completing one block of barracks, the commanding officer's quarters, and the officers' quarters for a
single company. Alexander was to engage a few mechanics
and one master builder, relying on soldiers from Cantonment
Belknap for labor. By the spring of 1845, he had recruited a
crew, and construction resumed on the barracks and quarters.[41]

General Jesup visited Fort Smith during the summer of
1845. After a prolonged and scrutinizing inspection of the
works, he pronounced the storehouse inadequate, and directed
Alexander to complete bastion number one and to convert it
into a storehouse for commissary and quartermaster supplies.
Alexander was also to change one officers' quarters into a hospital. In his report to the secretary of war of the Belle Point
inspection, Jesup wrote that, since Fort Smith was the head of
steamboat navigation on the Arkansas, it was "an important

[41] Scott to Spencer, February 14, 1843. Jesup to Alexander, October
24, 1844. Alexander to Jesup, October 2, 1845. National Archives, War
Department, Quartermaster General, Letters Sent File.

point for a depot of supplies for a force operating on that frontier as well as for the posts in advance on Red river, and Fort Gibson." Jesup said that because of its position Fort Smith had a decided advantage over any other station in the Southwest as a supply depot. The works, he admitted, had been commenced on too vast a scale, and consequently too much money had been expended. The buildings which had been started were, however, necessary, and the amount needed to complete them "could not be more judiciously applied to the public service than in finishing them."[42]

Before General Jesup left Fort Smith, he directed Alexander to contract out the work on converting bastion number one into a storehouse and on erecting the post hospital, thus marking a change in the construction pattern at Fort Smith. Augustus A. Blumenthal of St. Louis, low bidder on the contract, brought a crew which completed the bastion storehouse on February 2, 1846. Blumenthal's goal was to have the hospital completed by August 1, and to achieve this he sent to St. Louis for additional workmen. His energetic laborers stimulated the artisans and soldiers working on the barracks and officers' quarters, which were completed and ready for occupancy on May 15, 1846.[43]

Command and garrison force changes had occurred at Fort Smith. In the spring of 1844, Colonel Taylor was sent to command the reorganized First Department, which now included Louisiana, with headquarters at Fort Jesup. On May 23, Colonel Arbuckle returned to command the Second Military Department with headquarters at Cantonment Belknap.[44]

[42] Jesup to Stanton, July 9, 1845. Jesup to Marcy, January, 1846. National Archives, War Department, Quartermaster General, Letters Sent File.

[43] Alexander to Jesup, May 1, 1846. Alexander to Jesup, June 1, 1846. National Archives, War Department, Quartermaster General, Letters Received File.

[44] Arbuckle to Adjutant General. June 4, 1844. National Archives, War Department, Adjutant General's Office, Letters Received File.

Four companies of the 6th Infantry from Jefferson Barracks had arrived at Belle Point on September 17, 1842, to relieve the 4th Infantry.[45] Major William Hoffman was the new commander of the Fort Smith (Cantonment Belknap) garrison. Companies D and F of the 6th were to replace Company E, which had served as the Belle Point garrison force and which was now assigned to duty in Florida. Companies E and G of the 6th Infantry were assigned to Fort Gibson.[46]

Thus, with the new Fort Smith ready for occupancy after eight years of construction, the first garrison consisted of the officers and men of companies D and F, 6th Infantry, which evacuated Cantonment Belknap and moved to the new station on May 15, 1846.[47]

[45] Alexander to Jesup, October 11, 1842. National Archives, War Department, Quartermaster General, Letters Received File.

[46] Hoffman to Adjutant General, September 19, 1842. National Archives, War Department, Adjutant General's Office, Letters Received File.

[47] Alexander to Jesup, June 1, 1846. National Archives, War Department, Quartermaster General, Letters Received File.

# CHAPTER TEN

# Portals of Croesus

D URING THE FIFTEEN YEARS between 1846, when Fort Smith was completed and garrisoned by 6th Infantry troops, and the outbreak of the Civil War in 1861, the new post was the focus of the Southwestern frontier. It served as a base for arming and equipping military units for service in the Mexican War. It was headquarters for exploration and reconnaissance parties ranging over the Southwest to the Pacific. It was a strategic funnel through which poured thousands of California-bound emigrants. It served also as communications center for the army in the Southwest, as headquarters for regimental and 2nd and 7th Military Department officials, and as administrative office for Indian affairs west of Arkansas. With all these important functions, Fort Smith was also the mother post for new military stations across the Southwest. Its officers supervised the construction of new army installations, and Fort Smith nourished these posts with supplies and troops.

Fortuitously, the new Fort Smith was completed just at the outbreak of the Mexican War. Even before Congress declared war on Mexico in May, 1846, a build-up of United States military strength in the Southwest placed a serious strain on the resources of the new station. Captain Edmund Alexander, the post quartermaster, was hard-pressed to supply the commissary stores, ordnance, and equipment requested by units moving through Fort Smith bound for the Río Grande. River steamers rushed replenishment stores to Belle Point from Cincinnati, St. Louis, and New Orleans. At times, Alexander had to purchase flour, pork, and other subsistence stores locally in order to fill requests.[1]

Several changes in the Fort Smith garrison during 1846 demonstrated the pressure of manpower needs on the Río Grande. On July 13, the War Department directed Major Benjamin L. E. Bonneville, commandant at Fort Smith, to march his two 6th Infantry companies to the Mexican border. This added to Alexander's duties in that, with Bonneville's departure, he had to serve also as post commandant.[2] Then, on August 10, the War Department transferred Company D of the 1st Dragoons from Fort Gibson to Fort Smith as the garrison force. When, on October 1, Alexander received orders directing him to report to his regiment, the 3d Infantry on the Mexican border, Lieutenant John W. T. Gardiner, officer in charge of the garrison Dragoon company, took on the additional duties of post quartermaster and commandant.[3]

The Fort Smith garrison changed again on May 10, 1847, when Gardiner was ordered to take the field with his Dragoon company. The new garrison was a battalion of Arkansas volunteers held at Fort Smith as a ready reserve to rush to Mexico if General Zachary Taylor needed reinforcements. The state troops remained at Fort Smith as the garrison force until they were relieved on October 31, 1848; the United States maintained control of the military stores and command at Fort Smith by assigning as quartermaster and commandant Lieutenant Franklin Flint of the 6th Infantry, who held this post

[1] Alexander to Jesup, June 7, 1846. National Archives, War Department, Quartermaster General, Letters Received File.

[2] Alexander to Jesup, September 30, 1846. National Archives, War Department, Quartermaster General, Letters Received File.

[3] Special Order 23, 2nd Military Department, October 1, 1846. National Archives, War Department, Quartermaster General, Letters Sent File.

until November 3, 1848. Besides fulfilling his station duties, Flint was also active in enforcing federal laws regulating trade in Indian Territory. As before, Fort Smith citizens bitterly protested interference with their contraband traffic. Flint's biggest haul occurred in July, 1848, when, with the assistance of a detachment of Arkansas volunteers, he seized a flatboat and several smaller craft loaded with whisky bound for the Indian nations. Flint turned the contraband over to the United States marshal at Fort Smith, and was denounced by local people for his "high handed methods."[4]

With the close of the Mexican War, the War Department began redeploying troops. The 5th Infantry Regiment and two companies of the First Dragoons were assigned to the 2d Military Department with headquarters at Fort Smith. The infantry and cavalry units were distributed among the posts under the department's jurisdiction. Fort Gibson received four infantry companies and a company of Dragoons; Fort Washita was garrisoned with a Dragoon company and two infantry companies; two of the 5th Infantry companies were assigned to both Fort Towson and Fort Smith. Six companies of the 5th Infantry arrived at Fort Smith on October 31, 1848, and, after a rest and replenishment of supplies and equipment, marched to their new stations. Companies B and E comprised the Fort Smith garrison. Captain Caleb C. Sibley of E. Company relieved Lieutenant Flint as post commander, naming Lieutenant John C. Robinson to assume Flint's quartermaster duties. During 1848, the War Department reorganized its military jurisdictions. Fort Smith and its satellite posts were changed from the 2d to the 7th Military Department. Fort Smith was designated headquarters for the new department, with Colonel Mathew Arbuckle reassigned as its commander. Late in the year, Quartermaster General Thomas Jesup named

[4] *Fort Smith Herald*, July 16, 1848.

Captain Arthur B. Lansing to take over the stores at Fort Smith as quartermaster for the 7th Military Department.[5]

Soldiers of the 5th Infantry performed the customary garrison duties, unloaded steamers at the government landing, stowed commissary, quartermaster, and ordnance goods in the Fort Smith warehouses and magazines, and performed construction duties on the expanding post. A typical day in the life of a private might run as follows.

> The soldier at sunrise found himself in ranks. Hurrying into his room . . . he made his bed, swept his quarters and set his belongings in order so as to be ready for inspection twenty-five minutes after reveille. After he had eaten his breakfast, he cleaned his musket or his rifle, polished his breastplate, cartridge box and buttons, brushed his hat, pompon and clothing, and generally prepared himself for parade at nine o'clock. At that dress ceremony, he saw the national colors raised to the top of the flag pole, heard the "Star Spangled Banner" played, beheld his officers move to the front and doff their hats to the commanding officer and then he himself, while yet in ranks, marched with his company in review. After the ceremony was over he changed his dress uniform for the more comfortable one of fatigue, if he was not detailed for guard that day. If on guard, he prepared himself more thoroughly in dress uniform for inspection, paying particular heed to his rifle and the cleanliness of his person. At guard mounting which took place immediately after parade the soldier awaited the results of inspection to see whether he would be selected as the neatest and most immaculate man in ranks. If he were so selected he was appointed orderly at headquarters and was not required with the others to walk post and guard prisoners at work. If he was not on the guard detail for the day, he attended drill

[5] *Ibid.,* October 25, November 1, and November 15, 1848. General Order 49, Adjutant General's Office, 1848. Lansing to Jessup, January 31 and February 9, 1849. National Archives, War Department, Quartermaster General, Letters Received File.

shortly after guard mount. Throughout the remainder of the day he helped in his fatigue uniform to make the post cleanly and to repair and construct those parts of the garrison that were in need of such labor. . . . [He] shod the horses, fixed the chimneys, mowed the grass, picked up and carted away the debris, repaired the boots, sawed and planed the wood, fitted and nailed the lumber into buildings and performed all manner of chores for the garrison. Dinner was usually at one o'clock; the roll call of retreat, when the national colors were lowered, was at sunset; and tattoo, another roll call, was at nine o'clock. The soldier was in bed at nine-thirty when taps was sounded by the drum.[6]

Almost every year after its occupation in 1846 saw some change at Fort Smith. Shortly after the 6th Infantry arrived at the new Fort Smith as its first garrison in 1846, Captain Alexander negotiated an agreement with Augustus A. Blumenthal, the contractor from St. Louis, to convert bastion number two, the northwest blockhouse, into a storehouse. Alexander was unable to recruit enough workmen to open the quarry, and so Blumenthal's men razed the foundations of an uncompleted barracks and the commanding officer's quarters for stone to complete the new storehouse. The Missourians finished the job on September 30, 1846.[7]

In the same year, the new post obtained a stone magazine. Colonel Arbuckle issued a contract for the structure, to be erected on the foundation of the southeast bastion, declaring that the magazine was "absolutely necessary for the safe keeping and preservation of the large quantity of ammunition on hand, as well as that recently received on account of Mexican hostilities."[8]

[6] William A. Ganoe. *History of the United States Army*, 193–94.

[7] Alexander to Jesup, June 20 and September 30, 1846. National Archives, War Department, Quartermaster General, Letters Received File.

[8] Alexander to Jesup, September 25, 1846. National Archives, War Department, Quartermaster General, Letters Received File.

Fort Smith garrisons were usually temporary. Units were often assigned there to provide the men a rest from some arduous assignment, and an early reassignment was expected. Through the years, the garrison force included infantry, cavalry, and artillery units. Dragoons were increasingly billeted at Fort Smith, and in 1847 a contract was signed to construct a stable of two buildings with ninety-three stalls. When the 1st Cavalry was assigned to Fort Smith in 1858, the capacity of the stables was doubled.[9]

One essential building lacking at Fort Smith was a guardhouse. In 1847, Department Quartermaster Lieutenant Gardiner reported to General Jesup that garrison commanders were forced to use tents and irons to hold military prisoners, "and, the vicinity of the town of Fort Smith renders it very desirable to provide a more secure place for the prisoners."[10]

As the months passed and there was no word from Washington to go ahead, Arbuckle urged the need for a strong guardhouse, pointing out that, with the 5th Infantry expected momentarily and the closeness of the town "with its many temptations to the soldiers," in his opinion it would be "prejudicial to good order and military discipline" not to have a strong guardhouse. Lieutenant Flint, who had replaced Gardiner, proposed that he, with garrison labor, be permitted to construct the military jail out of hewn logs, a single window covered with an iron grill, and a log floor. Jesup delayed Flint's request for a guardhouse because funds for material were lacking, but in October, 1848, he approved a brick guardhouse as well as a request from Flint that he be permitted to erect a four-room brick office building for department, regimental, and garrison officers.[11]

[9] Gardiner to Jesup, December 29, 1846. Montgomery to Jesup, January 4, 1859. National Archives, War Department, Quartermaster General, Letters Received File.

[10] Gardiner to Jesup, January 17, 1847. National Archives, War Department, Quartermaster General, Letters Received File.

On April 9, 1849, a fire broke out in the enlisted men's barracks. The post had no fire engine, but officers organized a bucket brigade with water drawn from wells on the station. Several townspeople joined the firefighters, but the blaze burned freely, gutting the interior and destroying the roof. Only the brick walls stood amid the smoldering ruins. An army survey board ruled that the fire had begun from an attempt to purge a soot accumulation from one of the chimneys; straw had been burned to clean the flues, and heat from the burning soot had ignited a wooden girder in the garret.[12]

For temporary shelter, the troops erected a shed near the parade ground and pitched their tents under it. For permanent barracks, Colonel Arbuckle wanted to construct a one-story building, believing that workmen could salvage sufficient brick and stone from ruins for the new structure.[13] Jesup approved Arbuckle's recommendation, but Captain Alexander Montgomery, who became department quartermaster at Fort Smith soon after the fire, objected to the type of one-story barracks Arbuckle had proposed. Montgomery claimed that he had seen "Barns in Pennsylvania of much more tasteful and imposing appearance," and attempted to persuade Jesup to order the barracks rebuilt according to the original plan. He hoped Jesup would see what "a grotesque appearance" a single-story building would present when confronted by "the lofty Quarters occupied by the officers." He was opposed to expending public money and material on a barracks which, when completed, would present "no higher architectural pre-

[11] Flint to Jesup, February 28 and October 6, 1848. National Archives, War Department, Quartermaster General, Letters Received File.

[12] Burns to Jesup, April 8, 1849. Lansing to Jesup, April 10, 1849. National Archives, War Department, Quartermaster General, Letters Received File.

[13] Arbuckle to Jesup, April 13, 1849. National Archives, War Department, Quartermaster General, Letters Received File.

tension than a respectable cow-house."[14] But Jesup supported
Arbuckle, and the secretary of war approved the plan to erect
a single-story brick barracks, which was completed in late
1851.[15]

As late as 1858, Montgomery was still requesting authority
to convert the enlisted barracks into a two-story structure,
saying that a second story "will improve the appearance of the
building." Standing as it did opposite both the two-story
officers' quarters, "it presents a singularly squat and Barn-like
appearance; in strong contrast with its neighbors over the
way; by no means complimentary to the taste of its projec-
tion, and reflecting but little credit upon the Quarter Master's
Department, which is supposed to be responsible for its design." In this, as in earlier requests, he was unsuccessful.[16]

The officers' quarters included apartments for dependents,
but no provision had been made for sheltering families of enlisted men, either on or off the post. Those noncommissioned
officers and the few privates with families usually made arrangements with Fort Smith householders for room and board.
Ordnance Sergeant William H. Niles sheltered his family in
one of the dilapidated buildings of old Fort Smith.[17]

Montgomery, distressed that the post had no quarters for
families of enlisted men, worked through the years to obtain
authority from the War Department to construct some sort
of suitable apartments. He worked also to improve the lot of
the laundresses. In 1857, he reported to Jesup that the Fort
Smith garrison had two companies of 186 enlisted men and

[14] Montgomery to Jesup, October 6, 1849. National Archives, War
Department, Quartermaster General, Letters Received File.
[15] Montgomery to Jesup, August 16, 1850. National Archives, War
Department, Quartermaster General, Letters Received File.
[16] Montgomery to Jesup, and Montgomery to Crossman. [no date
or month] 1858. National Archives, War Department, Quartermaster
General, Letters Received File.
[17] Andrews to Craig, November 11, 1852. National Archives, War
Department, Quartermaster General, Letters Received File.

eight washerwomen, a group of sixteen enlisted men with one woman, and three staff noncommissioned officers. Montgomery asked for authority from the Quartermaster Department to construct ten cabins for his "non-commissioned staff and laundresses." He urged that the expense would be minimal inasmuch as garrison details would perform the work. Jesup refused, declaring that there was no authority to build a quarters for laundresses. Montgomery found, under paragraph 963 of Army Regulations that "to every six non-commissioned officers, musicians, privates, servants, and washerwomen there shall be allowed at this latitude 256 square feet of quarters." Jesup would not relent.[18]

Fort Smith's expanding role in opening the Southwest was enhanced by the discovery of gold in California in 1848 and the westward rush that got under way the following year. Late in 1848, John F. Wheeler, editor of the *Fort Smith Herald*, and other town leaders saw the possibilities of Fort Smith as a point of departure for the overland trek to the California gold fields. Wheeler urged a town meeting to draft a petition for the Arkansas legislature requesting that body to lay before the Congress a memorial that the federal government survey a road up the Arkansas and Canadian valley to Santa Fe. Wheeler predicted that this route would be "the best and shortest route" to the Far West, and said that the advantages of a highway opened for the accommodation of emigrants included terrain over which wagons would roll relatively free of mountains. Even more important, it abounded in "the best of range, the grass springing up from one month to six weeks earlier" than on the more northerly Santa Fe Trail.[19]

[18] Jesup to Montgomery, July 18, 1857. National Archives, War Department, Quartermaster General, Letters Sent File. Montgomery to Jesup, August 8, 1857. National Archives, War Department, Quartermaster General, Letters Received File.

[19] *Fort Smith Herald*, August 23, 1848.

John Rogers appointed a five-man committee to draft the petition preamble, which stated that a national road, commencing at Fort Smith and running west along the valley of the Canadian in nearly a direct line to Santa Fe and on to California, was the most direct, trouble-free route possible. Such a road would be of tremendous value not only to the people of Arkansas but also "to those of every portion of the Union, as a National means of developing the resources of the important territory lately acquired from Mexico, and the vast country bordering on the Pacific, and of reducing them to a state of civilization and improvement." The Fort Smith petitioners asked the Arkansas legislature to place this request before Congress at the beginning of the next session.[20]

The Arkansas General Assembly drafted a memorial asking Congress to open a military road from Fort Smith to California by way of Santa Fe, and forwarded it to the members of the Arkansas congressional delegation, who in turn placed it before the second session of the 30th Congress, where it was referred to committee. Additional steps were taken by Senator Solon Borland of Arkansas, who wrote Secretary of War William L. Marcy, on January 10, 1849, asking that a detachment of mounted troops be detailed to escort "the party or parties, of citizens, desirous to trade or migrate in the direction of New Mexico, Oregon, and California." According to the senator's informants, a large group of emigrants were scheduled to rendezvous at Fort Smith in the early spring. Borland said that these people believed that the route westward from Fort Smith to Santa Fe through the valley of the Canadian was "shorter and better" than the Santa Fe Trail, heretofore followed by emigrants and traders. He pointed out that the emigrants would feel far better about the success of their venture if they were assured of a military escort. Since they

[20] *Ibid.*, September 27 and October 25, 1848.

planned to assemble at Fort Smith early in April, prompt action by the War Department was necessary. Borland deemed it superfluous to reiterate the reasons which "gave interest to the proposed expedition," saying that it was of "great importance to our country, alike in a military point of view, and as a means of developing, and making available, the true character and value of our new western acquisitions."[21]

Marcy referred Borland's letter to Adjutant General Roger Jones with the comment that he had a twofold interest in the enterprise. Besides being eager to secure information regarding the route from Fort Smith to Santa Fe, he was desirous of "affording proper facilities for such explorations" as suggested by Senator Borland. Marcy hoped to open "new avenues" for emigration to the lands recently acquired from Mexico, and believed that it would be beneficial to the country's interest for the War Department to authorize a military escort from Fort Smith as requested by Borland.[22]

Communications from Washington to Colonel Arbuckle during the first three months of 1849 informed him of the steps he was to take in providing military escort for California-bound emigrants gathering at Fort Smith. He was "to organize a suitable party to accompany the expedition as far as Santa Fe." There being no Dragoons at the moment in the 7th Military Department, an officer with a thirty-man Dragoon detachment from Company F at Fort Scott was to report to Fort Smith. Lieutenant James H. Simpson of the Topographical Engineers had been detailed to accompany the expedition to the Pacific coast. The troops from Fort Smith were to accompany the emigrants only as far as Santa Fe. From the Río Grande to California, a detachment drawn from New Mexico posts would supply the emigrant escort. Ar-

[21] Borland to Marcy, January 10, 1849. National Archives, War Department, Secretary of War, Letters Received File.
[22] *Fort Smith Herald*, February 21, 1849.

buckle was authorized to notify the citizens at Fort Smith when his troops would be ready to march.[23]

With the growing certainty that overland caravans launched from Fort Smith would receive the services of a military escort, John F. Wheeler proclaimed to California-bound emigrants the advantages of gathering at Belle Point. A sample of his promotional journalism appeared in the September 20, 1848, issue of the *Fort Smith Herald*:

## HO FOR CALIFORNIA! ! !

A company is now forming in this place for California, which will start about 1st of April next. There is already from 15 to 20 names of heads of families, living in this place, and vicinity enrolled. Persons wishing to attach themselves to this company, will have an opportunity of doing so, by applying either to Mr. J. R. Kannady, Capt. John J. Dillard, or John F. Wheeler. Every able bodied male emigrant, will be required to furnish himself with a good rifle gun, and plenty of ammunition, also to each emigrant, rations for the journey, consisting of 180 lbs. of flour, 100 lbs. of bacon, and the transportation of same in wagons, to be drawn by horses, mules, or oxen, and no wagon to haul more than 2,000 lbs. The whole party to rendezvous at Fort Smith, by the 1st of April next, and choose their officers, and make all the necessary arrangements for the trip.[24]

Wheeler's goal was to displace Independence, Missouri, as the most popular point of departure for the Far West. He distributed extra issues of the *Herald* throughout the Mississippi valley, the Ohio River towns, and East coast cities. That Fort Smith was becoming known as a supply center and point of departure for overland travel was indicated by the response. Soon after January 1, 1849, gold seekers from Little Rock,

23 Adjutant General to Arbuckle, January 22, 1849. National Archives, War Department, Adjutant General's Office, Letters Sent File. *Fort Smith Herald*, February 21, 1849, and April 25, 1849.

24 *Fort Smith Herald*, September 20, 1848.

Batesville, Clarksville, Fayetteville, and other nearby towns began gathering at Belle Point. The largest organized group was the Fort Smith California Emigration Company. By March, every steamer docking at Fort Smith was packed with emigrants. Leaders of a Memphis group arrived on the *Orella No. 2* on March 20, met with Fort Smith merchants, and proceeded to purchase supplies, equipment, wagons, and teams for their one hundred members. A sixty-member company arrived from Holly Springs and Pontotoc, Mississippi. The *Pontiac* docked with two emigration companies, one from Cincinnati, the other from Nashville. The *Sallie Anderson* and *Alert No. 2* brought the Havillah Emigrating Company from New York and a Philadelphia company. The bustle and excitement along the Arkansas infected many of the local citizens with gold fever, and several river towns were nearly depopulated as the Western Rover Company and other overland groups were organized.[25]

By the first week of March, 1849, Fort Smith town was ringed with the camps of California-bound emigrants. Companies were organized, and members purchased rations, equipment, wagons, and teams from dwindling stocks of Fort Smith merchants. Wheeler gathered information about camping and life on the trail from Fort Smith officers and published it for the benefit of the argonauts. They were urged to "run into no excess, and pay particular attention to the state of . . . [their] stomach and bowels." The army officers warned that it was "very unhealthy to remain at one camp more than a week," and, recommended that the camps be moved every three or four days.[26]

Emigrant leaders met regularly with Colonel Arbuckle for briefing on the escort's departure plans. Arbuckle advised that the companies should be ready to depart Fort Smith soon

[25] *Ibid.*, February 21, March 21, and March 28, 1849.
[26] *Ibid.*, March 28, 1849.

after April 1 if the Poteau and other rivers were in good condition for ferrying, and said that the military escort would
precede the emigrant trains by several days to insure selection
of the best route. Thus, if the groups started around April 10,
they should overtake the escort 120 miles west of Fort Smith.
Arbuckle recommended that the companies be organized according to the military system, and suggested Captain John
J. Dillard, an emigration company officer from Fort Smith
who had served in the Mexican War, as an ideal choice for
caravan master.[27]

Arbuckle revealed to the emigrant leaders that the route he
planned to open to the Río Grande followed the south bank
of the Canadian. His men, who would escort the groups for
protection against Indian attack, smooth the roads on steep
grades, and mark fords, would generally follow the watershed
between the Canadian and the Washita and thus avoid bot-
toms and numerous creek crossings. Arbuckle had already
sent Lieutenant Frederick T. Dent of the 5th Infantry with
a detail of a corporal and three privates to reconnoiter the best
route. The military escort, commanded by Captain Randolph
B. Marcy of the 5th Infantry, would include a company of
infantry from Fort Towson, a Dragoon force from Fort Scott,
and Lieutenant James H. Simpson of the Corps of Topographical Engineers. The force was to accompany the caravan
to Santa Fe, from which point a force from New Mexico posts
would see the argonauts on to California. Lieutenant Simpson
would remain with the column all the way to the Pacific.[28]

On March 15, Lieutenant Joseph Updegraff led Company
D of the 5th Infantry into Fort Smith. His unit, drawn from
the Fort Towson garrison, consisted of three noncommissioned officers and twenty-two privates. Eight days later,
Lieutenant Dent and his reconnoitering detail returned to Fort

[27] *Ibid.*, March 14, 1849.
[28] *Ibid.*

Smith.[29] On March 27, Updegraff's company, with Dent as guide, crossed the Poteau to open the California Road. At the end of March, Marcy arrived at Fort Smith from Fort Towson. On April 3, Lieutenant John Buford and thirty Dragoons from Fort Scott rode into Fort Smith. Marcy waited for Simpson until April 4, when the column commander and the Dragoons struck out along the road marked by Dent and Updegraff. Three days later, the *Sallie Anderson*, with Lieutenant Simpson aboard, docked at Belle Point. The column's topographer pushed off to catch up with Marcy. Wheeler noted his departure by writing that the results of Simpson's Western survey would determine whether the "Great National Railroad is to run through this State or not."[30]

Great anticipation and excitement were rampant in the emigrant camps. Two days before Dent and Updegraff crossed the Poteau, the sixty-five members of the Knickerbocker Exploring Company moved out. Observers counted four hundred wagons moving through Fort Smith during April, 1849. Captain Lansing, department quartermaster, wrote Quartermaster General Jesup:

> The Emigrants are moving off in detached bodies—very slowly, and without good organization. There seems to be a want of harmony among them, and I apprehend the Expedition will not be without disaster—They have more to fear from themselves; their want of concert; than from bands of hostile Indians. Indeed, they need not apprehend much difficulty with the Indian tribes—for, moving in large (though unwieldly) bodies, well armed and well escorted, and assured (as I have heard) but lately, by a deputation of Southern Comanches, that they should pass unmolested, they will, doubtless traverse the prairies in safety.[31]

[29] *Ibid.*, March 28, 1849.
[30] *Ibid.*, April 11, 1849.
[31] Lansing to Jesup, April 6, 1849. National Archives, War Department, Quartermaster Department, Letters Received File.

Throughout the spring and summer of 1849, gold-seeking caravans organized at Fort Smith, crossed the Poteau, and coursed westward along the California Road. Emigrants from Ohio, Kentucky, Tennessee, Georgia, North Carolina, and other Eastern states formed into groups at Belle Point. Leaders of a company of New York men reported that they had shipped their gear and equipment to the Pacific coast by ship and intended to travel to California with pack mules.[32]

Fort Smith waited for some word from the caravans. Reports passed along the California Road revealed that Captain Marcy's column reached Santa Fe on June 30. In letters to interested parties at Belle Point, Marcy said that all emigrants who had left Fort Smith before May 18 had arrived safely on the Río Grande and were moving west with their new escort. He did add that one caravan had been attacked by Indians twenty-five miles west of the Río Grande, beyond his escort territory, and that two emigrants had been slain. To the delight of Wheeler and other Fort Smith promoters, Marcy wrote that emigrant companies from Independence had not reached Santa Fe and that, judging from scouts' reports, he believed it would be another two weeks before they arrived. He said that he had heard of a good route from Fort Smith to Valverde, near Socorro on the Río Grande, which would supposedly shorten the distance to California by three hundred miles. He planned to trace it out on his return journey to Fort Smith, which, he expected, would require forty days.[33]

Emigrants also sent letters to Fort Smith for publication in the *Herald*. Of these, Wheeler of course printed only the ones which reflected credit on Fort Smith as a launching point for overland travel and which scorned Independence. The general tone of the letters was that all companies formed at Fort Smith were well and in fine spirits. "*They had not lost, but two*

[32] *Fort Smith Herald*, May 16, 1849.
[33] *Ibid.*, September 5, 1849.

*oxen of 500.*" A letter from an emigrant on the Independence route to the Río Grande said that "Never had he seen such suffering. Hundreds of oxen had died, and large numbers of wagons had been abandoned."[34]

The California Road received a boost in late July, 1849, when Lieutenant Abraham Buford visited Fort Smith after having spent the winter of 1848 at Socorro, New Mexico. He claimed that "the direct and best route to California, is from Fort Smith *up the south side of the Canadian* to Socorro on the Rio Grande, thence by pack mules down the Gila, or by Cooke's road through Socorro, to the Pima village on the Gila." According to Buford, wagons could travel Cooke's road with ease. Grass was plentiful, and supplies could always be purchased at reasonable prices along the road. Buford did not think that the emigrants should go west by way of Santa Fe—it was out of the way, and grass was short in that region. Moreover, Santa Fe merchants asked high prices for forage and provisions. Socorro, about 120 miles southwest of Santa Fe, could be just as easily reached from Fort Smith.[35]

Emigrant companies forming at Fort Smith during the late summer plotted a course up the California Road to utilize the Socorro route. The local Marion Rangers and the Little Rock and California Association departed Belle Point in August with a sketch of Buford's proposed itinerary.[36]

Captain Marcy returned to Fort Smith on November 16, 1849, to announce that he had developed a direct route for the California traffic. He said that his line of march was from Doña Ana on the Río Grande, twelve miles from San Diego, where Cooke's road to California began, and that he struck directly for Fort Washita and found the country "generally smooth and level—the road firm and good." The distance from

[34] *Ibid.*
[35] *Ibid.*, July 25, 1849.
[36] *Ibid.*, August 22, 1849.

Doña Ana to Fort Washita was 727 miles; by chain measurement, it was 820 miles from Fort Smith to Santa Fe.[37]

Interest in the California gold fields continued strong into 1850, and the spectacle at Fort Smith was repeated. Steamers packed with emigrants began arriving in March, each carrying large quantities of traveling stores, weapons, and other equipment for the westward trek. The town's business tempo was brisk through September, mules, wagons, and other travel needs being in great demand. Each year thereafter until 1861, emigrant companies cleared Fort Smith for the overland passage. During the decade of the 1850's, an estimated five thousand persons passed through Belle Point, most of them following Captain Marcy's Doña Ana Road.[38]

The Arkansas border country, caught up in the excitement of the gold rush, apparently paid little attention to the election of 1848, but its result involved Fort Smith's future in high-level politics. Mexican War hero General Zachary Taylor, who was elected president, had at least two old army scores to settle. One was with Colonel Mathew Arbuckle, growing out of command controversies within the 7th Infantry Regiment. The other was his acknowledged scorn for Fort Smith as a military post in the American defensive system. At last General Taylor had the supreme authority to accomplish what had apparently been only an ambition until this time. Taylor could settle both scores by closing Fort Smith and abandoning the Belle Point station, thereby forcing Colonel Arbuckle, the department commander, to move from his comfortable headquarters suite at Fort Smith to the more primitive accommodations at Fort Gibson. In earlier times, the tough, hardy Arbuckle would have accepted punitive orders without a murmur, but he was old and tired with nearly thirty years service on the Southwestern frontier. For Arbuckle, what

---

[37] *Ibid.*, November 21, 1849, April 13, 1850, and April 30, 1850.
[38] *Ibid.*, April 13, 1850, and April 20, 1850.

would have been only an inconvenience ten years earlier was now a punishment.

General Order 19, issued May 31, 1850, directed the commandant of the 7th Military Department to dispose of the military stores and garrison at Fort Smith and to abandon the post. A new fort was to be constructed in western Indian Territory at a point near Marcy's road to Doña Ana, situated strategically to protect overland caravans from attack by the Kiowas and Comanches.[39]

The War Department order reached Belle Point on June 24, and generated a loud and sustained protest. Citizens of the town gathered in mass meeting. A five-man committee drafted a set of resolutions to be forwarded to the Arkansas congressional delegation, advising Congress that "this post ought not be abandoned, as it is the most central point for Headquarters Seventh Military Department, being the highest point of navigation on the Arkansas, where military stores, munitions of war can be stored for all the posts, west on Marcy's road, the Santa Fe road, and the Rio Grande." Congress was urged to take steps to insure "that the post of Fort Smith be kept up, and that at least one Company of Dragoons or Infantry be stationed there for the purpose of acting as escorts, expresses, &c." Fort Smith citizens made it clear that they were not opposed to the construction of the new post, as directed by General Order 19, as long as Fort Smith also was kept operational. They recommended that the new post "be named Fort Arbuckle, in honor of . . . Colonel Arbuckle, who has rendered important service on this Frontier for upwards of 30 years."[40]

Mayor N. Spring appointed Wheeler, Solomon F. Clark,

[39] General Order 19, May 31, 1850. National Archives, War Department, Adjutant General's Office, Letters Sent File. Marcy to Adjutant General, August 23, 1850. National Archives, War Department, Adjutant General's Office, Letters Received File. *Fort Smith Herald*, July 20, 1850.
[40] *Fort Smith Herald*, June 29, 1850.

and B. T. Duval to see that the resolutions were forwarded to Washington. Wheeler sought to strengthen the cause of keeping Fort Smith operational by reporting conversations with army officers at the post, who seemed to think that it would be unwise to abandon Fort Smith, which "must be kept up as a Military Depot, for the storing of supplies and munitions of war, for the new posts, now being established on the route to California, and Santa Fe."[41]

Wheeler said that the abandonment of Fort Smith would be wasteful.

The public buildings, for Military Purposes, at this place, are the largest, and best buildings on the Western Frontier. There are two large, elegantly finished brick buildings, two stories high, 40 by 100 feet, covered with slate, a gallery on each side, two stories, supported with pillars of brick. A large building, which burned down in 1849, now nearly rebuilt, for soldiers' quarters, 65 by 60 feet, for two companies of men. The carpenter's work is all ready to put together, and the brick made for the brickwork. Two large two story stone buildings for Commissary, & Quarter Master's Stores, a brick guard house, and a stone magazine, all surrounded with a stone wall three feet thick. There are also two large stables on the public grounds, capable of containing 200 horses, besides out houses &c.

These improvements have been left to go to waste and destruction by withdrawing the last company of infantry for Fort Gibson, where there were already three companies and where there are no more use for them, than there is here. The barracks at that place are built of wood, are old, and many of them rotting down.

A more healthy place for troops we venture to say, is not to be found in the United States than Fort Smith. During the time the 2 companies of the 5th Infantry were stationed here, which is nearly 2 years, there were not exceeding half

41 *Ibid.*, June 29, and July 6, 1850.

a dozen deaths, including those brought here with disease, contracted while in Mexico. Not a case of Cholera was among them last season, though the soldiers were called upon to remove freight from boats that had that disease upon them.

The troops were doing well here, and were needed, if for no other reason, than to take care of the public property; but the desires and caprices of 2 or 3 men had to be gratified; and Uncle Sam has to foot the bill.[42]

Colonel Arbuckle, who had been at Hot Springs attempting to overcome the infirmities of old age, returned to Fort Smith on July 16, and was distressed to learn that Fort Smith was to be abandoned. Writing to Quartermaster General Jesup on August 4, Arbuckle attributed the order to the machinations of Senator Borland. He said that word reaching him from Washington said that the senator had been using his influence to oppose the Doña Ana route to California because he believed that the road would "tend to depopulate western Arkansas" and that a military post at Fort Smith could be expected to facilitate emigration over this route. In opposition to Borland's view, Arbuckle argued that Fort Smith was the depot from which supplies were forwarded to the posts in the 7th Military Department. Because navigation on Red River above the log raft could not be relied upon, garrisons along the northern border of Texas had also to look to Fort Smith for subsistence. As the man who probably knew more about the area than any other person, Arbuckle regarded Fort Smith "as a post of the utmost importance as a military depot." As such, it must be occupied by a small command "to preserve the buildings, keep up the fences, receive stores and supplies, and expedite transportation." Arbuckle advised Jesup that he had written the secretary of war and General Scott on this subject. Besides urging them to keep Fort Smith garrisoned,

[42] *Ibid.*, July 6, 1850.

Arbuckle had pointed out that "its abandonment will be high-ly deterimental to the economy and interest of the service." He asked Jesup to enlighten him as to the reason behind the order to abandon the post.[43]

Arbuckle and the citizens of Fort Smith were informed of the real source of the order to abandon Fort Smith. Arkansas Senator W. K. Sebastian and Representative R. W. Johnson were informed by the secretary of war that the directive had originated with President Zachary Taylor, whose "personal opinion of the propriety of this measure" had guided the War Department.[44] Representative Johnson informed the people at Fort Smith that he had been the first to discover "the ill-judged and destructive orders issued concerning the removal and abandonment of Fort Smith." He had tried to get the order suspended, but was informed that it was impossible be-cause it had been issued by the "special direction of General Taylor."[45]

In compliance with General Order 19, Captain Montgom-ery, 7th Military Department quartermaster, began to liqui-date the stores at Fort Smith. First, he outfitted Captain Marcy's column, which had the duty of constructing the new post in western Indian Territory. He loaded thirty-one wag-ons with subsistence, ordnance, and quartermaster stores. Two pieces of artillery, caissons, and a traveling forge went with the train. The garrison force at Fort Smith was divided. One company was to go with Marcy to construct the new fort; the other was assigned to Fort Gibson.[46]

On July 2, 1850, Captain Caleb C. Sibley formed Company

[43] Arbuckle to Jesup, August 4, 1850. National Archives, War De-partment, Quartermaster Department, Letters Received File. Jesup to Arbuckle, August 23, 1850. National Archives, War Department, Quar-termaster Department, Letters Sent File.
[44] Fort Smith Herald, September 6, 1850.
[45] Ibid.
[46] Ibid., May 11, June 29, and August 3, 1850.

E and took passage for Fort Gibson on the *J. B. Gordon*. The *Fort Smith Herald* noted that "not even a corporal's guard" would remain behind to look after the large amount of public property—"here is another exhibition of government economy." The withdrawal of troops had left about "half a million dollars worth of public property exposed."[47]

Captain Montgomery remained in charge of the buildings and remaining stores with no men to assist him. If this was economy, Wheeler said, it was "saving at the spile and losing at the bung-hole." But the editor admired Montgomery's "spunk"—each morning he hoisted the colors, and in the evening lowered them; on July 4, he girded his sword and, assisted by citizens, fired the "National Salute."[48]

President Taylor died on July 9, 1850. The Arkansas congressional delegation immediately urged the War Department to reactivate Fort Smith, and were assured that "it was not the War Department's policy to abolish the fort entirely, but that it would be retained as a depot of Military supplies, and as the headquarters of the Military division embracing it." General Scott intimated to Congressman Johnson that, with Taylor dead, the new secretary of war, Charles M. Conrad, was disposed to order Fort Smith reoccupied.[49]

On February 12, 1851, the adjutant general directed Colonel Arbuckle to reoccupy Fort Smith by withdrawing Company E of the 5th Infantry from Fort Gibson. Headquarters for the 7th Military Department was also to be transferred from Fort Gibson to Fort Smith. Captain Sibley marched his unit into Fort Smith on March 14. It was a fitting if belated reward for Colonel Arbuckle to return to the comforts of Fort Smith—he died on June 11, 1851.[50]

[47] *Ibid.*, July 6, 1850.        [48] *Ibid.*        [49] *Ibid.*, September 6, 1850.
[50] Adjutant General to Arbuckle, February 12, 1851. National Archives, War Department, Adjutant General's Office, Letters Sent File. Page to Belknap, June 11, 1851. National Archives, War Department, Order Book, 7th Military Department.

# CHAPTER ELEVEN

# Mother Post for the Southwest

AFTER RECOVERING from President Taylor's abandonment order in 1850, Fort Smith settled down to nearly eleven years of uninterrupted existence as a frontier military station. Its status as permanent army post was due to its designation as department quartermaster depot, supplying Western forts, outfitting reconnaissance expeditions, and serving field forces engaged in Indian campaigns. There were troops at Fort Smith during most of the 1850's, but many of the units were transients. Troops in from the field rested and recuperated there while awaiting reassignment, and new troops from Eastern recruit depots were funneled through Fort Smith. At Belle Point, they rested, were equipped, at times received some training, and were then assigned to forts tributary to Fort Smith.

Fort Smith's garrison was constantly changing during the decade before the Civil War. After the War Department canceled the 1850 abandonment order, Fort Smith's garrison was Company E of the 5th Infantry Regiment from Fort Gibson, which reoccupied the Belle Point post in March, 1851. In the spring of 1851, the 5th Infantry was ordered to Texas, and Company F of the 7th Infantry Regiment, which reached Fort Smith on May 14, served as the garrison until May 8, 1854. During the summer of 1853, Company M of the 2d Light Artillery shared garrison duties with the 7th Infantry. From

May 8, 1854, until December 8, 1855, Fort Smith had no garrison force, although troops were there most of this period; while awaiting reassignment, they unloaded army cargoes from river steamers and assisted the department quartermaster in supplying Western posts. In response to a protest from the people at Fort Smith town, the War Department ordered companies B and F of the 7th Infantry to Belle Point on December 8, 1855. These two companies continued as the garrison force until August 1, 1857, when they were replaced by 7th Infantry companies D and H. On February 8, 1858, the 7th Infantry companies were pulled out of Fort Smith and ordered to join the Army of Utah because of troubles with the Mormons. A detachment of the 7th Infantry remained at Belle Point until March 1, when the companies garrisoning the advance posts arrived and embarked on the boats that were to carry them as far as Fort Leavenworth. Seven months later, units of the 1st Cavalry became the garrison, and continued until April 23, 1861, when the post was occupied by Arkansas Confederate troops. For a time during 1860, Companies E and F of the 2d Light Artillery joined the 1st Cavalry as the garrison.

In the 1850's, Fort Smith's military department affiliation shifted nearly as often as its garrison force. At the time of the reoccupation of Fort Smith in March, 1851, by Company E of the 5th Infantry Regiment from Fort Gibson, Fort Smith was again designated headquarters for the 7th Military Department. This office was soon returned to Fort Gibson until it was restored to Fort Smith in 1852. In 1853, the adjutant general ordered the merging of the 7th Military Department into the Department of the West, with headquarters at St. Louis. Then, in 1859, the limits of the Department of Texas, commanded by General David E. Twiggs, with headquarters at San Antonio, were extended northward in a corridor flanked by New Mexico and Arkansas to the southern boundary of Kansas Territory. At the same time, Fort Smith was attached to the Department of Texas.

During the 1850's, Fort Smith's role as communications center for the Southwest was broadened by technological developments and expanding stage, steamboat, and mail enterprises. The system of military roads radiating from Fort Smith carried an ever increasing flow of traffic, the California Road being the most heavily traveled. Small river steamers quickened the movement of goods, people, and mail along the Arkansas. When Major Bradford established Fort Smith in 1817, he complained that his letters required from six weeks to three months to reach Washington. In the 1850's this time had been reduced to about two weeks. Then, in 1858, the Missouri River and Western Telegraph Company installed a line from St. Louis to Belle Point, revolutionizing communications on the Southwestern frontier—military messages now reached Washington from Fort Smith in a few hours.

Also in 1858, Fort Smith became the focus for the Overland Mail. Even before 1850, local stages provided triweekly mail service between Fort Smith and the East. Soon after the rush to California mining camps began, Fort Smith citizens petitioned Congress to establish mail service by way of Belle Point to southern California.[1]

Overland Mail service began in 1858. Stage routes from Memphis and St. Louis merged at Fort Smith. In September, the first Butterfield Overland Mail stage passed through Fort Smith on a route southwest to El Paso and on to California, requiring fifteen and one-half days for the trip. Concord stages, ferried across the Arkansas on flatboats at Van Buren, carried mail and passengers to Fort Smith. West from Belle Point to California, the Overland Mail used "Thorough-brace

---

[1] *Fort Smith Herald*, June 29, 1850.

Wagons." A passenger on the first Butterfield Overland Mail stage through Fort Smith wrote in 1858:

> Fort Smith is a thriving town of about 2,500 inhabitants, and they boast that every house is full. There are two newspapers, both of which were, I believe, started by Judge Wheeler, who was a passenger by the overland mail route from St. Louis. As several other routes over the plains pass through this place, and have contributed much to its growth, the people evinced much interest; and the news that both the St. Louis and Memphis stages had arrived spread like wildfire. Horns were blown, houses were lit up, and many flocked to the hotel to have a look at the wagons and talk over the exciting topic, and have a peep at the first mail bags.[2]

As the department quartermaster depot, Fort Smith drew its stores from New Orleans and St. Louis. Arkansas River steamers—provocatively named *Pontiac, Swallow, Trustee, General Shields, Phillip Pennywit, Cotton Plant, St. Francis, Autocrat, Orella No. 2, Sallie Anderson, Alert No. 2,* and *Dispatch*—delivered barrels of salt pork, flour, and sugar, and great stacks of bacon at the Belle Point wharf. That the tedious ration of salt pork and beans had been altered was indicated by the additional commissary stores delivered to Fort Smith each year. Pickled onions, molasses, dessicated vegetables, rice, potatoes, salt, candles and twenty-gallon kegs of "good whiskey" were issued from Fort Smith's storehouses. The whisky was only for the officers' mess—the daily issue of a gill of whisky for enlisted men had been abolished in 1838.

The stores at Fort Smith included uniforms and accouterments, weapons, ammunition, tents, tools, and all those items required by a frontier army. The variety of units—infantry, cavalry, and artillery—traveling through Fort Smith or de-

---

[2] Walter B. Lang (ed.). *The First Overland Mail: Butterfield Trail,* I, 45–46.

pendent upon it required that the quartermaster keep on hand
a wide range of equipment and supplies. Captain Henry J.
Hunt and his Battery M, 2d United States Artillery, had been
part of the coastal defense force operating the big guns at Fort
Moultrie, South Carolina. In May, 1853, Battery M was reassigned to the light artillery for service at Fort Washita. In
July, the company stopped at Fort Smith, where they converted to horse artillery by receiving guns, caissons, limbers,
harness, and a traveling forge.[3]

In the mid-1850's, a severe drought made steam navigation
on the Arkansas so uncertain that the Fort Smith department
quartermaster had to use his wagons to haul government stores
to Belle Point from grounded vessels along the river. Captain
Samuel G. French, department and depot quartermaster at
the time, recommended to the War Department that, because
of the vital need of always having sufficient stores on hand for
supplying Western posts tributary to Fort Smith, he be permitted to take two preventive steps. First, if supply steamers
were unable to reach Belle Point, he asked for authority to
purchase commissary goods locally. He pointed out that it
would be a wise move from the standpoint of economy; it cost
the government ten dollars a barrel for flour delivered to Belle
Point from New Orleans, whereas he could purchase flour
locally for eight dollars a barrel. Second, he recommended
that the Fort Smith quartermaster's transportation equipment
include a fleet of keelboats, complete with towlines, anchors,
and poles, each capable of hauling thirty or forty tons of
freight, to be used as reserve transportation for bringing goods
to Fort Smith when steamers were unable to ascend the river.
The War Department authorized French to purchase two
keelboats. These craft, each drawing only ten inches when
loaded, came out from Pittsburgh in August, 1855.[4]

[3] Inspection Returns, Battery M, 2d Artillery, June 30 and August
31, 1853. National Archives, War Department, Reports Received File.

In order to distribute supplies to the posts west of Belle Point, the department quartermaster had to maintain a large transportation pool at Fort Smith. The army freight wagons were heavy-wheeled vehicles with wide steel tires, each with a cargo capacity of about two thousand pounds. Between seventy-five and a hundred of these wagons were in constant use on the supply circuit. In the early days, when Western roads were little more than blazed traces, oxen drew the wagons. As roads improved, six-mule teams were increasingly used. The lead mules were usually small; the middle mules, of medium size; the wheel mules "invariable were fine large animals." The driver—or mule skinner—rode the near wheel mule, driving the whole team with a single rein—the jerk line—a cracking whip, and language suitable for his animals.

The army horses, oxen, and mules required vast quantities of forage and grain each year. Fort Smith's increasing importance as a Western supply depot is shown by the rising volume of purchases of stock feed. In 1848, forage stores contained about two thousand bushels of oats and three thousand bushels of corn in addition to hay and fodder. By 1851, the amount had increased to ten thousand bushels of oats and thirty thousand bushels of corn.[5]

Military men differed in their preferences for draft animals. Colonel Mathew Arbuckle, department commandant, chose oxen. Captain Alexander Montgomery, quartermaster at Fort Smith for most of the 1850's, favored mules. On several occasions he attempted to dispose of all oxen at Fort Smith, claiming that they were highly susceptible to murrain and citing

[4] French to McClelland, July 10, 1855. French to Tompkins, July 17, 1855. French to Jesup, September 28, 1855. Kilburn to Gibson, July 29 and July 30, 1855. National Archives, War Department, Quartermaster General, Letters Received File. Gibson to French, August 7, 1855. National Archives, War Department, ACS, Letters Sent File.

[5] *Fort Smith Herald*, July 26, 1848. Bids Submitted to Montgomery, September 1, 1851. National Archives, War Department, Quartermaster General, Letters Received File.

Captain Randolph B. Marcy's experience. When Marcy's expedition left Fort Smith in 1850 to build Fort Arbuckle, so many oxen in his train had died from murrain within forty-eight hours after crossing the Poteau that he had to return to Fort Smith for more animals. Montgomery believed that although the initial expense for mules was greater, they were cheaper in the long run. The rough roads out of Fort Smith crippled oxen, which required several weeks to recover before they could be used again. According to Montgomery, oxen could make only about twelve miles a day, whereas mules traveled twice that distance without being pushed.[6] He claimed that oxen had to be four years old before they were able to do heavy army work; by the time they were eight years old, they were on the downgrade and had to be sold to Fort Smith butchers. He said that he knew of mules that had gone through the Seminole and Mexican wars and that were still being worked; he reported instances of the army's using the same mules for fifteen or twenty years. Quartermaster General Thomas S. Jesup approved the changeover to mules. Each spring, Montgomery bought, for from $50 to $75 each, small Spanish mules from drovers who passed Fort Smith on their way to Fort Leavenworth. He also obtained large, heavy mules from Missouri and Arkansas breeders for about $125 each. By 1860, the mule herd at Fort Smith numbered about five hundred.[7]

Montgomery employed a crew of eighty civilian teamsters to supply Fort Arbuckle, Fort Cobb, and Fort Washita. Each teamster received $25 a month; the two wagon masters, $60 a month. During 1860, Montgomery's teamsters hauled a hundred tons of freight to Fort Washita, 150 tons to Fort Arbuckle, and three hundred tons to Fort Cobb. The following

[6] Montgomery to Jesup, October 4, 1850. National Archives, War Department, Quartermaster General, Letters Received File.

[7] Jesup to Montgomery, November 4, 1850. National Archives, War Department, Quartermaster General, Letters Sent File.

MOTHER POST FOR THE SOUTHWEST 221

year, Montgomery was directed by the War Department to dispose of the livestock and to supply the Western posts by contract freighting. R. C. Armistead won the contract, for an average cost of $1.47 per hundredweight for each hundred miles.[8]

The duties of the Fort Smith quartermaster increased each year. In addition to his regular and growing responsibilities of supplying and equipping units moving through Fort Smith and servicing those posts in the Fort Smith constituency, he had also to provide quarters and assistance for the department paymaster who made the circuit of Western military stations every two months. Moreover, the quartermaster had a continuing association with the affairs of Indian Territory. Late-emigrating parties of Choctaws, Seminoles, and other Eastern Indians drew rations and supplies from his stores as they passed by way of Belle Point to the Indian nations west of Fort Smith. Each year, agents for the Five Civilized Tribes received substantial sums of federal money to distribute to their governments and private citizens. These funds, in specie and at times amounting to as much as $125,000, passed through Fort Smith; the quartermaster provided armed escorts to government officials transporting the money to Tahlequah, Doaksville, North Fork Town, and other Indian Territory towns. For several years, the quartermaster also provided both offices and quarters for the superintendent of Indian affairs, his staff, and their families until increased military use of the facilities at Fort Smith made it necessary for them to move off the posts in 1857.[9]

Twice during the 1850's, the Fort Smith quartermaster was

[8] Hindman to Floyd, March 28, 1860. Vinton to Jesup, March 1, 1860. National Archives, War Department, Quartermaster General, Letters Received File.

[9] Denver to Thompson, June 22, 1857. Thompson to Floyd, June 23, 1857. National Archives, War Department, Quartermaster General, Letters Received File.

called on to outfit expeditions for duty on the Western plains and beyond the Rocky Mountains. On July 29, 1857, the War Department ordered the Fort Smith garrison—two companies of the 7th Infantry—to move without delay by land via Fort Leavenworth to Fort Laramie. The quartermaster loaded eleven mule-drawn wagons with gear and rations for 120 men for twenty days; the column reached Fort Leavenworth in eighteen days, and arrived at Fort Laramie on September 26, 1857.[10] Then, in early 1858, because of troubles with the Mormons, the War Department reinforced the Army of Utah with the 1st Cavalry Regiment, the 6th and 7th Infantry regiments, and Batteries A and M of the 2d Artillery stationed at Fort Smith, Fort Washita, Fort Arbuckle, and Fort Belknap. Montgomery had to supply the troops and furnish them transportation via the Arkansas and Mississippi to Jefferson Barracks. He chartered river steamers for infantry, artillery, cavalry, and nine laundresses. After all these troops had left, the Fort Smith garrison for a time consisted of Montgomery, the ordnance sergeant, and a 7th Infantry detachment commanded by Lieutenant Edward J. Brooks.[11]

Fort Smith's role as mother post for the Southwest was demonstrated in the founding of Fort Wayne in 1838, of Fort Washita in 1842, of Fort Arbuckle in 1850, of a string of Texas posts in 1851, and of Fort Cobb in 1859. The troops, orders,

[10] Inspection Returns for Companies B and F, 7th Infantry Regiment, August 31, October 31, 1857. National Archives, War Department, Reports Received File. Lynde to Montgomery, July 31, 1857. Montgomery to Jesup, August 6, 1857. National Archives, War Department, Quartermaster General, Letters Received File.

[11] Simmons to Montgomery, February 5, 1858. National Archives, War Department, Quartermaster General, Letters Sent File. General Order No. 1, January 8, 1858. National Archives, War Department, Adjutant General, Letters Sent File. Page to Montgomery, February 8, 1858. National Archives, War Department, Quartermaster General, Letters Received File. Inspection Returns for Companies D and H, 7th Infantry Regiment, February 28, 1858. National Archives, War Department, Reports Received File.

building plans, supplies, equipment, and ordnance—all came from Fort Smith. Once each post was constructed and garrisoned, a military road—its lifeline over which coursed supplies, rations, reinforcements, and communications—was built connecting it with Fort Smith.

Soon after Captain Marcy's report on his reconnaissance of the California Road via Doña Ana reached the War Department, Marcy was directed to construct a new post west of Fort Smith near the junction of the Santa Fe and Doña Ana roads. For the expedition, Captain Montgomery loaded thirty-one ox-drawn wagons with quartermaster, ordnance, and commissary stores. When Marcy's supply column rolled out of Belle Point on July 30, 1850, it included two pieces of artillery, a caisson, and traveling forge. After temporarily occupying a site on the Canadian River, Marcy selected a spot on Wild Horse Creek, a tributary of the Washita. Troops from Fort Washita and Fort Towson joined him to work on the new post, which was named Fort Arbuckle. Marcy claimed that Fort Arbuckle was strategically situated to protect overland traffic, and that traffic taking that route could save about sixty miles between Fort Smith and Doña Ana.[12]

The construction of Fort Arbuckle was part of a broad War Department plan to advance the frontier into western Texas and to provide protection for emigrants passing along the Doña Ana Road from Fort Smith to the Southwest. The 5th Infantry Regiment, garrison force for posts in the 7th Military Department, was ordered to Texas in April, 1851, to establish a string of military stations on or near Marcy's route to Doña Ana. Suggested locations were at the Brazos crossing, at the Pecos crossing, and at some point between the Pecos and Doña

[12] General Order 19, May 31, 1850. National Archives, War Department, Adjutant General's Office, Letters Sent File. Marcy to Adjutant General, August 23, 1850. National Archives, War Department, Adjutant General's Office, Letters Received File. *Fort Smith Herald*, August 3, 10, 17, and 24, and September 14 and 21, 1850.

Ana. The 7th Infantry Regiment, a battalion of which was at
Fort Leavenworth, was ordered to the 7th Military Department to garrison those posts evacuated by the 5th Regiment.[13]

The War Department designated Fort Smith as the supply
depot to outfit and provision the 5th Infantry Regiment. Captain Montgomery was instructed to furnish the Texas expedition with at least four-months' supply of subsistence and quartermaster stores. Both wagons and wall tents were scarce at
Fort Smith. Montgomery ordered tents, flies, and poles from
the Philadelphia depot. He had only twenty-five freight
wagons free at the time and, needing 125 for the expedition, he
ordered a hundred from the St. Louis depot. Montgomery's
workers carefully packed and weighed each wagon to make
certain that no cargo exceeded the allowed twenty-five hundred pounds. Government freighters hauled the stores to the
Red River. Montgomery engaged the Black and Butt Freighting Company of Preston, Texas, to transport 5th Infantry
supplies from Preston to the Brazos at a cost of three dollars a
hundred pounds. Assuming that Fort Smith would be responsible for supplying the new Texas posts, Montgomery established an advanced depot at Preston. His plan was to move
stores from Fort Smith to that point by government train.
Black and Butt agreed to relay the supplies to the west Texas
stations. Montgomery believed that this arrangement would
reduce the size of the supply train maintained at Fort Smith.[14]

Throughout 1851, equipment and troops for the army
build-up in western Texas poured through Fort Smith. Three
companies of 5th Infantry Regiment reinforcements from
Corpus Christi were exposed to cholera while aboard trans-

[13] General Order 18, March 31, 1851. General Order 19, April 11,
1851. National Archives, War Department, Adjutant General's Office,
Letters Sent File.
[14] Montgomery to Hunt, May 4, 1851. Hunt to Jesup, May 14, 1851.
Montgomery to Stanton, June 1, 2, and 14, 1851. National Archives,
War Department Quartermaster General, Letters Received File.

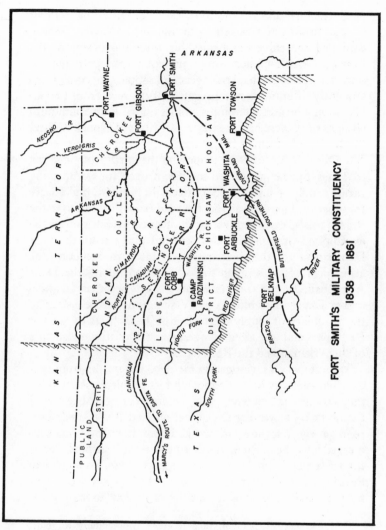

FORT SMITH'S MILITARY CONSTITUENCY, 1838–1861.

port steamers, and by the time they docked at Belle Point several had been stricken with the disease. Montgomery equipped the three companies for their movement to the Brazos, the able-bodied troops prepared to depart, but his teamsters refused to haul their gear and supplies to Texas. Consequently, Montgomery segregated all the men from Corpus Christi in a quarantine camp six miles out of Fort Smith until all signs of cholera had passed. In early July, Colonel William G. Belknap returned from the Brazos and complimented Montgomery for his work in moving the initial troop column to Texas, but he questioned the use of oxen for transporting future supply trains to the Southwest. In his view, mules were far superior. He reported that the road from Fort Smith to the Brazos was strewn with carcasses of oxen, which slowed the expedition. Montgomery also received praise from the War Department for the contribution he made to executing the army plan of establishing military stations along the Doña Ana Road. At the same time, he was advised that Quartermaster Department officers in Washington were considering the possibility of supplying the line of Texas posts by way of Red River, and was asked to investigate the relative advantages of the Arkansas and the Red routes.[15]

Montgomery's investigation included statements from persons acquainted with the region and its problems. Abel Warren, a trader on Red River, told Montgomery that because of the obstacles to regular navigation on Red River—swift current, generally shallow bottom, and ubiquitous snags and submerged logs—he relied on the Arkansas as the transport avenue for trade goods for his post. His merchandise, consigned to Fort Smith via steamer, was transported to his Red River post by pack train. He advised that the only way to supply the

[15] Montgomery to Stanton, June 14, 1851. Montgomery to Jesup, July 11 and September 5, 1851. National Archives, War Department, Quartermaster General, Letters Received File.

posts established in Texas was by wagon train from Fort Smith.[16]

Doaksville merchant Wiliam L. Poalk declared that the feasibility of sending army supply boats up Red River was "very uncertain and exceedingly precarious." He could recall years in which eleven months passed without a single boat docking at Towson landing, and said that, most of the year, merchants at Doaksville, Pine Bluff, Clarksville, and Preston were compelled to transport their goods by wagon from Shreveport. Poalk described this road as "one of the worst . . . in the whole country."[17]

When Montgomery learned that officials in Washington were determined to establish the principal depot for supplying the western Texas posts on Red River, probably at Fort Towson landing, he reported that in his judgment only shallow-draft Mackinaw boats could be relied upon for moving goods on that stream. His investigation showed that only on rare occasions had the army been able to supply posts on Red River and its tributaries by water transportation. In 1842, a large Quartermaster Department keelboat had ascended the Red and the Washita from Fort Towson to Fort Washita. Montgomery said that only two steamers had ever ascended the Red and its tributaries as far as Fort Washita. One made the passage in February, 1844; the other, in February, 1846. Only one of the steamers had been able to return to Towson landing. The other, caught in a rapid fall on the Red, was grounded and abandoned. Rivermen said that the river's strong current made ascent by keelboats extremely difficult.[18]

Montgomery reported that ten steamers reached Fort Smith

[16] Montgomery to Jesup, June 27, 1851. National Archives, War Department, Quartermaster General, Letters Received File.

[17] Poalk to Montgomery, June 28, 1851. National Archives, War Department, Quartermaster General, Letters Received File.

[18] Montgomery to Jesup, September 15, 1851. National Archives, War Department, Quartermaster General, Letters Received File.

for every one that docked at Towson landing. Steamers drawing eight or nine feet reached Fort Smith from New Orleans
and Cincinnati, but no craft with a draft of more than four and
a half feet had ever reached Towson landing. Most of the
goods reaching the upper Red River towns were delivered in
freight wagons, but not more than one ton in five thousand
came into Fort Smith in wheeled vehicles.[19]

In Montgomery's opinion, the question of whether Towson
landing or Fort Smith should serve as the depot for supplying
the new posts became, "Would the difference in land transportation compensate for the difference in facilities of water
transportation?" He did not believe that it would. The distance from Towson landing to the Brazos via Preston was 263
miles; from Fort Smith to the crossing of the Brazos via Fort
Arbuckle, 302 miles—an advantage of only thirty-nine miles
for Towson landing. Montgomery felt that, although the distance that wagons would have to haul supplies to the advance
posts was slightly less for the projected depot on the Red, this
advantage would not compensate for the difficulty and higher
transportation cost involved in delivering to Towson landing.
He believed that consideration should be given also to a number of other factors incidental to steamboating on the Red.
"The greater risk of losses by accidents of navigation, the
greater risks of delays in delivery and consequent embarrass-
ment of the troops to be supplied, and the very probable con-
tingency of having to transport by wagon from Shreveport
125 miles to Towson landing over one of the worst roads in
all the South West."[20]

Montgomery, clearly attempting to protect the future of
Fort Smith as a Western supply depot, wrote War Department officials that he was convinced that the establishment of
a depot at Towson landing would be attended with no ma-

[19] *Ibid.*
[20] *Ibid.*

terial benefits to the service. At the same time, he said, it would
be a needless and wasteful expenditure of public funds. Even
worse, it could very probably entail disastrous losses and much
suffering among the troops dependent on the new depot.[21]

To make a stronger case for Fort Smith as the principal
Western depot, Montgomery pointed to the emergence of
the counties of northwestern Arkansas and southwestern Missouri as wheat-growing areas. Farmers were sending many
wagon loads of wheat and flour to Fort Smith and Van Buren.
Montgomery was satisfied that he could supply the flour required by the troops on the advance line at much cheaper rates
than the New Orleans depot could with flour purchased at
Cincinnati and New Orleans. With the source of supply close
at hand, the risk of spoilage would be greatly reduced.
Further, he observed, the day was not distant when the Commissary Department would be able to secure in the Fort Smith
and Van Buren markets the pork and bacon needed to feed
the troops on the frontier. Montgomery also drew on the experience and knowledge of the late Colonel Arbuckle, who
was reported to have said that when the road was completed
from Fort Smith to the Brazos, "it would be more convenient,
far more certain, and equally as cheap to the Government to
supply the Posts on the Brazos, using the navigation of the
Arkansas River."[22]

The advocates of a Red River supply depot to serve the west
Texas posts won out, at least temporarily, and Fort Smith's
supply constituency consisted of only the Indian Territory
posts. Captain Montgomery was belatedly informed that on
July 2, 1851, the War Department had redefined the military
departments. The boundaries of the 7th and 8th Military Departments were altered, and the forts established by the 5th
Infantry Regiment south of Red River were transferred from

21 *Ibid.*
22 *Ibid.*

the 7th to the 8th Military Department.[23] By 1852, it was obvious that the War Department scheme to supply west Texas posts by way of the Red was faltering, and from time to time the Fort Smith quartermaster was called upon to rush subsistence stores to the frontier stations in that region.[24]

Fort Cobb, in the heart of the Kiowa-Comanche range, was founded in 1859. The genesis of this post goes back to the spring of 1858, when a Texas Ranger force led by Captain John S. Ford crossed Red River into the Leased District, struck an unsuspecting Comanche village, and killed about seventy-six Indians. Ford's raid was in retaliation for alleged Comanche depredations in Texas.[25]

The 7th Infantry Regiment, garrison forces for Fort Smith and Indian Territory posts, had only recently been ordered to Utah. A small detachment had been left at Fort Smith for quartermaster duty; at Fort Arbuckle, the garrison consisted of only five men. Comanche war parties, angered by Ford's raid, were reported to be planning an attack on Fort Arbuckle to obtain arms for a retaliatory strike against the Texans. Indian Agent Douglas Cooper mustered a force of Choctaws and Chickasaws to defend the post. On June 22, 1858, he sent a messenger to Fort Belknap in Texas; with forced marches in summer's heat, a relief column—Company E of the 1st Infantry, under Lieutenant James E. Powell—reached Fort Arbuckle in seven days to replace Cooper and his Choctaw-Chickasaw battalion.[26]

The Comanches continued active, and so the War Depart-

[23] Page to Montgomery November 20, 1851. National Archives, War Department, 7th Military Department, Order Book.
[24] Montgomery to Jesup, October 2, 1852. National Archives, War Department, Quartermaster Department, Letters Received File.
[25] Walter P. Webb. *The Texas Rangers*, 151–60.
[26] *Arkansas Intelligencer*, July 9, 1858. Cooper to Rector, July 21, 1858. National Archives, Office of Indian Affairs, Southern Superintendency, Letters Received File.

Old U. S. Jail, Fort Smith, Ark.

Barracks erected in 1851, later used as courtroom and jail by Judge Parker. Shows structure before upper floor and jail wing addition.

Fort Smith federal courthouse and jail, 1889.

Prisoners guarded by U.S. deputy marshals on steps of Fort Smith courthouse, 1879.

Execution scene, gallows at Fort Smith, 1879.

"The Hanging Judge,"
Isaac Parker.

Judge Parker's court, Fort Smith, 1891.

Fort Smith in 1865, scene of the Fort Smith Council.

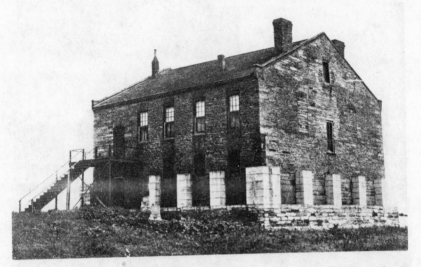

Commissary Building, Fort Smith, erected in 1846, one of extant structures being restored.

Workmen restoring foundations of original Fort Smith buildings on Belle Point.

Foundations of original Fort Smith buildings on Belle Point.

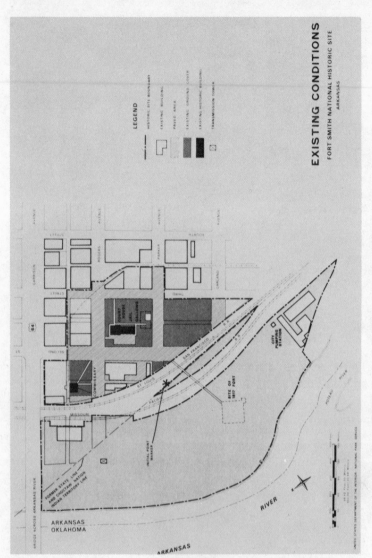

Fort Smith National Historic Site, Arkansas, 1979.

ment ordered several companies of the 1st Cavalry into Indian
Territory. Major William H. Emory assumed command at
Fort Arbuckle in September, 1858, and immediately called
on Captain Montgomery at Fort Smith for supplies and fifty
mules for a pack train to sustain a cavalry campaign against the
Comanches.[27]

Before Montgomery could fill Emory's request, the Comanches were hit again by a surprise attack. On the night of
October 1, Major Earl Van Dorn and four companies of the
2d Cavalry from Texas struck a Comanche village near Rush
Springs, smashing the settlement, killing fifty-six warriors and
two women, taking three hundred horses, and burning 120
lodges.[28]

Rather than intimidating the Comanches, the Van Dorn
raid only increased their fury and determination for vengeance. To strengthen the Indian Territory posts, the War Department issued General Order 21 on November 6, 1858, ordering two companies of the 1st Cavalry to take posts at each
of Fort Smith, Fort Washita, and Fort Riley. Captain Delos
B. Sacket's A and B companies, the Fort Smith garrison group,
reached Belle Point from Fort Leavenworth on December
18.[29]

The Comanche menace died down during the winter, but in
the spring the warriors resumed their raids on Southwestern
settlements and emigrant trains. Sacket's cavalry was ordered
to take the field on June 13, 1859, with directions to rendezvous with troops from Fort Washita. The combined force was
to operate in the Antelope Hills area of the Canadian valley.

[27] Montgomery to Jesup, November 1, 1858. National Archives, War
Department, Quartermaster General, Letters Received File.
[28] Rupert N. Richardson. *The Frontier of Northwest Texas, 1846–
1876*, 193.
[29] General Order 21, November 6, 1851. National Archives, War
Department, Adjutant General's Office, Letters Sent File. *Fort Smith
Herald*, December 25, 1858.

Montgomery furnished Sacket's train and recruited civilian teamsters to drive the wagons.[30]

After Sacket's departure, Fort Smith's garrison was a detachment of 1st Cavalry left behind to assist Montgomery in unloading military stores from steamers, repairing wagons, and keeping trains in the field to provision and equip the troops in the Comanche campaign. Field officers pointed to the need for a permanent base for operations on the Kiowa-Comanche range. On July 27, 1859, the War Department issued General Order 4, directing the construction of a new post in the Leased District on or near the Washita adjacent to a reserve selected for relocating the Texas Indians. Major Emory was placed in command of the projected post, to be known as Fort Cobb. The garrison was to consist of four companies of the 1st Infantry from Texas and of Companies D and E of the 1st Cavalry from Fort Arbuckle. When Captain Sacket completed the Antelope Hills operation, he was to take his cavalry force to Fort Arbuckle. The garrison force for Fort Smith would be Companies E and F, 2d Light Artillery. The General Order specified that Fort Cobb would be supplied by the Fort Smith depot, and that the limits of the Department of Texas were to be extended northward to the southern boundary of Kansas Territory, encompassing all Indian Territory and including Fort Smith. General David E. Twiggs commanded this department, with headquarters at San Antonio.[31]

Just as the Fort Smith quartermaster gathered and shipped supplies, equipment, and building materials for constructing new posts and provisioned them once they became operational, he served also as custodian for posts west of Belle Point

[30] Montgomery to Jesup, July 2, 1859. National Archives, War Department, Quartermaster General, Letters Received File.

[31] General Order 4, August 19, 1859. National Archives, War Department, Adjutant General's Office, Letters Sent File.

abandoned by the army. In 1854, the War Department decided to abandon Fort Towson. Captain Samuel G. French,
Fort Smith quartermaster at the time, was ordered to visit the
station "to examine the public buildings and sell them." French
was at Fort Washita when these instructions arrived. Captain
Braxton Bragg, who commanded Fort Washita, gave French
a mule "with a hard saddle." With no escort, French started
for Towson. It was a lonely ride—he did not meet even one
person on the trail. Spending the night with an Indian family,
he reached Fort Towson the next day and met with a committee of Choctaws and their agent Douglas Cooper. Accompanied by the committee, French examined the buildings at
Fort Towson and concluded that it would be folly "to sell or
destroy such property, for it would bring nothing," but he
recommended that it be deeded to the Choctaws for an
academy.[32] Secretary of War Jefferson Davis approved
French's recommendation, and General Jesup directed that
the Fort Towson buildings be turned over to the Choctaws
with the understanding that the War Department reserved
the right to use the post as required for future military purposes.[33]

The Fort Smith quartermaster performed a similar function
in closing Fort Gibson. Situated near the mouth of Grand
River in the southern part of the Cherokee Nation, this post
was the source of contention with the Cherokee leaders. For
years, the National Council had urged the federal government
to close Fort Gibson. An 1854 Cherokee memorial charged
that the fort, with the community of tavern keepers, loose
women, and frontier renegades it supported, had become a
curse to the Indians. Tribal leaders asserted that the Cherokee
Nation was a civilized community, that there was no need for

[32] French to Cooper, December 27, 1854. National Archives, War
Department, Quartermaster General, Letters Received File.
[33] Jesup to French, November 30, 1854. National Archives, War Department, Quartermaster General, Letters Sent File.

the post, and that the garrison should move west, where it was needed. The War Department finally succumbed to prolonged pressure and on May 7, 1857, issued General Order 6, directing that Fort Gibson "be abandoned without unnecessary delay." Of the four garrison companies of the 7th Infantry Regiment, two were assigned to Fort Smith, one to Fort Washita, and the fourth to Fort Arbuckle. Regimental headquarters and the regimental band were also moved to Fort Smith. Lieutenant William L. Cabell and twenty men remained at Fort Gibson to guard the ordnance, medical, quartermaster, and commissary stores until these could be removed to Fort Smith. The abandonment of Fort Gibson was completed on September 1 by the removal of the last ammunition and supplies; it was turned over to Daniel W. Coodey for the Cherokee Nation.[34]

Other duties of the Fort Smith quartermaster included maintaining existing military roads connecting satellite posts and opening new ones. The last road constructed west of Fort Smith before the post became a Confederate bastion grew from an order received at Belle Point in June, 1860, from the San Antonio headquarters for the Department of Texas. Captain Montgomery was directed to draw a detail of two officers and forty men from Fort Cobb, survey the most direct route between Fort Smith and Fort Cobb, and open a road connecting the posts. Montgomery sent a wagon train to Fort Cobb with provisions and road-building equipment, ran the survey, supervised construction of the road, and reported it completed and open for traffic on December 28, 1860.[35]

[34] Drew to Davis, January 24, 1854. National Archives War Department, Secretary of War, Letters Received File. General Order 6, May 7, 1857. National Archives, War Department, Adjutant General's Office, Letters Sent File.
[35] Montgomery to Johnston, November 8 and December 28, 1860. National Archives, War Department, Quartermaster General, Letters Received File.

In the decade preceding the Civil War, Fort Smith was an important base of operations and outfitting point for several government surveys, including the Whipple reconnaissance beginning in 1853, the Beale expedition of 1858, and several local surveys carried out by Captain Randolph B. Marcy. Fort Smith also served the Texas Boundary Commission. When the work of this commission was completed in 1859, Captain Thomas Pitcher, in charge of its military escort, came to Belle Point to draw from Montgomery those supplies, ammunition, and mules necessary to equip his detachment for its return to Santa Fe.[36]

Popular pressure from Fort Smith town and other Western communities for a transcontinental railroad influenced Congress to appropriate, on March 3, 1853, $150,000, to be used by the secretary of war in making surveys to ascertain the best railroad route from the Mississippi River to the Pacific. Secretary of War Jefferson Davis ordered northern, central, and southern surveys. The southern survey, along the 35th parallel beginning at Fort Smith, was in charge of Lieutenant Amiel W. Whipple. His party of twelve scientists and engineers reached Fort Smith on the *Umpire No. 3* on July 2, 1853, and spent two weeks at Belle Point assembling wagons, draft animals, and subsistence and ordnance supplies, including a small field piece, for the trip west. Before Whipple's column departed, H. B. Mollhausen, expedition topographer and artist, made two drawings of Fort Smith.[37]

In 1858, Lieutenant Alexander E. Steen and a detachment of the 3d Infantry reached Fort Smith to escort an expedition commanded by Edward F. Beale, whose assignment was to

[36] Montgomery to Jesup, December 3 and December 19, 1859. National Archives, War Department, Quartermaster General, Letters Received File.

[37] Muriel H. Wright and George Shirk (eds.). "The Journal of Lt. A. W. Whipple." *Chronicles of Oklahoma*, XXVII (Autumn, 1950), 235–83.

survey a route for a wagon road west from Fort Smith along the Canadian to the Colorado River. Among the items drawn by Steen from the Fort Smith stores were two field pieces. Van Dorn's raid had stirred up the Comanches, so that travel was extremely hazardous west of Belle Point. Steen's column departed Fort Smith on October 28, 1858.[38]

Marcy was the most active explorer in the region west of Fort Smith. One of his more important surveys was the Red River Expedition of 1852. Accompanied by Captain George B. McClellan, a military escort, and Indian guides, Marcy explored and mapped the country between the mouth of Cache Creek and the sources of Red River. He drew his subsistence supplies for the Red River Expedition from the Preston Depot, forty miles south of Fort Washita, but received equipment, ordnance, and wagons from Fort Smith. Another Marcy survey, made in 1854, grew out of an act by the Texas legislature authorizing the federal government to select and survey from vacant state lands reservations for Texas Indian tribes. The War Department ordered Marcy to accompany Indian Agent Robert S. Neighbors in selecting and surveying the reservations. Marcy reached Fort Smith on May 17, 1854, on the steamer *Mattie Wayne* to organize the expedition. The Fort Smith quartermaster supplied him nine wagons, twenty-seven oxen, eleven horses, and two mules as well as subsistence and ordnance. From Belle Point, Marcy proceeded with his military escort to Fort Belknap, where he was to meet Neighbors and begin the survey.[39]

The political thunder generated by the elections of 1860, the threatened secession by Arkansas and other slave-holding states, and the resulting possibility that the federal government

[38] Beale to Steen, October 26, 1858. Steen to Montgomery, October 26, 1858. Montgomery to Sheen, October 27, 1858. National Archives, War Department, Quartermaster General, Letters Received File.

[39] French to Jesup, May 15, 1854. National Archives, War Department, Quartermaster General, Letters Received File.

might lose control of its Southern military posts—nine of this had noticeable effect on the War Department, which continued to garrison and supply the military stations in the troubled zone. Throughout 1860 and into early 1861, Fort Smith was supplied by steamers from St. Louis, Cincinnati, and New Orleans. The Belle Point station was attractive to secessionists not only because of its strategic location but also because its storehouses and magazines were packed with subsistence, quartermaster, and ordnance stores. Arkansas state troops seized Fort Smith several weeks before the Little Rock convention adopted an ordinance of secession.

# CHAPTER TWELVE

# Fort Smith and the Civil War:
# A Confederate Post

FORT SMITH AND THE SOUTHWEST soon felt the effect of the election of 1860 and the sectional turmoil that followed. South Carolina withdrew from the Union on December 20, and by February, 1861, the other six states of the lower South had seceded. Delegates from these states convened at Montgomery, Alabama, and adopted a constitution on February 7. Eleven days later, Jefferson Davis was inaugurated provisional president of the Confederate States of America. At the same time, the upper South was taking steps to join the new political community. On the same day that delegates at Montgomery adopted a constitution, the Choctaw Council declared their support of the Southern cause. Even before Arkansas seceded, local separatist groups moved quickly to seize the United States Arsenal at Little Rock and other federal property in the state. At Napoleon, quartermaster and ordnance stores from the St. Louis army depot, consigned to Captain Montgomery at Fort Smith, were "seized by certain individuals pretending to act for the State of Arkansas."[1]

Because of these seizures of federal property and the likelihood that Arkansas would soon join the Confederacy, the War Department directed the evacuation and abandonment of Fort Smith. General Winfield Scott ordered General William S.

[1] McKinstry to Williams, February 12, 1861. *War of Rebellion: A Compilation of the Official Records of the Union and Confederate Armies*, Series I, Volume I, 646.

Harney, commander of the Department of the West, to move the Fort Smith garrison—Companies D and E, 1st Cavalry—to Fort Leavenworth. Before abandoning the post, the troops were to remove all public property except subsistence stores, which were to be sent to Fort Washita. In view of the seizure of the Little Rock Arsenal and the stores at Napoleon, Scott was satisfied that it was unsafe to send supplies up the Arkansas for Fort Arbuckle, Fort Cobb, and Fort Washita. Henceforth, these posts would be supplied via Fort Scott from St. Louis or Fort Leavenworth.[2]

News that the War Department planned to abandon Fort Smith alarmed local citizens. On February 22, they wired a protest to the secretary of war:

> We, the undersigned, citizens of Arkansas, learn with deep regret that the post of Fort Smith is to be abandoned by the General Government. It is fair to suppose that this order has been determined upon in consequence of the actions of a mob in Little Rock and the unfortunate course of the governor in demanding from the United States officer the arsenal. The late decision of the people at the ballot-box has proved beyond question the almost unanimous voice in the counties adjoining Fort Smith for Union as against violence, mob law, and secession. We, therefore, in the name of the people, the whole people, ask a suspension of this movement until the decision of the State by its convention is known.[3]

This appeal caused Scott to telegraph Harney to "stop the march of the troops from Fort Smith." By mid-March, when Arkansas appeared closer to withdrawing from the Union, Scott decided to make preliminary preparations for evacuating federal troops from military stations west of Fort Smith.[4]

[2] Thomas to Harney, February 13, 1861. *Ibid.*, 654.
[3] Wolfe to Secretary of War, February 22, 1861. *Ibid.*, 655.
[4] Scott to Harney, February 22, 1861. *Ibid.*, 656.

Scott ordered Colonel Emory, former commandant at Fort Cobb who was then in Washington, to return to Indian Territory and to group the 1st Cavalry companies from Fort Arbuckle and Fort Cobb at Fort Washita. This order was not binding if, in Emory's judgment, the safety of the troops and the interests of the United States demanded otherwise. At the same time, the adjutant general's office telegraphed Harney to move Company E of the 1st Infantry from Fort Arbuckle to Fort Washita and to alert the troops at Fort Cobb to be ready to abandon the post. The next day, Harney relayed this message to Captain Montgomery at Fort Smith. Montgomery was to see that express riders carried copies of the dispatch to the commandants at Fort Arbuckle, Fort Cobb, and Fort Washita.[5]

Some officials in Washington opposed General Scott's plan to evacuate Fort Cobb, saying that it would expose the reservation Indians to attack by the wild tribes of the area. Scott reluctantly promised to maintain a garrison at Fort Cobb. Emory, about to depart Washington for Indian Territory, was informed of the change in plans regarding Fort Cobb. If the Fort Smith officers called on him for aid in protecting the depot stores at Belle Point, he was to provide assistance with troops from Indian Territory posts; if Arkansas seceded, he was to withdraw all troops from the territory.[6]

Emory proceeded by rail from Washington to Memphis, where he boarded a steamer for Fort Smith. Low water sixty miles below Dardanelle grounded the vessel. Emory had anticipated the possibility of being detained, and before leaving Little Rock he sent a copy of General Scott's instructions to the Fort Arbuckle commander. The latter was instructed to commence transferring his troops to Fort Washita; if Texas

[5] Williams to Montgomery, March 19, 1861. *Ibid.*, 656–57.
[6] Townsend to Emory, March 21, 1861. *Ibid.*, 659.

troops threatened Fort Washita, he was "to march to its support with his whole force."[7]

On April 2, a slight rise on the Arkansas enabled the steamer to resume the run to Fort Smith. From Belle Point, Emory sent an express rider with instructions for the commanding officer at Fort Cobb. He was to rush two of his four companies to Fort Washita and hold the others at Fort Cobb until further orders; he was to use surplus wagons and teams for transferring to Fort Washita all ordnance and other public property not required at Fort Cobb.[8]

On April 12, 1861, Confederate batteries opened fire on Fort Sumter. On April 14, the fort surrendered. Several hours before the capitulation, Colonel Emory telegraphed a report to the War Department on the border situation and left Fort Smith for Fort Washita. Emory's report disclosed that ammunition stores were low at Fort Smith and its satellite posts in Indian Territory, and asked that a shipment be sent overland from the Fort Leavenworth. Another problem facing Emory was the widespread resignations among 1st Cavalry officers, who were tendering their services to the Confederacy; in four companies, only two officers remained. Emory had instructed Captain Samuel D. Sturgis, commandant at Fort Smith, that as soon as he heard that Arkansas had seceded, he was to pull his troops out of Fort Smith, retire into Indian Territory, and post his men on the Arkansas River at the crossing of the Texas Road.[9]

Reports filtering through to Belle Point from Little Rock told of a call by Governor Henry M. Rector for five thousand troops. Former United States Senator Solon Borland was placed in command of this force, whose first mission was to

[7] Emory to Townsend, April 2, 1861. *Ibid.,* 659–60.
[8] Emory to Commanding Officer at Fort Cobb, April 6, 1861. *Ibid.,* 662.
[9] Emory to Townsend, April 13, 1861. *Ibid.,* 656–66.

march on Fort Smith. Borland supervised enrollment of the volunteer troops, issued them weapons from the Little Rock Arsenal, and chartered steamers to carry them to Belle Point. As soon as Captain Sturgis heard of these preparations at Little Rock, he ordered his men to pack their gear, load all available wagons with commissary, quartermaster, and ordnance stores from the warehouses, and prepare to evacuate Fort Smith. Even though Emory's orders directed him to hold Fort Smith until he heard that Arkansas had seceded, Sturgis considered his position untenable. Besides being faced with the task of resisting Borland's force with his own two companies of cavalry, he was confronted by "the entire population of the surrounding country . . . ready at a moment's warning to take up arms against us." Resistance could result only in his men's being taken prisoner and the loss to the government "of all the arms, horses, means of transportation, &c. at the post." Sturgis directed Captain Montgomery, the ordnance sergeant, the hospital steward, the sick, and the laundresses to remain and eventually to proceed to department headquarters at St. Louis. On April 23, Sturgis' scouts reported that Borland's steamer transports had reached nearby Van Buren. By nine o'clock that evening, the Fort Smith commandant led his cavalry companies and wagon train across the Poteau. The column reached Fort Washita on April 30.[10]

Colonel Borland's transports, the *Frederick Notrebe* and *Tahlequah*, with three hundred Arkansas volunteers and eight pieces of light artillery aboard, stopped at Van Buren long enough for the expedition commander to assure the editor of the *Press* that his command was "fully provided with all the munitions of war necessary for taking possession of Fort Smith." There was great excitement in Van Buren, whose citizens rushed to the wharf to view the conquering host. Before proceeding to Belle Point, Colonel Borland ordered the

10 Sturgis to Williams, May 21, 1861. *Ibid.*, 650.

local militia company, the Frontier Guards, to turn out and join his troops.[11]

The steamers made the short run to Fort Smith, crewmen tied up at the wharf, and the Arkansas Volunteers led by Borland and Edmund Burgevin, adjutant general of Arkansas, marched into Fort Smith. Borland declared Montgomery and the others left by Captain Sturgis prisoners of war and took possession of the fort in the name of the state of Arkansas.[12]

For several days, reinforcements poured into Fort Smith. Captain Perkins' Crawford County Cavalry Company was among the first to arrive; the steamer *Leon* docked with more troops from Little Rock. Borland's command had increased fourfold. The town's streets were jammed with armed men, as yet only Arkansas Volunteers and not Confederate troops until May 6, when the Arkansas convention adopted an ordinance of secession. Meanwhile, Borland and his Little Rock troops returned to their homes, and Napoleon B. Burrows of the 8th Arkansas Brigade took command at Fort Smith. For a time the fort was garrisoned by two Sebastian County companies and Perkins' and Foster's companies from Crawford County.[13]

Action by the Arkansas convention at Little Rock brought about an early change in the command at Fort Smith. Three generals were designated to command state troops: James Yell, major general; N. Bart Pearce and Napoleon Burrows, brigadier generals. Burrows was placed in command of Eastern Division troops, and Pearce was to head the Western Division with headquarters at Fort Smith.[14]

General Pearce reached Fort Smith on May 20. The next

11 *Van Buren Press*, April 24, 1861.
12 Gatlin to Thomas, April 24, 1861. *Official Records*, Series I, Volume I, 650.
13 *Van Buren Press*, April 24 and May 1, 1861.
14 *Ibid.*, May 13 and May 22, 1861. John M. Harrell. *Confederate Military History of Arkansas*, 17.

day, he launched Fort Smith's first Civil War offensive when he sent a three-company force—one of infantry, and two of cavalry—to intercept a Union train of thirty wagons reported to be en route from Fort Cobb to Fort Leavenworth. This was a part of Emory's column which had collected troops, equipment, ordnance, and stores from Indian Territory posts for the march to Kansas. In addition to having 750 men in eleven companies, including Sturgis' two cavalry companies from Fort Smith, Emory's group included 150 women, children, and teamsters. Texas Confederate cavalry racing from the south and Pearce's westward-moving column failed to catch the Union force, which reached Fort Leavenworth on May 31.[15]

Fort Smith served as a Confederate military post until September 1, 1863. Because of the station's strategic location, storage facilities, and transportation and communications network, the Confederate command continued its use as a prime supply depot. In this period also, the post took on additional functions. The most important of these was serving as defensive bastion for protecting Confederate states west of the Mississippi. Confederate planners, believing that their river defenses could check Union attempts to penetrate the South via the Mississippi, expected Federal armies to move along the western frontier, drive through the Grand River valley or along the Telegraph Road from southeastern Missouri, and strike the Confederacy's rear with eastward-moving columns along the Arkansas and Red. Fort Smith became the command center for Confederate troops protecting the approaches to Arkansas, Texas, and Louisiana from the northwest.

Essential to Fort Smith's role as a defensive bastion for insulating these states from Union invasion was the incorporation of Indian Territory into the Confederate orbit. The region between Kansas and Texas and west of Arkansas to the

15 Emory to Townsend, May 19, 1861. *Official Records*, Series I, Volume I, 648–49.

100th meridian had been carved up by United States treaties negotiated between 1820 and 1837 with the Cherokees, Creeks, Seminoles, Choctaws, and Chickasaws assigning each of these tribes a national domain. These Indian groups were self-governing and, because of their remarkable progress in the arts of civilization, came to be known as the Five Civilized Tribes. The land of Indian Territory was esteemed as a geographic buffer indispensable for protecting trans-Mississippi Confederate states from invasion. Indian Territory's principal waterways—the Arkansas and the Red—and its major highways—the Texas and the Butterfield roads—were vital for Confederate communications and transportation.

The abundant resources of Indian Territory also attracted Confederate interest. Beef, hides, horses, grain, salt, lead, and tribal manpower—all made the region attractive to Southern leaders. Indian slaveholders generally dominated tribal affairs, and had already expressed sympathy for the Southern cause and receptivity to joining the Confederacy. Robert M. Jones, a Choctaw planter who owned five hundred slaves, was one articulate advocate of the South. The Confederate government named Albert Pike of Arkansas commissioner to negotiate treaties with the Five Civilized Tribes. His base of operations was Fort Smith. During the spring and summer of 1861, he obtained agreements with the Cherokees, Creeks, Seminoles, Choctaws, and Chickasaws whereby each abjured its association with the United States and joined the Confederacy. Among other commitments made by the leaders of the Indian nations, they agreed to raise troops for Confederate service. Anti-Confederate elements in the Creek, Cherokee, and Seminole nations later became a source of difficulty for the Southern cause in the West.[16]

[16] The text of the Confederate treaties negotiated by Albert Pike with the Cherokees, Choctaws, Chickasaws, Seminole, and Creeks can be found in *Official Records*, Series 4, Volume I.

Leroy P. Walker, secretary of war for the Confederacy, selected General Ben McCulloch to build a frontier army at Fort Smith to guard the Southern rear from Union invasion. Three regiments comprised McCulloch's initial force: two of cavalry, and one of infantry, one each drawn from Texas, Louisiana, and Arkansas. McCulloch was authorized to call on Arkansas for state troops and on Indian Territory for two regiments. Newly commissioned Brigadier General Albert Pike was assigned to McCulloch's staff with instructions to raise regiments from among the Cherokees, Creeks, Seminoles, Choctaws, and Chickasaws, which were to be supplied with arms and equipment drawn from Fort Smith.[17]

McCulloch's levy for Arkansas state troops was raised by orders issued by General N. Bart Pearce, who called on each county in his jurisdiction to raise four companies of volunteers. As each company was organized, the captain was to report with his troops to Fort Smith. Nearly two thousand state troops, including the crack Pulaski Light Artillery, answered Pearce's call. All around Fort Smith and north to Mayesville, Pearce and McCulloch set up "Camps of Instruction" to train the Arkansas volunteers.[18]

By early summer, the three Confederate regiments composing McCulloch's brigade reached Fort Smith. The 3d Louisiana Regiment, commanded by Colonel Louis Hébert, arrived on June 7 and set up camp near the Poteau one and a half miles from Fort Smith. They were followed by Colonel Thomas Churchill's 1st Arkansas Mounted Rifles and Colonel Elkanah Greer's South Kansas and Texas Regiment from Dallas.[19]

Fort Smith's storehouses and magazines, emptied by Sturgis'

17 Cooper to McCulloch, May 13, 1861. *Official Records*, Series I, Volume III, 575–76.

18 *Van Buren Press*, May 22 and June 5, 1861.

19 McCulloch to Walker, June 12, 1861. *Official Records*, Series I, Volume III, 590–91.

retreating cavalry column and by Colonel Borland's volunteer army from Little Rock, were filled again by early summer. A heavy shipment of ordnance and subsistence stores came to Belle Point when the Arkansas convention voted to turn over to the Fort Smith quartermaster all Union material seized before secession at the Little Rock Arsenal and from Federal supply steamers on the Arkansas. Confederate supply officers at the New Orleans depot added to the stores at Belle Point by shipping uniforms, tents, ordnance, subsistence stores, and weapons. With the stores on hand and bumper wheat, oat, and corn crops in the western Arkansas counties, McCulloch believed that he could equip and supply his frontier army and maintain it in the field for several months.[20]

The second Confederate offensive launched from Fort Smith grew out of a Union buildup in Missouri. Soon after McCulloch reached Fort Smith, he warned Secretary of War Walker that, with pro-Union sentiment ascendant in Missouri, he believed that an invasion by way of northwestern Arkansas was imminent. He preferred to strike the invader on the border rather than to wait for him closer to the Arkansas. On June 14, a messenger reached Belle Point with a note from pro-Southern Missouri Governor Claiborne F. Jackson telling of his forced evacuation of Jefferson City. He warned that Union forces were pressing him and urged McCulloch to advance a column into southern Missouri. McCulloch advised Walker of this development and proposed that he be allowed to send his brigade north, check the Union drive, capture Fort Scott, and "subjugate that portion of Kansas." This, he said, "would give heart . . . to our friends in Missouri, and accomplish the very object for which I was sent here, preventing a force from the North invading the Indian Territory."[21]

[20] McCulloch to Walker, May 20 and May 23, 1861. *Ibid.*, 579–83. *Van Buren Press*, June 5 and 19, 1861.
[21] McCulloch to Walker, June 14, 1861. *Ibid.*, 594–95.

Before McCulloch had received an answer, Jackson and his men were routed from Booneville by twenty-four hundred Union troops. Union forces also occupied Springfield in southwestern Missouri, less than eighty miles from the Arkansas border, where it was reported that General Nathaniel Lyon and a nine thousand-man army were moving to join the Union vanguard. On June 26, Walker authorized McCulloch to march north, seize Fort Scott, and extend service to Jackson insofar as "it will subserve the main purpose of your command." On June 30, McCulloch crossed the Arkansas with his staff; within a week, he was followed by his brigade. Before leaving Fort Smith, McCulloch ordered Captain Joel Foster and his Crawford County Guards to serve as the garrison force. He also issued a proclamation calling all men of "Western Arkansas to arms for the emergency," explaining that he wanted the certainty of sufficient reserve troops to roll back the Union troops.[22]

On July 3, McCulloch's column linked with General Sterling Price and his 1,700 Missouri State Guards near Maysville. Sweeping into Neosho, they captured 137 Union troops, joined Governor Jackson near Carthage, and rolled the advance Union column back to Springfield.[23]

Major W. Clarke, the Fort Smith quartermaster, fed a steady supply of ordnance and subsistence to McCulloch and energetically collected arms, clothing, food, and ammunition to sustain the Missouri offensive. Steamers delivered arms and ammunition to the Belle Point landing. Clarke rushed the stands of arms to McCulloch's camps in southern Missouri and northern Arkansas to replace the shotguns and antiquated muskets most of the troops had carried north. He introduced Confederate money into western Arkansas by purchasing

22 *Van Buren Press*, July 3, 1861.
23 McCulloch to Walker, July 5, 1861. *Officials Records*, Series I, Volume III, 39.

from local farmers grain and forage for cavalry mounts and mule teams pulling the supply wagons. Clarke also supplied and equipped the troops moving north through Fort Smith to strengthen McCulloch's frontier army. On July 27, Colonel Greer's Texas regiment finally reached Fort Smith. Clarke arranged for transporting the six hundred Texans across the Arkansas and supplied material and equipment for shoeing the horses for the march to Missouri. He sent Foster's Crawford County Guards north to join McCulloch when they were relieved as the Fort Smith garrison by a company of Arkansas state troops from Sevier County.[24]

McCulloch was unable to carry out his plan of striking at Fort Scott because intelligence that Union forces in Missouri were regrouping forced him to concentrate his men for border defense. By July 30, McCulloch and Price had moved into Cassville; on August 2, their scouts contacted Union patrols thirty-five miles southwest of Springfield. Four days later, the Confederate army moved up and camped on Wilson's Creek. On August 9, Generals Nathaniel Lyon and Franz Sigel led their forces out of Springfield to storm the Southern camp. Union forces were defeated in a fierce contest on August 10, known as the Battle of Wilson's Creek, which cut heavily into the ranks of both armies and in which General Lyon was killed. Surviving Union commanders retreated with their battered troops to Rolla. The Confederates moved into Springfield on August 11.[25]

McCulloch's victorious column returned to Arkansas in late August. Troops flooded into Fort Smith to join citizens in celebrating the Wilson's Creek victory. Parades, dances, speeches, and barbecues feted the officers and men of McCulloch's command. It was well that the people of western

[24] *Van Buren Press*, July 17, 24, and 31, 1861.
[25] McCulloch to Walker, August 10, 1861. *Official Records*, Series I, Volume III, 104.

Arkansas rejoiced so lavishly on this occasion; very soon they were to have little but gloom, privation, and eventual scorn for the Confederate cause. An omen of faltering Southern fortunes resulted from the enforcement of a directive from the Arkansas State Military Board. About the time the conquering army returned to Belle Point, General Pearce was instructed to muster his state troops and to poll them on the question of volunteering for Confederate service. General William J. Hardee was to receive all troops who elected to change from state to Confederate service. Officers addressed the troops urging that they change. To the man, Pearce's state troops refused, and Hardee was shocked that the vote against entering Confederate service was "unanimous."[26]

Spokesmen for the Arkansas state troops explained that the men were weary of military service. Most of them had been in the army for from two to five months and had "never received any pay or clothing, and when the board said they could honorably leave the service, and left it to their choice, being naked and barefooted, the natural impulse to each individual was, 'I must go home.'" Soldiers in the ranks declared: "We are as good Southern men as any persons. We have fought the enemy and driven him away. We are needy and will go home, and when another call is made, we will have clothes and shoes, and will again do battle for the South."[27]

The state troops were mustered out on August 31. Secretary Walker directed Confederate officers in Arkansas to reinforce McCulloch's frontier army by raising five regiments of infantry each from Louisiana, Texas, and Arkansas for "three years or during the war." Men responded to the call, eighty Texans reporting from Lavaca County on good horses and armed with Mississippi rifles. Major Clarke attempted to rustle

[26] McCulloch to Walker, August 31, 1861. Pearce to Walker, October 10, 1861. *Ibid.*, 689, 715–16.
[27] Pearce to Walker, October 10, 1861. *Ibid.*, 715–16.

equipment, arms, and uniforms for the new brigade, but the increasing scarcity of goods on the frontier taxed his energy and ingenuity. Judah P. Benjamin, who replaced Walker as Confederate secretary of war on September 17, had advised Clarke that uniforms for the recruits would have to come from local sources. The Fort Smith quartermaster appealed to citizens and merchants for assistance in clothing the men of the new Arkansas brigade:

> It will require the combined efforts of all patriotic citizens in aid of the Quarter Master's Department, to supply sufficient comfortable clothing to our gallant troops, during the coming winter. With the view of furnishing the troops on the Arkansas frontier, the Merchants of the state are requested to inform this Office, at an early day, of the quantity and prices of such articles as they can supply.

Clarke explained that his goal was to provide each man with two suits of winter clothes, two blankets, and each company with tents.[28]

Clarke's repeated appeals called for socks, shirts, drawers, coats, shoes, pants, hats, and caps, and announced that contributions of any of the enumerated articles would be received at Fort Smith quartermaster storehouse. All citizens were urged to designate receivers to pack, mark, and forward their donations to Clarke's office. Clarke offered to pay for goods if the owner required, but he was having difficulty getting local people to accept his Confederate currency, and he added, "None other than those who are patriotic enough to receive the money of their *Government*, need respond to this announcement."[29]

Clarke needed heavy cloth for uniforms. Bolts of this fabric

[28] Proclamation of General Ben McCulloch to the Citizens of Arkansas, Texas, and Louisiana, September 10, 1861. *Ibid.*, 700. *Van Buren Press*, September 18, 1861.

[29] *Van Buren Press*, September 18, 1861.

were scarce in western Arkansas; merchants' shelves at Fort Smith and Van Buren were bare. Clarke pointed out that Van Buren had a cotton mill "engaged to its fullest capacity, in turning out a superior article of cotton yarn." He asserted also that there was a large quantity of wool in the western counties "if the people will only set about manufacturing it."[30]

By October 1, fabric and blankets were still scarce at Fort Smith, and so Clarke sent agents across Arkansas to buy up stocks. He explained that his plan was to set up a uniform factory at Fort Smith to work the cloth his agents purchased "for the making of clothes . . . to the extent of our ability to make them up." Employment would be given to all "cutters and seamstresses" who would apply. Even Confederate currency was scarce at Belle Point at this time; so Clarke explained that funds were not on hand to pay for the goods or labor in making uniforms, and that a "strict indulgence of a few weeks" was requested.[31]

At the same time, Clarke was busy with other supply and communication chores. Each week he sent a train of supply wagons from Fort Smith to Confederate frontier army units guarding the northwestern Arkansas boundary. The wagons had been returning empty to Fort Smith. Clarke soon ordered the drivers on the return trip to bring down lead from the Granby mines, to be melted into shot and minié balls for supplying local troops and also to be forwarded to Memphis in the form of pig lead to alleviate the shortage among Confederate armies in Kentucky and Tennessee. To expedite communications with Richmond, Clarke supervised the stringing of a telegraph line between Fort Smith and Little Rock.[32]

Throughout the autumn of 1861, units of McCulloch's fron-

30 *Ibid.*
31 *Ibid.*, October 1, 1861.
32 Clarke to Benjamin, October 14, 1861. *Official Records*, Series I, Volume III, 718. *Van Buren Press*, October 25, 1861.

tier army moved up and down the Telegraph Road linking Fort Smith with the Missouri-Arkansas border. On several occasions, Federal movements toward Springfield caused a burst of preparation and movement from Fort Smith. In October, McCulloch's scouts sent word that General John C. Frémont was leading an army of thirty thousand on Springfield. Frémont entered Springfield on October 27, but he was relieved by General David Hunter five days later. Believing the season too advanced for a campaign, Hunter withdrew from Springfield. When patrols brought this intelligence to Cassville, where McCulloch had taken position, he and General Price decided that it was unlikely that the Federal army in Missouri would attempt a southward thrust until spring. McCulloch's troops went into winter quarters in a string of camps extending from Cross Hollows to Fort Smith. Texas and Arkansas troops established camps around Fort Smith, but a threatened smallpox epidemic forced relocation of most of the men to near Van Buren before the end of the winter.[33]

The only action involving Confederate troops from Fort Smith during December and January, 1861–62, grew out of the determination of the anti-Confederate community, made up of Creek, Seminole, and Cherokee Indians, led by Creek Chief Opothleyaholo, to remain neutral. Confederate leaders, equating the Indian declaration of neutrality with sympathy if not support for the Union, regarded the village a menace to Confederate security. On two different occasions, Confederate Indian and Texas troops, led by Colonel Douglas Cooper, attempted to drive the villagers from Indian Territory. Each time, Opothleyaholo's fighters had defeated the troops. Cooper's appeal for reinforcements led to the assignment of Colonel James McIntosh and sixteen hundred troops of the 1st Cavalry Brigade to assist Cooper. On December 17, 1861, McIntosh

[33] McIntosh to Cooper, December 7, 1861. *Official Records*, Series I, Volume III, 703.

rode west and the day after Christmas, he crushed Opothleyaholo's warriors at the Battle of Chustenalah. Indian survivors
of the debacle fled to Kansas. McIntosh returned to Fort
Smith on January 1, 1862.[34]

The year 1862 was a time of disaster for Confederate fortunes in the West. The sustained attrition of Southern might
and resources in that sector made the conquest of the Confederate bastion at Belle Point a rather simple, innocuous military exercise on September 1, 1863. It all began with a determined Union thrust toward Fort Smith in January, 1862.
General Samuel R. Curtis and fast-moving cavalry columns
drawn from his Army of the Southwest at Rolla probed Confederate positions near Springfield. Price's Confederate Missouri army near Springfield called on McCulloch for help,
and Hébert's brigade was ordered north. Curtis forced Price
to abandon Springfield on February 12. Union cavalry pursued Price all the way to the Arkansas border, where the Confederate commander dropped down the Telegraph Road into
northwestern Arkansas, made a stand on Little Sugar Creek,
and for the moment checked his tormentors.[35]

While Curtis was preparing a drive along the western border to the Arkansas, plans were being made for a Union invasion of Indian Territory. On May 5, General James G.
Blunt assumed command of the Department of Kansas, and
quickly gathered an invasion force to thrust into Indian Territory along Grand River valley. Blunt's army of six thousand,
known as the Indian Expedition, consisted of the 2d Ohio
Cavalry, 6th Kansas Cavalry, 1st Kansas Battery, Rabb's 2d
Indiana Battery, and five infantry units. Blunt placed Colonel
William Weer in command of this invasion force.[36]

[34] *Van Buren Press*, January 9, 1862.
[35] Price to Jackson, February 25, 1862. *Official Records*, Series I,
Volume VIII, 756–57.
[36] Wiley Britton. *The Civil War on the Border*, I, 295.

Before the double-pronged Union invasion of the approaches to Fort Smith got under way, several changes occurred in the management of the Confederate Army of the West, headquartered at Belle Point. On January 10, 1862, Secretary of War Benjamin organized the Trans-Mississippi District of Department No. 2 to include all of Arkansas, Louisiana north of the Red River, Indian Territory, and most of southwestern Missouri. General Earl Van Dorn, commander of a division in the Confederate Army of the Potomac, was sent to Arkansas to command the new department. Obsessed with the need for action, Van Dorn cancelled all leaves, ordered officers and men in his jurisdiction to report to their units at once, and prepared to take the initiative.[37]

McCulloch's division, Price's Missourians, and all other Confederate troops on the Arkansas as well as Pike's Indian regiments were ordered north to trap Curtis' army in the rough hill country of northwestern Arkansas. General Sigel's Union corps retreated through Bentonville on March 6. McCulloch and Price attempted to cut him off but failed. Van Dorn then concentrated his armies near Elkhorn Tavern in an effort to turn Curtis' army out of its strong position behind Little Sugar Creek. In the bloody two-day struggle that followed on March 7–8, known as the Battle of Pea Ridge, Union artillery pulverized Confederate lines with scathing shot, shell, and canister; Union cavalry-infantry assaults splintered Van Dorn's brigades and killed and captured a number of Confederate officers. The vaunted Confederate offensive became a shameless retreat to the fastnesses of the Boston Mountains. One survivor wrote: "The retreat was more disastrous than a dozen battles. The [3d] Louisiana Regiment had only two hundred and seventy men in a body on the retreat; other regiments in the same proportion. Our physicians, wounded, and

[37] Special Orders No. 8, January 10, 1862. *Official Records*, Series I, Volume VIII, 734.

nurses were taken prisoners, and the ambulances sent for the wounded seized."[38]

The Union victory at Pea Ridge sealed the doom of the Confederate cause in the West and cut mightily into the human resources of the Army of the West. General Ben Mc-Culloch, the border's finest soldier, was among those slain. In their retreat, Confederate troops had abandoned great quantities of subsistence and forage stores, muskets, ammunition, heavy guns, and tents. Survivors falling back to Fort Smith deserted in great numbers, and many joined the Union army. Gloom permeated the border people, and never again would Confederate recruiters meet with much success in northwestern Arkansas.

Van Dorn reorganized the depleted companies in each brigade and prepared to pull his army out of western Arkansas. His plan was to march down the Arkansas and strike into southeastern Missouri. Van Dorn drained Clarke's reserve supplies at Fort Smith and even plundered a substantial quantity of subsistence and ordnance stores which had recently arrived for distribution to General Pike's Confederate Indian regiments. His troops looted boxes of clothing, shoes, and other supplies awaiting trans-shipment to Indian Territory. They helped themselves "to nearly the whole, and to almost all the tents"; hardly a box reached Indian Territory from Fort Smith which had not been opened and "part of the contents abstracted." Van Dorn added to the scorn and contempt border people felt for him as a military commander by ordering his men to take down the telegraph line connecting Fort Smith and Little Rock.[39]

After Van Dorn's withdrawal from Fort Smith, all of Mc-

[38] W. H. Tunnard. *A Southern Record: The History of the Third Regiment, Louisiana Infantry*, 146–47.

[39] Van Dorn to Johnston, March 18, 1862. *Official Records*, Series I, Volume VIII, 789–91. Pike to Randolph, May 4 and June 26, 1862. Pike to Davis, July 31, 1862. *Ibid.*, Series I, Volume XIII, 821, 841, 861.

Culloch's old army that remained on the border was Pike's Indian Brigade, Woodruff's Arkansas Battery, and two Texas cavalry regiments. Because Pike was known to lack sufficient strength to meet the Federal troops in a pitched battle, Van Dorn instructed him to impede any enemy advance "by felling trees, burning bridges, removing supplies of forage and subsistence, attacking his trains, stampeding his animals, cutting off his detachments, and other similar means."[40]

The Arkansas delegation to the Confederate Congress was dismayed to learn that Van Dorn had pulled his army out of western Arkansas. On April 15, 1862, they petitioned President Jefferson Davis to countermand the virtual abandonment of the Arkansas frontier, which had "been brought to the verge of ruin." They charged that Van Dorn had begun a

> retreat down the Arkansas River with all his forces except General Pike's . . . [brigade] of Indians (which he declines to have anything to do with), broke up the military depot at Fort Smith, causing the material, much of it General Pike's, to be shipped down the Arkansas River, leaving General Pike unsupported with either men or supplies at the usual depot and base of operations. All this was done at much loss and cost, to the alarm and terror of all that section of country, and without excuse . . . as the enemy were in no condition to pursue . . . .

The delegation asked that President Davis establish a Trans-Mississippi department, that Van Dorn be removed as district commander, that General Braxton Bragg or a man from the Southwest be designated his replacement, that the public property removed from Fort Smith and Little Rock be returned, and that the telegraph line be restored. They requested also that the troops now on the Mississippi be returned to the frontier, and that "a goodly supply of arms, ammunition, and

[40] Maury to Pike, March 21, 1862. *Ibid.*, 795–96.

military stores" be rushed to Arkansas before the Mississippi was lost to the Confederacy.[41]

General Van Dorn was never able to accomplish his invasion of southeastern Missouri. General Albert S. Johnston ordered him to move his army across the Mississippi to Memphis and join the Confederate force massing at Corinth to oppose the Union advance up the Tennessee valley. Van Dorn was sensitive to the storm of criticism his actions had provoked, and he explained to President Davis and Arkansas congressmen that it was not his intent to abandon western Arkansas. He had sent General Thomas C. Hindman "to organize the troops . . . and put them in the field."[42]

Hindman attempted to restore some order in the chaos of frontier military affairs. Arriving in Arkansas from Corinth on May 30, 1862, he assumed command of the Trans-Mississippi District. Reports reaching Fort Smith told of a massive invasion of the southern border country. Weer's Union column was reported moving down the Grand toward Fort Gibson. Curtis' Union army, which had smashed Van Dorn at Pea Ridge, was en route to Helena. Cavalry sweeps from southern Missouri Union bases probed as far south as Fayetteville. Hindman believed that these were harbingers of a large-scale invasion. To cope with the threat, he ordered General Pike, who had established his headquarters at Fort McCulloch deep in the Choctaw Nation, to move north and defend the approaches to Fort Gibson. Hindman placed Colonel Charles Carroll in charge of the District of Northwestern Arkansas, with headquarters at Fort Smith. Hindman proclaimed martial law at Fort Smith and its tributary area, and authorized Major Pearce, former Arkansas state general now in Confederate service, to "impress all articles necessary for either of the de-

[41] Johnson to Davis, April 15, 1862. *Ibid.*, Series I, Volume XIII, 814–16.
[42] Van Dorn to Davis, June 9, 1862. *Ibid.*, 831–32.

partments [commissary and quartermaster] over which he is placed when reasonable prices are refused."[43]

Action developed first on the Indian Territory front. Weer's Indian expedition drove through the Cherokee Nation to the Locust Grove–Fort Gibson road junction. Pike's slowness in moving north caused Hindman to place Colonel J. J. Clarkson in charge of defending the Cherokee Nation. Clarkson's force, operating with Colonel Stand Watie and his Cherokee Mounted Rifles, were surprised at Locust Grove and soundly defeated, the "men routed without arms, and many minus their hats" made a frantic retreat to Fort Smith. Clarkson lost a hundred men and his train, which carried more than fifty kegs of precious powder from Fort Smith's nearly empty magazines. Major Pearce told Hindman, "Had the loss been Clarkson, without that of the train and powder, I think that the Confederacy would have been the gainer." Weer's men took Tahlequah, the Cherokee Nation's capital, captured Cherokee Chief John Ross, and then returned to Kansas.[44]

In August, Hindman inspected his army preparatory to launching an offensive into southern Missouri. His striking force consisted of 3,600 cavalry, 2,500 infantry, and about three thousand Indian cavalry. Hindman's inspection revealed that the troops had only fourteen cannons, little camp equipment, and small arms that scarcely "deserved the name." In the Fort Smith ordnance shop, 250 stands of arms were being repaired which, when serviceable, would be issued; in the meantime, five hundred infantrymen lacked weapons. The Belle Point magazines were "exceedingly destitute of caps and powder." To make matters worse, the volatile Pike had resigned as commander of the Department of Indian Territory. Hindman named Colonel Douglas Cooper to replace him.[45]

[43] Special Orders 17, June 17, 1862. *Ibid.*, 835–36.
[44] Pearce to Hindman, July 5, 1862. *Ibid.*, 963–65.
[45] Hindman to Holmes and Hindman to Cooper, November 3, 1862. *Ibid.*, 40–41, 46–47.

Despite the condition of his army, Hindman sent General James S. Rains and five regiments north from Fort Smith to join Carroll's troops already in northwestern Arkansas. After crossing the Arkansas, Cooper placed companies on the river at Carey's Ferry covering the Texas Road and north of Fort Gibson and led a cavalry force to join Rains' troops. Confederate cavalry swept into southern Missouri and captured Cassville, Newtonia, and Neosho. Union forces fell back, and the Confederate thrust appeared to be developing a momentum which would be difficult to check. What Hindman failed to realize on this and on a subsequent occasion was that Union strategy was to draw his army far from its supply base at Fort Smith and then to overwhelm it with superior artillery and infantry. On October 4, the Union forces struck. Generals John S. Schofield and James G. Blunt closed in on Newtonia and found Hindman's army dispersed on a line running south to the Arkansas border. Fast-moving Union columns mauled the extended Confederates, marking the mobile assault line with dead and wounded men, abandoned supplies and ordnance, and prisoners. With most of his subsistence stores captured and destroyed and only ten rounds per man remaining in the ordnance train, Hindman pulled his troops back to Fort Smith.[46]

Hindman reorganized his forces, supplied them from the meager Belle Point stores, and then recrossed the Arkansas on November 29 and 30 to check the Union advance, which extended to Cane Hill and Fayetteville. The Union Army of the Frontier and Hindman's troops collided at Prairie Grove, where a desperate battle followed. The Confederates were driven back and again forced to retreat to Fort Smith. Food and forage were so scarce in the Belle Point area that Hindman sent his cavalry units a hundred miles downriver to revive

[46] Cooper to Rains, October 2, 1862, and Hindman to Holmes, November 3, 1862. *Ibid.*, 46–51, 296–300.

both horses and men. In the days after the Prairie Grove defeat, Hindman lamented that his Army of the Frontier seemed to "diminish in strength daily by desertions and a frightful increase of sickness." He blamed the desertions to "non-payment of the troops and consequent sufferings of their families." To defend Fort Smith, Hindman placed his infantry in camps ringing Belle Point. He sent one infantry regiment with a section of artillery across the river near Van Buren, and posted Colonel R. P. Crump and the 1st Texas Partisan Regiment at Dripping Springs, nine miles north of Van Buren, to patrol all roads leading to Fort Smith.[47]

Hindman expected that the Union army which had smashed his troops at Prairie Grove would follow the familiar pattern and withdraw into Missouri for the winter, but Schofield determined to torment the Confederates once more in 1862. Union divisions drove across the mountains, crashed through Crump's pickets, and stormed Van Buren on December 28. They captured several Confederate steamers loaded with grain for Fort Smith, destroyed the ferry, and shelled enemy positions on the south bank of the Arkansas. Hindman believed that the artillery barrage was a prelude to crossing the river in force. Convinced that he could not hold Fort Smith, he turned the troops to loading wagons and emptying the post's storehouses and magazines. Hindman ordered Cooper's brigade, the 1st Texas Partisans, and the 1st Arkansas Cavalry to remain in the general area and to harass the invaders; under cover of darkness on December 28, he led his own troops and train out of Fort Smith bound for Clarksville.[48]

Schofield found it impossible to subsist his troops south of the Boston Mountains; so he ordered Blunt to evacuate Van Buren, and the Union column marched north to Missouri on

[47] Hindman to Anderson, December 25, 1862, and February 15, 1863. *Ibid.*, Series I, Volume XXII, Part One, 138–46, 171.
[48] Hindman to Anderson, February 15, 1863. *Ibid.*, 172–73.

December 30. The Union commanders left Colonel William A. Phillips and a force near Mayesville and Colonel La Rue Harrison at Fayetteville. From his Little Rock headquarters, General Theophilus H. Holmes sent General William Steele to attempt to revitalize faltering Confederate frontier defenses. Steele arrived at Fort Smith by steamer on January 8, 1863. Hindman had forewarned him that the country was "exhausted" and that the few troops he would lead were "undisciplined, ill-equipped, and demoralized." Steele said that when he reached Fort Smith "everything was of the most gloomy description." The "continuous occupation" of the region by large numbers of Confederate soldiers since the beginning of the war "had utterly exhausted its resources." The withdrawal of Hindman's corps just before his arrival had left the people "desponding, hopeless, and, with a few honorable exceptions, throughly demoralized." He found that the only troops at Fort Smith were a hundred men from the 1st Arkansas Cavalry, a 150-man remnant of 1st Texas Partisan Rangers, and understrength companies of the 26th Arkansas Infantry. When Steele inspected the Texans, he noted that the men lacked proper clothing and averaged less than one blanket to a man. In the Fort Smith hospital were fifteen hundred sick and wounded from the Prairie Grove campaign whose condition was "wretched." Hindman's troops left only a few supplies, principally poor beef and corn meal. Cooper's brigade at Canadian Depot in Indian Territory faced hunger. The commander of Indian troops reported that he had only five hundred pounds of flour on hand and "very little of anything else." His mules were so exhausted that they could scarcely pull an empty wagon.[49]

What under different conditions would have been good news, but with extremely limited subsistence stores only increased Steele's problems, was the tidings that his command

[49] Steele to Anderson, February 15, 1864. *Ibid.*, 28–36.

was to be reinforced by Colonel John W. Speight's Texas Brigade. Rations were so short at the end of January that Steele ordered Speight to move his infantry regiments and battery to Red River near Doaksville, where subsistence was more plentiful.[50]

Steele's task of mounting an effective Confederate defense on the Arkansas to check Union invaders was compounded by the fact that the country around Fort Smith was infested with small parties of Union raiders. Colonel James Stuart at Fayetteville used wide-ranging squads drawn from his 10th Illinois Cavalry to harass Steele's communication and supply routes. Union recruiters added to Stuart's striking force by enrolling citizens into the 1st Arkansas (Union) Infantry Regiment. Confederates called these turncoats "Mountain Federals." Stuart's men carried out several daring raids, as did a force of Union partisans led by Martin Hart. While Speight's brigade was en route to Fort Smith, a Union raiding party struck Speight's rear guard fifteen miles south of Belle Point and captured twenty Texans.[51]

Fifty Union raiders plundered farms along the Fort Towson road twenty miles south of Belle Point, and a smaller band robbed and killed several citizens within sight of Fort Smith. Steele's couriers riding to Little Rock headquarters had to have heavily armed escorts. On several occasions, cavalry from the Union base at Fayetteville escorted an artillery group to the Arkansas, where their howitzers blasted steamers attempting to deliver food, medical supplies, and ordnance to Fort Smith. In February, Stuart approached the Arkansas below Fort Smith with a hundred men, who slipped across the river in skiffs, raided several Confederate camps, captured

[50] Steele to Newton, January 15, 1863. *Ibid.*, Series I, Volume XXII, Part Two, 773.

[51] Steele to Anderson, February 15, 1864. *Ibid.*, Series I, Volume XXII, Part One, 28–36.

seven prisoners, and returned to the north bank with only one casualty—a Union trooper drowned in the crossing. The sorry condition of the Confederate horses slowed Steele's cavalry patrols and enabled the raiders to escape uncontested. Corn, necessary to build up the horses, was scarce at Fort Smith and, because of the general lack of subsistence stores, was used to feed the troops.[52]

With all his disappointments and limitations, Steele maintained his optimism that the tide would turn. He demanded corn and forage to rehabilitate the cavalry mounts. He pleaded for ordnance, declaring that his men were "almost destitute of ammunition of every description." He pointed out to Confederate supply officers that attempts to provision Fort Smith by way of the Arkansas was extremely risky with Stuart's cavalry and artillery active on the river's north bank. He asked that subsistence and other needs be sent from Texas along the Butterfield Road. Steele also asked for troops to add to Speight's Brigade, his reserve force then south of the Red River near Clarksville. The Confederate high command denied Steele reinforcements, and on March 30, 1863, ordered Colonel Speight to move his brigade east of the Mississippi.[53]

Steele did receive some command assistance through the assignment of General William L. Cabell, a professional soldier with prewar experience on the Arkansas frontier, to Fort Smith to take charge of Colonel Carroll's brigade. His first missions were to attempt to persuade the northern Arkansas deserters to return to their Confederate units and to drive the Union troops from Fayetteville. He failed in both.[54]

During the spring and summer of 1863, startling reports reached Fort Smith. Colonel William A. Phillips struck at

[52] Stuart to Schofield, February 14, 1863. *Ibid.*, 228–29.
[53] Steele to Holmes, March 31, 1863. *Ibid.*, Series I, Volume XXII, Part Two, 809.
[54] Britton. *Civil War on the Border.* II, 54.

Fort Gibson on April 13, drove off the Indian defenders, occupied the post, and renamed it Fort Blunt. Steele suspected
that Fort Blunt would become a base to support operations
against Fort Smith. This suspicion was confirmed on June 25
when one of Blunt's tough subordinates, Colonel James H.
Williams, left Baxter Springs with two thousand men, four
guns, and two hundred wagons. His mounted companies included detachments from the 2d Colorado and 3d Wisconsin
Infantry and the 9th and 14th Kansas cavalry regiments. Two
of the heavy guns were manned by the 2d Kansas Battery.[55]

Anticipating Blunt's vanguard as the ultimate attack force
on Fort Smith, Steele determined to trap and destroy the invasion train before it could reach Fort Blunt. He ordered
Colonel Stand Watie and General Cabell to set up an ambush
on the Cabin Creek crossing of the military road from Baxter
Springs in the upper Cherokee Nation. Watie reached the
spot first and positioned his riflemen—he had no artillery.
Cabell was marching northeast from Fort Smith with cavalry
and artillery. Heavy rains drenched the region, and creeks
and rivers ran bank full. Although slowed by the mud, the
Union column progressed by keeping to the ridges and higher
ground. On July 1, the Union force reached the crossing and
the first Battle of Cabin Creek occurred. High water on
Grand River made it impossible for Cabell to cross and join
Watie. Cherokee sharpshooters stopped the invaders and held
them in check until the Union artillery was moved up. Gunners swept the ambush positions with deadly fire from six- and
twelve-pounders. Watie ordered a retreat, and Williams' column crossed.[56]

When Steele learned that Williams' column had fought its
way out of the Cabin Creek ambush, he determined to attack

[55] Phillips to Blunt, July 7, 1863. *Official Records*, Series I, Volume
XXII, Part One, 378–82.
[56] *Ibid.*

Fort Blunt and destroy the Union force before it moved on
Fort Smith. Cabell's Arkansas brigade was to join Cooper's
brigade at Honey Springs in Indian Territory and to march on
Fort Blunt. Union spies reported Steele's attack plan, and
Blunt decided to move quickly on Honey Springs and hit
Cooper before Cabell could arrive from Fort Smith. On July
15, he moved troops and artillery toward Cooper's position;
two days later, he met the Confederate commander head on.
Cooper had one battery of four light guns and defective pow-
der, compared to Blunt's ten cannons. Again Cabell was slow
in arriving, and Blunt drove Cooper's army from the Honey
Springs battlefield, further softening the Confederates for
Blunt's thrust on Fort Smith.[57]

Despite the Honey Springs defeat, Steele persevered in his
determination to take Fort Blunt. After assigning a special
detachment to guard the magazines and detailing the 26th
Arkansas Infantry to garrison duty, he rode out of Fort Smith.
By July 28, his army of sixty-five hundred men and seven cannons had taken position at Honey Springs. Steele calculated
that his Union rival had five thousand men and sixteen pieces
of artillery, with reinforcements expected from Kansas. He
had requested from Texas depots reinforcements and fresh
powder to replace the faulty explosive sent earlier. Dispatches
from the Red River told him that an ordnance train and a
column led by General Smith P. Bankhead were en route. The
assault on Fort Blunt would begin when Bankhead's force arrived. While he waited, Steele regrouped his regiments on the
western approaches to Fort Smith and along the Texas Road
to guard his line of supply and communication. Desertions
cut deep into the ranks. Men left by squads, platoons, even
companies. As many as two hundred, including several officers, left in a single night. Many of these had gone over to the

[57] Blunt to Schofield, July 26, 1863. *Ibid.*, 447–62.

foe; most of the deserters had been raised in northern Arkansas.[58]

On August 19, Steele learned that a Union column was advancing from southern Missouri along the western border of Arkansas on Fort Smith. To counter this advance, he ordered Cabell to move with a brigade back to Fort Smith. Cabell posted his men at McLean's Crossing on the Poteau, nine miles southwest of Belle Point. He sent pickets across the Arkansas to check the progress of the southward-moving Union column and put men to work obstructing the fords and roads leading to the landings across from Fort Smith.[59]

Union spies reported this division of Steele's army to General Blunt. It was known also that Steele's defenses on the Canadian were further reduced by his having dispersed his cavalry units over a wide area to forage the horses wherever they could find grass. Steele had only fifteen hundred men immediately available. Steele was aware that Blunt had about five thousand, of which three thousand were foot soldiers, and believed that he could call in his own scattered cavalry units before the Union infantry reached his position. The inventive Blunt determined to exploit this division and dispersal of Confederate troops by moving the Union infantry in wagons. As soon as he was reinforced by the Union column that had caused Steele to rush Cabell to Fort Smith, Blunt struck. Union forces moved so quickly on Steele's Canadian line that on August 23 he had to evacuate and move down the Texas Road. His main column reached Perryville on August 25, when word arrived that Bankhead's Texans were finally on the way to join him.[60]

[58] Steele to Blair, August 7, 1863. *Ibid.*, Series I, Volume XXII, Part Two, 597.
[59] Cabell to Duval, December 7, 1863. *Ibid.*, Series I, Volume XXII, Part One, 604–609.
[60] Blunt to Schofield, August 27, 1863. *Ibid.*, Series I, Volume XXII, Part Two 597–601.

Steele implored Bankhead to push his men. "The Federal cavalry is still harassing us, and the artillery and infantry reported not far behind. Hurry up." The fast-moving Union column drove Steele's Confederate army through Perryville on August 26. To escape a pitched battle, Steele marched his men all night; on August 28, he met Bankhead on the Middle Boggy River. Steele's plan was to move the combined force to Fort Smith and relieve Cabell.[61]

Having divided the Fort Smith defense, Blunt ordered his men to burn Perryville, a Confederate depot. Then he marched his column north and east toward Fort Smith. The distance from Perryville to Fort Smith was about a hundred miles, which Blunt's men covered in four days. On August 30, the Union vanguard was only four miles from Cabell's outer defensive perimeter. Cabell's scouts reported Blunt's strength, especially in artillery. Aware that the Union troops had driven Steele so deep into the Choctaw Nation that he could not possibly relieve him, Cabell decided to abandon Fort Smith. Desertions had reduced his force. Presently, he mustered 1,250 men, of which he could depend on only about half in battle. Troops loaded all available wagons with military stores, and wagonmasters put the train in motion on the Waldron Road across the Devil's Backbone. At nine on the evening of August 31, Cabell ordered a general retreat from Fort Smith.[62]

At daylight on September 1, Blunt ordered his troops to the attack. Skirmishers found no Confederates at McLean's Crossing but only indications of a general evacuation by way of Waldron Road. Blunt sent a cavalry force with four 2d Indiana Battery guns to harass the retreating Confederates, and then proceeded into Fort Smith and took possession of

[61] Steele to Bankhead, August 26, 1863. *Ibid.*, 981–82.
[62] Steele to Duval, December 7, 1863. *Ibid.*, Series I, Volume XXII, Part One, 604–609.

the post. Captain J. M. Mentzer and Company K of the 2d Kansas Cavalry garrisoned Fort Smith and raised the "stars and stripes to the breeze."[63]

[63] Blunt to Schofield. September 3, 1863. *Ibid.*, 601–603.

# CHAPTER THIRTEEN

## Fort Smith and the Civil War: A Union Post

GENERAL JAMES BLUNT found it easier to win battles than to command a frontier military station, deal with wartime civilian problems, and buck army politics. To the chagrin of officials high in the military hierarchy, he frequently shared his views on military affairs with President Lincoln. Blunt's contempt for obstructive official channels, his energy, and his penchant for action—all contributed materially to his brilliant field operations but eventually brought about his downfall as frontier commander.

Blunt's first action after formally taking possession of Fort Smith was to deploy his troops in a defensive perimeter about Belle Point to check any attempted reconquest by frontier Confederate forces. At the time, Blunt's army consisted of twenty-three hundred well-armed and well-equipped troops, including a Negro infantry regiment. When the 2d Colorado Cavalry and other reinforcements reached Fort Smith, Blunt extended his defenses by establishing small approach posts at Clarksville, Van Buren, and Roseville. Since this was conquered territory, Blunt had also to supervise civilians. Hundreds of Arkansas citizens, some of them from as far away as eighty miles, came to Fort Smith to assert that they had been pro-Union all along but had supported the Confederate cause only because they had been forced to do so. Confederate deserters came in too, many of them volunteering to serve in the Union army; Blunt's officers generally administered the Federal Loyalty Oath and sent the deserters on their way. One Fort Smith official asserted that, if not a majority, at least a large minority of the people of western Arkansas seemed to rejoice at the Union conquest, their only fear being that Union forces could not hold the area.[1]

On September 18, Blunt set out for Fort Scott to supervise gathering a supply train and reinforcements for his army on the Arkansas. He left Colonel William Cloud in charge, with instructions to maintain pressure on the enemy. General Frederick Steele's Union army drove through to Little Rock on September 10. Cloud led a cavalry column downriver to open communications with Steele's headquarters. On the two hundred-mile sweep from Fort Smith to Little Rock, Cloud's men captured two Confederate steamers and found additional evidence that the "Mountaineers" were for the Union. Cloud believed that thousands of these men were ready to take up arms for the United States "as soon as they can be furnished." He said that several hundred citizens had pleaded with him "to stand by them and keep them from being taken by the [Confederate] conscript officers or from being taken into the Rebel Army," from which many of them had deserted.[2]

On the sortie from Fort Smith, Cloud had led his cavalry, the 2d Kansas, supported by two guns of the 2d Indiana battery. At Dardanelle, he checked on reports that two hundred Confederates had gathered there. En route he had been joined by three hundred soldiers in Confederate uniforms, who came in with "Stars and Stripes flying, and cheers for the Union." They told Cloud that they had fought him at Devil's Backbone on Cabell's retreat from Fort Smith and that now

[1] Cloud to Schofield, September 8, 1863. *War of Rebellion: A Compilation of the Official Records of the Union and Confederate Armies*, Series I, Volume XXII, Part One, 599–603. And Wiley Britton. *The Civil War on the Border*, II, 158.

[2] Cloud to McNeil, September 20, 1863. *Official Records*, Series I, Volume XXII, Part One, 603.

they wished to fight under him. Cloud absorbed them into his column, drove on to Dardanelle, and forced the Confederates from the town. Fifteen of the Confederates attempted to escape across the Arkansas and were shot in the water. Cloud's men captured two hundred head of cattle and a storehouse of wheat.[3]

Steele's conquest of Little Rock, coupled with Cloud's clearing the upper Arkansas, opened the river to Union steamers from Fort Smith to the Mississippi. Blunt immediately began pressing Department Commander Schofield with recommendations and requests for extending Union control in the Southwest. He recommended that Fort Smith and its satellite posts be supplied by steamers from Union depots on the Mississippi. In his view, an infantry detachment with two howitzers on each boat could protect transport and cargo steamers from riverbank ambush. In addition, Blunt recommended that the telegraph lines be restored between Fort Smith and St. Louis and between Fort Smith and Little Rock. It would be a simple matter to reestablish service: the poles were standing, and only the wire had to be strung. He urged that Colonel La Rue Harrison's 1st Arkansas (Union) Cavalry, then at Cassville, be ordered back into northwestern Arkansas. Harrison's men, who were from Benton and Washington counties, knew the area, and would be of great assistance in guarding the telegraph lines and ridding the region of Confederate raiders.[4]

Initially, Blunt's recommendations and requests were met with surprising promptness. By November 9, Fort Smith had telegraphic communications with St. Louis, and a few weeks later with Little Rock. Blunt's ubiquitous demands were usually reasonable and his assessment of military situations correct;

[3] *Ibid*. Britton. *Civil War on the Border*. II, 159–60.
[4] Blunt to Schofield, September 11, 1863. *Official Records*, Series I, Volume XXII, Part Two, 525–26.

but these facts seemed only to irritate department and division commanders, who perhaps coveted his talent for quickly seeing a fault or flaw and moving to correct it and his promptness in offering a solution.

Blunt's aggressiveness, his support from high-level political figures, and perhaps even his military successes—all annoyed Department Commander Schofield. Thus, when General John McNeil, commander of the southwestern Missouri sector, immodestly requested that he be given Blunt's post as commander of the District of the Frontier, Schofield agreed. McNeil promised that what he lacked in "military knowledge" for the assignment at Fort Smith he would recompense for in energy and determination.[5]

On October 1, 1863, Schofield wired General-in-Chief Henry W. Halleck that he intended to send McNeil to Fort Smith to replace Blunt. Blunt's friends in Washington objected; but Schofield had his way, and Blunt was ordered to report to Fort Leavenworth. When the reassignment orders arrived, Blunt was about to depart Fort Scott with twelve hundred men and three hundred wagons loaded with military stores. His troops esteemed his leadership, and news of the command shift caused strong comment in the ranks. An officer at Fort Scott noted that "he [Blunt] is a brave officer, and has never met defeat. He is popular with the Army of the Frontier." Blunt disregarded Halleck's order, and proceeded with a small escort to Fort Smith. McNeil assumed command of the District of the Frontier on November 2, 1863. Eleven days later, Blunt reached Fort Smith with troops and supply train. Continuing to disregard his orders to report to Fort Leavenworth, Blunt ignored General McNeil and began raising Union troops in western Arkansas.[6]

[5] McNeil to Schofield, September 15, 1863. *Ibid.*, 535.

[6] McNeil to Schofield, December 1, 1863. *Ibid.*, 727–28. Wiley Britton. *Memoirs of the Rebellion on the Border*, 424.

The question of what to do with Blunt was presumably settled by a War Department general order issued on January 1, 1864, establishing the Department of Kansas, with jurisdiction over Kansas, the territory of Nebraska and Colorado, and Indian Territory, including Fort Smith. General Samuel R. Curtis was appointed commander of the district, with headquarters at Fort Leavenworth. A subsequent order created the Department of Arkansas, which included all the state except Fort Smith.[7]

This new arrangement inevitably pitted Curtis and his officers against General Steele and the Department of Arkansas officers. For several months partisans of Curtis and Steele at Fort Smith spent more time harassing one another than to driving the Confederates to the Red River, which was Halleck's goal. Halleck's directive that Steele be responsible for all troops in Arkansas except the garrison at Fort Smith confounded Blunt and Curtis. Most of Blunt's Army of the Frontier had been dispersed at Waldron, Van Buren, Roseville, and Clarksville as approach stations for guarding Fort Smith. Thus, Curtis assumed that the order assigning Fort Smith to his command included the "outposts of Fort Smith and the troops formerly commanded by General Blunt and General McNeil." If not, then he commanded "a post almost without a garrison, and country without troops to defend it." He considered Fort Smith important because it could "either restrain or take in flank" any Confederate raiders who sought to ford the Arkansas and strike into southwestern Missouri or southeastern Kansas.[8]

On February 10, Curtis visited Fort Smith and received a thirteen-gun salute. After inspecting the works, he wired Stanton and Halleck that, properly to garrison and support

[7] General Orders 1, January 1, 1864, and General Orders 14, January 6, 1864. *Official Records*, Series I, Volume XXXIV, Part Two, 7, 34.
[8] Curtis to Stanton, January 26, 1864. *Ibid.*, 162–64.

Fort Smith, the Department of Kansas would have to be enlarged to include the western tier of Arkansas counties. No fortifications guarded the approaches to the town, and the ferry for crossing troops was only a small flatboat. He ordered two "field forts" thrown up on the approaches to Fort Smith and improved arrangements for crossing the river. Further, he instructed local officers to requisition siege guns and ordnance to strengthen the Belle Point station. During his three-day stay at Fort Smith the officers honored him with a "grand review." A "large concourse of citizens and soldiers assembled at 6 p.m. [on February 11] at the east gate" of the post to officially welcome the general.[9]

On his return to Fort Leavenworth, Curtis wrote Halleck that the houses of the eighteen hundred persons in the town of Fort Smith were widely "scattered" and that the buildings on the adjacent military reservation, especially the post warehouses and magazines, were exposed to raids. Troops assigned to the District of the Frontier had been dispersed to hold other points, leaving about two thousand to garrison Fort Smith. Curtis informed Halleck that troops were already throwing up redoubts on three hills commanding land approaches to the town. These fortifications would "greatly economize the force required to protect the place and public stores." A compelling question for Curtis was whose troops would man the outer defenses he had ordered constructed—the entire perimeter system was in the Department of Arkansas except for the redoubt line along the Poteau. It was expected that the Confederates would take to the field as soon as the grass was green, and great efforts were being made to have the post ready to repel any assault. Curtis pointed out that the headquarters "the so-called Army of the Frontier" was at Fort Smith whereas its brigades were deployed on both sides of the line separating

[9] Curtis to Stanton, February 10, 1864. Curtis to Halleck, February 10, 1864. *Ibid.*, 292–93. *Fort Smith New Era*, February 13 and 20, 1864.

Arkansas and the Indian Territory. He told Halleck that he did not "desire the command of an inch of territory or a corporal's guard beyond my proper limits and the common safety seems to require," but that the order establishing his department had created an impossible command situation at Fort Smith.[10]

At Little Rock, General Steele had designated western Arkansas as the District of the Frontier in the Department of Arkansas and sent General John M. Thayer, a veteran of the Vicksburg and Little Rock campaigns, to take command. Thayer was puzzled. Clearly, the military reservation comprising Fort Smith was in Curtis' department. But what about Fort Smith town, which abutted the post's eastern edge? Was it included in Steele's or in Curtis'? The townspeople too were puzzled by the new arrangement, because only a few Department of Kansas troops were at the post. Most of those troops were outside the town in the approach defenses and within the limits of the Department of Arkansas. To settle the question, Thayer inquired of Little Rock headquarters, "Is the town of Fort Smith in the Department of Arkansas or Kansas?"[11]

Steele queried the War Department and was informed that the town was included in his department, and so he directed Thayer to set up his headquarters at Fort Smith town. Further to complicate matters, Curtis ordered Blunt "to resume command of so much of the District of the Frontier as is concluded within the boundaries of the Department of Kansas." When Halleck remained adamant, Curtis told Blunt "to try to preserve terms of courtesy and cooperation with General Thayer and other adjacent commanders."[12]

[10] Curtis to Halleck, February 15, 1864. *Official Records*, Series I, Volume XXXIV, Part Two, 339-40.

[11] Thayer to Greene, February 5, 1864. *Ibid.*, 247. *Fort Smith New Era*, February 6, 1864.

[12] General Orders 1, February 22, 1864. General Orders 8, February

By the time that Blunt received his new assignment from
General Curtis, Thayer had nearly emptied Fort Smith of
troops, ordnance, and subsistence. Most of the garrison units
were ordered to defensive points within the Department of
Arkansas. Blunt informed Curtis on March 8 that Fort Smith
had been "entirely stripped of everything, even to taking
down the telegraph wire." Not a man was left for him to command. He said that Thayer's action caused "great confusion in
everything, and terrible indignation among the troops." Blunt
believed that it would be easy for him "to take command of
all the troops heretofore belonging to the District of the Frontier, as the officers and men" were eager for him "to assume
command of them." Blunt predicted that these men, most of
whom had served under him in numerous battles, would
"cheerfully comply with whatever" he might "ask of them in
defiance of Thayer and Steele." Since Curtis' departure,
Thayer's conduct had been "not only unsoldierly and un-
gentlemanly, but infamous." Blunt promised to "lie quiet and
await" developments and not to force the issue until the question of the department boundary was settled.[13]

Halleck had further reduced troops in the Department of
Kansas by directing the transfer of the 9th Kansas Cavalry to
Steele's command. Curtis protested to Secretary of War Stanton, claiming that this took "all or nearly all the troops about
Fort Smith" which Blunt had used to check raids on Kansas
and Indian Territory. He urged that it was mandatory for the
government to assign to his department the western tier of
Arkansas counties and to restore those troops Blunt had
brought into the region and the reinforcements sent him.[14]

Halleck and the War Department were adamant on chang-

23, 1864. Curtis to Blunt, March 6, 1864. *Official Records*, Series I, Volume XXXIV, Part Two, 394, 408, 533-34.
[13] Blunt to Curtis, March 9, 1864. *Ibid.*, 537.
[14] Curtis to Stanton, February 27, 1864. *Ibid.*, 443-46.

ing department lines. Thayer resented Blunt's presence at
Fort Smith and wrote General Ulysses S. Grant that he hoped
he would advise the War Department not to give in to Curtis
and Blunt. Grant wired Stanton that Curtis' request to detach
the western tier of Arkansas counties was "decidedly unad-
visable." Blunt, stirred to action by Curtis' request, ordered
all officers in the District of the Frontier to report to him.
Steele instructed Thayer to ignore orders from Blunt and Curtis, and Thayer redeployed the troops of western Arkansas
well beyond Blunt's reach.[15]

As spring approached, Federal generals planned an offensive
up the Red River on Shreveport, with the intent of carrying
the war into eastern Texas. General Nathaniel P. Bank's army,
supported by Rear Admiral David Porter's gunboats, was to
advance up the Red from the Mississippi. Arkansas Department troops were to join Banks near Shreveport. Steele
planned to march from Little Rock with two divisions, joining Thayer's division made up of troops stationed around Fort
Smith. Thayer was instructed to leave only enough men at
Fort Smith to guarantee safety of his headquarters and the
townspeople. Blunt had voluntarily turned over to Thayer
"such transportation" as he might require from the wagons
and teams at Fort Smith. He had ninety wagons and teams
thirty-five miles southeast of Fort Smith gathering forage. On
his way to join Steele, Thayer encountered the forage train
and, "by a brilliant piece of strategy," incorporated it into his
column on the grounds that, besides being needed for transportation, the forage train was trespassing in his district. Blunt
protested to no avail. Most of Thayer's troops came from
Blunt's old Frontier Army, including the 6th, 12th, and 14th
Kansas Cavalry, the 1st Kansas Colored Infantry, and several

[15] Thayer to Grant, March 11, 1864. Steele to Halleck, March 12,
1864. Grant to Stanton, March 14, 1864. *Ibid.*, 566, 567, 602. *Fort Smith
New Era*, January 16, 1864.

artillery batteries. Many of these men deserted on the march to join Steele for the Red River campaign. Steele blamed these desertions on Blunt's influence, and said that Curtis was "most likely [Blunt's] accomplice" in attempting to sabotage the operation.[16]

While Thayer was absent, Colonel William R. Judson was in charge of the defense force for Fort Smith town, including the 13th Kansas Cavalry, a detachment from the 6th Kansas Cavalry, and a section of the 3d Kansas Battery. Blunt's troops at the post—by this time a battalion of the 11th U.S. Colored Infantry, two sections of the 2d Kansas Battery, and four companies of cavalry—worked with Judson's men to defend the Belle Point area. Judson furnished troops for police duty in and about the town and fatigue details for work in the quartermaster and commissary depots at Fort Smith; Blunt assigned men from the 11th Infantry to work on the fortifications. But relations became strained. In early April, Judson telegraphed Little Rock headquarters that his troops were unable to obtain commissary supplies from the Fort Smith depot except through a direct appeal to Blunt, and that he feared his troops would starve. Blunt's officers ordered that all stores coming in by boat and wagon train be deposited in the Fort Smith warehouses and magazines, where they controlled the issue of supplies. Judson's protest was forwarded to General Halleck, who used it as the basis for drafting a confidential memorandum to General Grant. He pointed out that at the time the Departments of Kansas and Arkansas were constituted, he had recommended that Fort Smith and the Indian Territory be included in Steele's command, "inasmuch as it must be defended by Steele's army and receive all supplies through Little Rock and Fort Smith." Halleck recalled that

[16] Thayer to Steele, March 15, 1864. Steele to Breck, March 29, 1864. Curtis to Halleck, March 26, 1864. *Official Records*, Series I, Volume XXXIV, Part Two, 618, 751, 764.

Secretary of War Stanton had concurred with him, but that the president, responding to pressure from Kansas Senator Jim Lane and others, directed that Indian Territory and Fort Smith be assigned Curtis' department. Halleck added that "General Blunt, who seems to be a very quarrelsome man," had been sent by Curtis to command the district. Since then, there had been "much difficulty and confusion, which may produce some serious results." So far as Halleck could see, the only way to solve this problem was "to attach Fort Smith and the Indian Territory to the Department of Arkansas and send General Blunt back to Kansas." If Grant agreed with his view, Halleck promised to see whether he and Stanton could get President Lincoln to "consent to the change." Grant moved promptly on Halleck's recommendation. On April 16, he telegraphed, "Please ask the President to authorize the transfer of Fort Smith and the Indian Territory to the Department of Arkansas." If this change was acceptable to the president, Grant wanted "General Blunt ordered back to report to General Curtis."[17]

President Lincoln approved, and, on April 17, the War Department issued a general order carrying out Halleck's recommendations. Blunt received his copy of the order on April 19, turned over his command to Colonel Judson, and proceeded to Fort Leavenworth. Judson issued an order announcing his assuming command of Indian Territory and the post of Fort Smith.[18]

A Confederate assault on the Belle Point station was expected during the late spring. Judson pushed completion of the outer defense system. Perimeter forts guarding the Van Buren, Fort Towson, Waldron, and Roseville roads were nearly completed and each fitted with two twelve-pounder

[17] Halleck to Grant, April 15, 1864. Grant to Halleck, April 16, 1864. *Ibid.*, Part Three, 161, 178.

[18] Lincoln Endorsement, April 16, 1864. General Orders 5, April 19, 1864. *Ibid.*, 178, 225.

brass guns. The Van Buren Road earthwork, with accommodations for five hundred men, was the largest. By late April, work had started on the supporting batteries at Fort Smith. Connecting the forts, a line of rifle pits, planned to extend from the Arkansas to and along the Poteau, was being excavated. The system was designed to hold six thousand men.[19]

On May 11, Union spies reported from north Texas that eight thousand Confederate troops were marching to attack Fort Smith. Judson sent his troops into the defenses, ordered all business houses closed, and impressed the male citizens into labor companies to work on the rifle pits. The alarm passed when Judson learned that the enemy force was only a "heavy scout" probing to determine how far north the Confederates could extend their outposts. The emergency did provide him with a large civilian labor force, and much progress was made on constructing the outer defenses.[20]

Thayer returned with his troops from the Red River campaign on May 16 and resumed command of the District of the Frontier. He placed Colonel Judson in command of the garrison at Fort Smith. Thayer pushed his troops to complete the Belle Point fortifications, and by the summer of 1864 the field forts were completed and manned and there was "a continuous line of rifle-pits, with an extensive abatis, from the Arkansas around to the Poteau River extending for 2 miles." The defenses were "about finished, and are strong, excellent works, with various appurtenances complete, quarters, magazines, water, &c." Thayer boasted that if he had "plenty of supplies" he could hold Fort Smith forever in the face of an attack by all of General Kirby Smith's troops.[21]

[19] Gerster to Curtis, April 9, 1864. Judson to Kimball, April 10, 1864. *Ibid.*, 112–13, and Part One, 861.
[20] Britton. *Civil War on the Border.* II, 342.
[21] General Orders 29, May 18, 1864. Thayer to Steele, May 28, 1864. Thayer to Curtis, June 11, 1864. *Official Records*, Series I, Volume XXXIV, Part Three, 654, Part Four, 84, 317–18.

Several changes had occurred in the Confederate command since the Union conquest of Fort Smith. After evacuating Belle Point, Cabell fell back through Waldron and then joined Sterling Price's army, which had been driven out of Little Rock by General Frederick Steele's Union force stationed at Arkadelphia. Confederate General Steele, commander of the District of Indian Territory, maintained his headquarters at Boggy Depot, convenient to the stream of flour, beef, clothing, and other items coming in from Texas. He claimed that he had been forced to adopt a "defensive policy" since he had lost Cabell's brigade to Price's army. He placed his troops on a crescent south and west of Fort Smith, with Bankhead's Texans at Riddle's on the Butterfield Road, and Cooper's Indian troops at Perryville. He assured the Confederate high command that he would take the offensive and attempt to recover Fort Smith as soon as two cavalry regiments and a battery arrived from the Texas Gulf coast. About the only offensive action he planned at the time was to send Colonel Stand Watie's Cherokee regiment to reconnoiter north of the Arkansas, raid into Kansas, and intercept supply trains moving south from Fort Scott to Union bases on the Arkansas.[22]

On November 1, 1863, General Richard N. Gano reported to Steele with about 250 reinforcements and a four-gun battery, and was placed in charge of the brigade formerly led by Bankhead. A most important command change occurred in January, 1864, when Steele was replaced by General Samuel B. Maxey as chief of the District of Indian Territory. Maxey immediately put into action the Confederate forces in the Indian Territory, and by the summer of 1864 his troops controlled all the land north to the Arkansas and east to the Poteau. His harassment tactics on the rim of Fort Smith forced

[22] Crosby to Cooper, September 15, 1863. Steele to Boggs, September 17, 1863. Cooper to McCulloch, October 9, 1863. *Ibid.*, Series I, Volume XXII, Part Two, 1016, 1019; Series I, Volume XXVI, Part Two, 303.

the Belle Point garrison into a state of siege. One favorite ruse was for Colonel Sampson N. Folsom to scatter his Choctaw Brigade along the Poteau and fire into the outer defenses. This lure would occasionally draw a cavalry column out of Fort Smith; Folsom's mounted men would then race down the Fort Towson Road and lead the pursuing Federal column into an ambush set by Colonel Jack McCurtain's Choctaws.[23]

After Thayer set up cavalry stations outside the post, Indian troops would slip in during the night, spook the horses, and drive them into Confederate territory. One sortie captured 117 Kansas Cavalry and much-needed weapons, including revolving pistols. Raiders annihilated hay-cutting details sent out to gather forage; horses at the post weakened because of limited feed. More and more of the cavalry at Fort Smith became foot soldiers. Thus, with almost no cavalry to chase the raiders away, they became more daring. They cut the telegraph lines from Fort Smith to St. Louis and from Fort Smith to Little Rock, and then ambushed men sent to restore service. Thayer put guards along the lines; the Confederate snipers made guard duty the deadliest and most dreaded assignment at Fort Smith, During late July and early August, 1864, sharpshooters from the Cherokee and Creek regiments spent several hours each day in the brush on the west bank of the Poteau firing into the outer defenses of Belle Point; their harassment kept several of the post's cannons busy throwing canister into the brush, but since the riflemen were constantly moving to new firing positions, few of the blind shots were effective.[24]

The rough hill country north of Fort Smith was infested with Confederate raiders and guerilla bands, who preyed on Telegraph Road traffic. Captain Buck Brown and his two

[23] Cooper to Scott, August 10, 1864. *Ibid.*, Series I, Volume XLI, Part One, 31–36.
[24] Thayer to Steele, July 30, 1864. Morehead to Judson, July 29, 1864. Maxey to Boggs, July 30, 1864. *Ibid.*, 24–29.

hundred partisans roamed the countryside in small bands, intimidating "Mountain Federals," robbing mail and supply trains, and cutting telegraph lines.

Raiders also cut off Fort Smith from the east. Their special targets were steamers attempting to supply Fort Smith. The speed for each craft was held down to enable troops marching along the bank to be in supporting range, thus making the steamers ideal marks for riverbank ambushes. Hidden sharpshooters picked off the howitzer crews aboard, and masked cannons blasted heavy shot into the steamers, wrecking machinery and sometimes causing the boats to sink. So many Union supply boats were shot up and crippled or burned during June, 1864, that Thayer asked General Curtis to "put on the route from Fort Scott . . . a lot of ox team trains." Inasmuch as Thayer's lifeline by water was threatened by increasing Confederate depredations, he had to depend more and more on Fort Scott as the supply depot for the District of the Frontier.[25]

One of the more dramatic coups on the Union supply line was the capture of the *J. R. Williams* by Colonel Stand Watie's Cherokee cavalry. The *J. R. Williams* was a river steamer kept at Fort Smith to ferry troops and supply trains across the river and to supply posts close to Belle Point. On the morning of June 15, 1864, she cast off for Fort Gibson with a cargo of flour, bacon, and Indian goods consigned to the Union faction of the Cherokee Nation; her military escort included one sergeant, twenty-four privates, and Lieutenant Horace A. B. Cook of the 12th Kansas Infantry. No cavalry rode the riverbank to alert the armed guard of trouble. Seventy miles above Fort Smith, on a great bend approaching Pleasant Bluff, Watie waited in ambush. He had positioned Lieutenant Henry Forrester of Lee's Texas Battery with three

25 Thayer to Curtis, June 11, 1864. *Ibid.*, Series I, Volume XXXIV, Part Four, 317–18.

guns behind "clusters of bushes, about one hundred yards apart." His cavalrymen were dismounted and hiding in the brush. Watie told Forrester to hold his fire until the boat was opposite his center gun. At Watie's command, sharpshooters cut down men on the deck as cannon fire smashed into the boat. One ball crushed the chimney four feet above the deck; a second ripped through the pilothouse, knocking most of it away; a third broke some steam pipes, releasing a cloud of white vapor that enveloped the boat and caused the pilot to ground the craft on a sand bar near the north bank. The survivors splashed ashore and ran for the woods. Watie's men got the steamer off the bar, ran her to the south bank, unloaded the cargo, and then burned the boat. Thereafter, Thayer sent supplies overland to Fort Gibson with a heavy escort that invited flying thrusts by Confederate raiders.[26]

Enemy bands kept constant pressure on Union outposts between Fort Smith and Little Rock. Roseville was garrisoned by three Kansas cavalry companies to guard several hundred bales of cotton awaiting shipment to Northern mills. Raiders hit the town and burned 133 bales of cotton and two gins but were unable to dislodge the Union troops. After the battle, a Union messenger rushed to Fort Smith for a surgeon to tend the wounded. Assistant Surgeon Stephen A. Fairchild and a twenty-five man cavalry escort answered the call. Ten miles west of Roseville they rode into an ambush; Fairchild and eleven others died.[27]

General Nathan Kimball, in charge at Little Rock in the absence of General Frederick Steele, became impatient with the efforts of his troops in the Department of Arkansas to clean out the Confederate raiders. He stormed, "I want those guerrillas captured, killed, or dispersed, and the telegraph line

[26] Thayer to Steele, June 22, 1864. *Ibid.*, 503–504.
[27] Judson to Kimball, April 4, 1864. Judson to Sanborn, April 15, 1864. *Ibid.*, Part One, 860–61.

kept in order." He directed his officers to "seize and impress all the horses belonging to rebels and their sympathizers, and drive every disloyal man out of the country. . . . hang or shoot every devil who . . . destroys the telegraph."[28]

Troops from Fort Smith finally captured four Confederate partisans—A. J. Copeland, James H. Rowden, John Norwood, and William Carey—who were tried and convicted by a military commission. The charge was that they and twenty other Confederates—all clad in Union uniforms and pretending to be members of the 14th Kansas Cavalry—had come upon a detachment of the 1st Arkansas Union Cavalry near Prairie Grove on April 7, 1864. Suddenly opening fire, the partisans gunned down ten Union soldiers and one civilian. The Fort Smith tribunal ordered them to pay the "extreme penalty of the law for murder and violation of the civilized rules of warfare."[29]

When the death sentences were first read, the accused seemed indifferent, one of them remarking, "Well, all right." But as the time for execution neared, they requested the services of a clergyman. On July 29, the prisoners were visited by Chaplain Francis Springer and, after religious services, their irons were removed. Escorted from the prison, they were placed in wagons, each seated on his own coffin. Chaplain Springer was with two of the condemned in the first wagon; Chaplains Wilson and McAfee, with the other two in the second vehicle. The "solemn procession" was then formed. The place of execution was south of Fort Smith town near the rifle pits. The prisoners were placed in a line, each by the side of his coffin. Three sides of a hollow square of infantry had been formed to keep the "multitude of spectators at a proper distance, leaving the side next to the prisoners open." After the judge advocate read the charges and findings of the

28 Kimball to Waugh, April 16, 1864. *Ibid.*, Part Three, 180.
29 *Fort Smith New Era*, August 6, 1864.

commission, the prisoners knelt with the chaplains; Springer offered a short prayer. Several persons shook hands with the condemned and bade them farewell. The judge advocate remained until their eyes were bandaged and hands tied. The execution squad aimed forty-eight rifle-muskets; Captain Jeremiah Frankhouse commanded "Fire!" there was a crashing volley; and "four lifeless bodies lay stretched on the ground." A local editor observed that the whole "terrible scene, from beginning to end, was conducted with the propriety due to a transaction so awful!"[30]

Rather than intimidating local Confederates, the Fort Smith executions seemed to urge them to more daring exploits, the most sensational of which resulted in the second Battle of Cabin Creek. Its results were far-reaching, and nearly forced the Union command to abandon Fort Smith. Confederate depredations on supply steamers on the Arkansas had forced the Belle Point depot to depend increasingly on wagon trains running on the military road from Fort Scott to the Arkansas. On August 18, 1864, Colonel William Adair of the 2d Cherokee Regiment rode into General Maxey's Fort Towson headquarters with a battle plan from General Stand Watie. He requested permission to sweep north of the Arkansas and cut the military road from Fort Scott to Fort Smith, lifeline for the District of the Frontier, and perhaps raid into southern Kansas. He pointed out that this was the key to recovering Fort Smith and the region because the Belle Point depot, besides provisioning troops in the Fort Smith defense system, was also the source of supply for Fort Gibson and other satellite posts on the upper Arkansas. General Cooper, Watie's immediate superior, asked that Watie's brigade of eight hundred Indian troops be joined by General Gano and his twelve hundred Texans and Howell's six-gun battery. Maxey received approval for the campaign from the Trans-Mississippi

[30] *Ibid.*

Department Command, and Watie and Gano set the expedition in motion.[31]

On the way north, Watie's column found a Federal hay-cutting detail at Flat Rock—troops from the 1st Kansas Colored Infantry were working in the meadows, guarded by 2d Kansas Cavalry units. Confederate cavalry struck a lightning sweep through the Federal defenses and overran the hay cutters. It had been charged that the Confederates were giving no quarter to Negro soldiers, and men of the 1st Kansas Colored Infantry were determined to sell their lives as dearly as possible. Concerning the Flat Rock episode, General Gano reported: "The sun witnessed our complete success, and its last lingering rays rested upon a field of blood. Seventy-three Federals, mostly negroes, lay dead upon the field." The Confederates captured eighty-five prisoners and the hay-cutting detail's horses and mules, put the torch to the wagons, equipment, and three thousand tons of hay, and then proceeded toward Kansas.[32]

On September 12, a Federal train of three hundred wagons with a 260-man escort, commanded by Major Henry Hopkins of the 2d Kansas Cavalry, left Fort Scott for Fort Smith. At Baxter Springs, Hopkins was reinforced with units from the 2d and 3d Union Cherokee Home Guards and proceeded down the Military Road, arriving at Cabin Creek Station at nine on the morning of September 18. Cabin Creek Station was a small Federal fort enclosed with a heavy log palisade and garrisoned by 170 Union Cherokees. A force of 140 Cherokees and Creeks had recently arrived from Fort Gibson to reinforce the station garrison. During the day, scouts advised Hopkins that a Confederate column was on the Military Road moving toward the crossing. Hopkins ordered the teamsters

[31] Maxey to Smith, August 18, 1864. *Official Records*, Series I, Volume XLI, Part Two, 1072.
[32] Gano to Cooper, September 29, 1864. *Ibid.*, Part One, 788–91.

to corral the wagons in a quarter circle behind the stockade with teams hitched, and put the men to work setting up a defense system of rifle pits and barricades outside the stockade. Late that evening, Confederate patrols brushed with Hopkins' pickets, and by midnight all Union forces were compressed into the defenses, the stockade, or about the wagons. Confederate cannons, flashing from the heights above the station, panicked the wagonmasters and teamsters, who cut mules from the wagons and rode bareback up the Military Road for Fort Scott. Several mule teams stampeded into the timber; some became tangled in their traces and snapped off wagon tongues; others bolted over the bluffs, pulling wagons crashing after them into the creek. Watie's men drove the Union troops from the wagon defenses and captured part of the train.

At daybreak, General Gano moved his artillery to positions from which his gunners hammered the breastworks and stockade walls for several hours. Major John Jumper's Seminole Battalion dismounted, infiltrated the timber, turned the Federal flank, and gained the Military Road, thus thwarting Hopkins' hopes of evacuating those wagons he still held. Hopkins, believing his situation hopeless, collected the surviving defenders stationed outside the palisade and retreated across Cabin Creek toward Fort Scott. Watie's men moved in on the stockade and bottled up those troops stationed inside. The second Battle of Cabin Creek ended at nine on the morning of September 19.

The Confederate commanders found that they had captured a million dollars' worth of goods—enough clothing to equip two thousand men and vast subsistence stores. The troops sorted the booty, concentrated it in 130 wagons, and rounded up 740 mules. They then shot all crippled mules and burned the Cabin Creek Station, three thousand tons of stacked hay, 120 damaged wagons, and all the goods they could not carry away. Expecting a Federal relief column from Fort

Smith and Fort Gibson, Watie and Gano turned their men and
the captured train toward the Canadian.[33]

On the approaches to Pryor Creek Crossing, Watie's scouts
sighted a strong Federal force. The Confederate commanders
decided that the precious booty in the captured train was more
important to Confederate interests than another engagement,
and so they made plans to elude the Federal column. Confederate Cherokee scouts, well acquainted with the country,
led the slow-moving train on a wide circle to another crossing.
Watie and a battalion kept one wagon, which, to make the
enemy believe that they were parking the supply train in
preparation for battle, they moved back and forth on a high
rock ledge for several hours. Before retiring, the Confederates
built a number of roaring fires along the ridge in view of the
Federal camp. The captured wagon train, well on its way
before the Federal troops discovered the deception, crossed
the Canadian into Confederate territory on September 27.
Confederate officials described Watie's and Gano's coup at
Cabin Creek "as brilliant as any one of the war."[34]

The civilian population suffered most from the Civil War
on the border. For years, armies had foraged their livestock,
poultry, and grain; guerrilla bands had plundered their households, violated their women, and carried off their valuables.
With the Union occupation of Arkansas and Indian Territory
to the Arkansas River, many local men joined the Union army.
Confederates harassed "Mountain Federal" families, burned
their houses and barns, and drove them into Fort Smith, Fort
Gibson, and other Union stations along the Arkansas. In the
spring of 1864, more than fifteen hundred "completely destitute" Unionists and three hundred Negro slaves collected at
Fort Smith. Feeding and clothing the refugees placed an added
drain on the Belle Point depot. General Thayer, seeking to

[33] *Ibid.*
[34] Cooper to Scott, September 27, 1864. *Ibid.*, 783.

move them north as quickly as possible, stressed to his superiors the urgency of getting the unfortunates "to some point where supplies are more [plentiful], for I cannot feed them here, and they must starve if I do not." During May, four steamers cast off from Fort Smith with 120 whites and three hundred Negroes aboard. The Negroes, mostly women and children, were slated to work on the plantations operated by the Treasury Department on the lower Arkansas and Mississippi.[35]

Running the Confederate ambush gauntlet between Belle Point and Little Rock was perilous for refugees evacuating the Arkansas valley, but no more so than by land on the Telegraph Road into southwestern Missouri or on the Military Road to Fort Scott. Reports of Confederate raiders lurking along the roads led Thayer to assign heavy cavalry and infantry escort to each refugee train. Because of the uncertainty of supply by land and water, Thayer had carefully to manage subsistence stores in the Belle Point warehouses; consequently, each refugee train was issued only bare minimum rations and almost no feed for the teams and cavalry mounts. Thus, the trains were slowed, adding to the refugees' distress. The country north of Fort Smith—desolated by rampaging armies, several battles, and guerilla strikes—was a wasteland. Confederate raiders burned the hay and grain reserves at Union military stations along the Telegraph and Military roads. Foraging parties sent out from the refugee trains "to glean whatever . . . grain might have escaped the rapacity of preceding troops" often returned empty-handed. Horses and mules "nearly famished"; daily they grew thinner and weaker, until finally many were unable to go farther "and were left on the road to shift for themselves or to die." In one night, a refugee train teamster asserted, the mules "ate off seventeen wagon tongues to which they had been tied, so keenly were they pinched with hunger."[36]

Throughout the summer and autumn of 1864, refugees continued to gather at Fort Smith. On August 6, the *Fort Smith New Era* reported that "a party of 1,500 persons" was about to leave Belle Point "to seek a temporary or permanent home in the North." "Many if not most" of the refugees had been ruined by the war.

> They belong of course to the loyal part of the people, for the secesh and their sympathizers, have either gone South or stay in the country under a pretence of loyalty. The late raid of the rebels . . . has driven all those who live in comparative security within 10 or 15 miles from town, within the line of fortifications, many escaping with little more than their lives. Among those leaving are many leading Union men who enjoyed the confidence and esteem of loyal men and who, with the wreck of their former competence, are compelled to start life among strangers. We bespeak a kindly welcome for them among their co-patriots of the North.

Two hundred government wagons, which had reached Fort Smith with subsistence stores in late July, were loaded with refugees and their effects and started for Fort Scott on August 8. Colonel William Cloud and the 2d Kansas Cavalry escorted the train.[37]

Confederate commanders on the frontier, eager to recover Fort Smith, nearly received it as a gift from Union General Edward R. S. Canby. On December 5, 1864, acting in his capacity of commander of the Military Division of West Mississippi, Canby directed General Frederick Steele to see

[36] *Official Military History of Kansas Regiments during the War for the Suppression of the Great Rebellion.* Josiah B. McAfee (comp.), 282. Judson to Sanborn, April 16, 1864. *Official Records*, Series I, Volume XXXIV, Part Three, 187.
[37] *Fort Smith New Era*, August 13, 1864.

that, in view of the approach of winter and high cost of keeping it up, Fort Smith and its dependencies were evacuated. District of the Frontier troops and supplies were to be concentrated at Little Rock. Before abandoning the Belle Point works, General Thayer was to destroy all public and private property in the area which might be of use to the enemy.[38]

Canby's order to abandon Fort Smith and withdraw all Federal troops from the frontier back to Little Rock aroused wide protest. Colonel La Rue Harrison, in charge at Fayetteville, wrote General Grenville M. Dodge, commander of the Department of the Missouri, "In the name and for the sake of the thousands of families who will be left to the tender mercies of assassins and robbers, in the name of this beautiful country which will be left a desert, in the name of humanity," to try to get Canby's order countermanded. Harrison hoped that Dodge would try to get President Lincoln to intervene to have Canby cancel his order and save the Unionists of northwestern Arkansas from destruction.[39]

Arkansas politicians protested also. C. P. Bertrand, former Little Rock mayor and a power in the emerging Reconstruction government, wrote Lincoln, on December 12, that he had been informed that General Canby had directed "the immediate evacuation of Fort Smith. . . . Do you know that this abandons one entire Congressional district and the whole of another, save two or three counties, and that two-thirds of the members and perhaps three-fourths of the Legislature, now in session here, are furnished from the district of the country thus to be abandoned and given up?"[40]

General Thayer, best prepared to give an expert opinion on the effect of Canby's order, declared: "When we leave Fort Smith the inhabitants will be left at the mercy of guer-

[38] Christensen to Steele, December 5, 1864. *Official Records*, Series I, Volume XLI, Part Four, 768.

[39] Harrison to Dodge, December 22, 1864. *Ibid.*, 917.

[40] Bertrand to Lincoln, December 12, 1864. *Ibid.*, 835–38.

rillas, and loyal people will be subjected to terrible suffering. Those who are not killed outright will be robbed of their subsistence, and in a short time will be in an actual state of starvation." Thayer reported that at least five hundred persons, black and white, lacked any means of transportation. "Humanity demanded" that the Union provide them a way of getting away. The only solution would be for the government to send "a train as large as can be spared" from Little Rock to assist in hauling public property and removing these people.[41]

Thayer explained to Little Rock headquarters that a speedy evacuation was impossible. First of all, a supply train en route from Fort Scott would not arrive at Belle Point until about January 1. Then too, Thayer had only a hundred wagons, of which ninety-five were hauling stores from steamers grounded by low water on the Arkansas below Clarksville. At Fort Smith he had twenty-seven guns but no artillery horses—the cannons had been emplaced in the field forts. Mules would have to be drawn from the quartermaster train to pull the field pieces. While Thayer's letter of explanation was on its way to Little Rock—it required a week to reach its destination —General Joseph J. Reynolds replaced Steele as commander of the Department of Arkansas and the 7th Army Corps. Reynolds ordered five transports upriver to haul troops and refugees to Little Rock. Thayer loaded the boats with people and stores, but more than a thousand refugees remained at Fort Smith. After organizing a guard force to protect the remaining refugees and public property, he sent most of his infantry and cavalry downriver toward Little Rock.[42]

The protest aroused by Canby's order to abandon Fort Smith caused a stir in Washington. President Lincoln directed General Grant to overrule the Western commander. On Jan-

[41] Thayer to Steele, December 17, 1864. *Ibid.*, 876–77.
[42] Thayer to Green, December 26, 1864. *Ibid.*, 934–35.

uary 10, 1865, a dispatch from Grant's headquarters reached Little Rock: "Should Fort Smith and posts in vicinity have been abandoned before receiving [this order] they will be reoccupied as early as the garrisons can be supplied." General Reynolds relayed the message to Thayer with instructions to recall those troops already on the way to Little Rock and to regarrison the Belle Point post and its satellite stations. Thayer was to send Reynolds all Negro units in the District of the Frontier.[43]

Reynolds persisted in defending Canby's order even though it had been overruled. He pointed out to officials in the War Department:

> Ft. Smith and dependencies cannot and have not afforded protection to citizens outside the picket-lines, and will not be able to do any more hereafter. In future operations expected of this department it is respectfully suggested, that the War Department will not count upon these garrisons for anything. They are a dead weight upon this department.[44]

Reynolds did attempt to stiffen the Fort Smith defense with a command change. On February 6, 1865, he replaced Thayer with General Cyrus Bussey, commander of a cavalry brigade at Little Rock, who reached Fort Smith on February 12. Bussey soon advised Reynolds that he could not depend upon the officers then at Fort Smith, charging that most of them were tainted by "alleged speculations, &c.," and asked that an infantry regiment with a staff of reliable officers be sent him. He urged that the shifting of units continue until all commands that had spent more than a few months at Fort Smith were rotated. Reynolds sent the 40th Iowa Infantry to Fort

[43] Halleck to Reynolds, January 3, 1865. Reynolds to Ryan, January 12, 1865. *Ibid.*, Series I, Volume XLVIII, Part One, 403, 496.

[44] Reynolds to Halleck, January 14, 1865. *Ibid.*, 515.

Smith and reassigned the 2d and 6th Kansas Cavalry and 12th and 13th Kansas Infantry.[45]

On March 4, General Bussey presided over the local celebration of the capture of Charleston. Guns were alerted to fire a "National Salute." A clear, cloudless day brought out off-duty soldiers and a large number of citizens, who assembled on the parade ground within the garrison walls. The 40th Iowa, with Colonel John A. Garrett at its head, was the first unit on the ground, "and marched into the Garrison with flying colors and martial music." Other regiments and crowds of citizens, from "the city and vicinity, with a sprinkling of ladies, kept pouring in, till many thousands were gathered around the platform in the center of the parade ground." A public meeting to commemorate the victory was called to order by Charles Miller as heavy guns roared in the distance.[46]

The Union army was winning the war in the East, but it was making little headway on the Arkansas frontier. Confederate pressure continued on Fort Smith, and the refugee problem persisted. Officers issued rations from the post commissary to the destitute, and sent them downriver or to Fort Scott or into southwestern Missouri as transportation was available. Many Fort Smith families had funds, but local merchants were out of flour and other necessities. To these families, quartermaster officers issued passes to allow them to make purchases at the commissary.[47]

In February, 1865, at a public meeting in Fort Smith town, citizens drafted a petition to President Lincoln. They told him that the "loyal people" of the town and countryside had for a considerable time been "destitute of the necessaries of life, from various causes, chief among which is the appropria-

[45] Bussey to Levering, February 15, 1865. *Ibid.*, 857–58. *Fort Smith New Era*, February 18, 1865.

[46] *Ibid.*, March 11, 1856.

[47] Thayer to Levering, February 7, 1865. *Official Records*, Series I, Volume XLVIII, Part One, 767.

tion for the use of the army of corn, wheat, beef, &c., and the want of protection against guerrillas . . . in carrying on farming operations." To remedy this situation, they called on Lincoln "either to cause sufficient supplies to be brought to this place, so as to allow citizens to purchase from the commissary stores, without curtailing the rations of the troops, or to order supplies to be shipped here on Government account, independent of the army, to be sold to the citizens under the superintendence of persons of known loyalty." Until a crop could be harvested, there were about "2,000 persons in this place and vicinity who need assistance." They wanted to cultivate their lands. Without assistance from the government, they would be compelled to leave Arkansas; but they were willing, if encouraged to do so by the national authorities, to band together to protect themselves against Confederate partisans and farm the land.[48]

Little Rock headquarters directed Bussey to raise companies of home guards and to issue them arms to protect men working in the fields. Bussey was authorized to sell at cost subsistence stores, corn, and oats to loyal families residing near the posts under his command if the purchasers were engaged in farming. Bussey was to deport to Little Rock those persons not engaged in occupations whereby they could support themselves. The number of destitute civilians fed by the military was to be reduced to the lowest number possible, "and the issue of provisions to such persons will cease entirely at the earliest moment practicable."[49]

As February faded into March, news that the army would encourage agriculture caused many Fort Smith citizens to begin "repairing fences and preparing to bring under cultivation as large a tract of garden land as possible." Troops from Fort Smith supervised the colonization of refugees on aban-

[48] Byers to Lincoln, February 9, 1865. *Ibid.*, 790–91.
[49] Levering to Bussey, February 14, 1865. *Ibid.*, 847–48.

doned plantations along the Arkansas. They organized farmer-defense companies and also provided some protection themselves. More than two hundred families were settled near Van Buren. A section of the rich Du Val plantation below Fort Smith was set aside for soldiers' gardens, and each company in the garrison was assigned sufficient ground to "raise all they needed in the vegetable line." Fourteen agricultural colonies were organized by Colonel Harrison in Washington, Benton, and Madison counties.[50]

During late March and early April, 1865, the Arkansas frontier hummed with plowing and planting. Armed citizens and Federal patrols roamed the farmsteads watching for Confederate raiders. Quartermaster officers at Fort Smith issued food and seed to destitute families and sold necessities to those with means. Then, on April 10, a telegram reached General Bussey at Fort Smith telling of the surrender of General Robert E. Lee and his Army of Northern Virginia the previous day at Appomattox Courthouse. Bussey issued orders for the firing of a national salute of two hundred rounds. As soon as it was dark, cannons began flashing the glad tidings across the Belle Point heights. Townspeople and country dwellers responded "with shouts of gladness and rejoicing."[51] The war on the border did not end at once, however; isolated incidents of violence continued along the Indian Territory–Arkansas border until June 23, when General Stand Watie tendered his sword to Federal commissioners at Doaksville in the Choctaw Nation.

[50] *Fort Smith New Era*, March 4 and 11, 1865.
[51] *Ibid.*, April 15, 1865.

# CHAPTER FOURTEEN

# Fort Smith's Epitaph

THE EDITOR OF THE *Fort Smith New Era* provided a résumé of the destruction brought by the Civil War to Belle Point when he wrote:

> The Garrison and the city of Fort Smith have been greatly injured by harsh severities of the war. Yard and garden fences have disappeared; fruit trees and shrubbery have been destroyed; and even the hallowed resting place of the dead have been spoiled. . . . Previous to the Rebellion, the Garrison grounds and buildings were said to have been kept in fine order, and constituted an attractive resort of leisure and fashion. [He went on to present a word portrait of the Union bastion as it appeared on the eve of Reconstruction.] The reservation embraces a tract of 300 acres, in the northwest corner of which are the public buildings raised for the accommodation of the officers and private soldiers on duty at the post. Most conspicuous among these government buildings are the two commodious brick edifices for headquarters offices, and temporary apartments for the families of the officers. Each of these houses is 100 feet in length and three stories high. They are fine structures of substantial and durable workmanship, and are separated from each other by an intervening space of about 80 feet. Each edifice is supplied with two ample porches in front and two in rear, running the entire length of the building. From the upper one of these long porches very fine views may be had of the adjacent forests, valleys, and moun-

tains—of the meanderings of the Poteau and Arkansas, and of the clear, calm skies, with their host of constellations that nightly perform their silent marches there. In front of these two main buildings and about 100 feet distant is a large two story brick edifice, [the editor considered the basement one story] Intended as barracks for the garrison. The barracks is the apex and the two buildings for headquarters, offices, etc., form the base of an isosceles triangle. These structures, together with a guardhouse, powder magazine, and a few wooden sheds, are encompassed by a stone wall enclosing an area of seven acres of ground. The wall has an average height of nine feet, with two feet thickness, and is perforated with embrasures for musketry. At the two angles of the wall nearest the river, and at the length of the wall from each other are two stout, dingy stone buildings. One of these is the quartermaster's office and storehouse, and the other is used for similar purpose by the commissary of subsistence. The entire premise is encompassed by the stone wall, and including the various edifices referred to, is called the "Garrison."[1]

The troops at Fort Smith had much to do in restoring local order and reconstructing the rebellious border country, but, grief-stricken by the news of President Lincoln's assassination, they interrupted their many tasks to attend a memorial funeral service on April 19, 1865. General Bussey said that his troops were so agitated by the assassination that they vowed "a willingness to re-enlist for twenty-years, if need be, to crush out the last vestige of treason in the country."[2]

On the morning of April 19, the troops joined fraternal orders and other citizens to form an "imposing procession," led by Bussey and the members of his staff. Muffled drums of the 18th Iowa regimental band sounded the funeral dirge. The

[1] *Fort Smith New Era*, July 22, 1865.
[2] Bussey to Pope, April 17, 1865. *War of Rebellion: A Compilation of the Official Records of the Union and Confederate Armies*, Series I, Volume XLVIII, Part Two, 110.

procession marched around the town and then into the garrison, where they gathered around the platform erected in the center of the parade ground. After the presentation of a resolution expressing the deep sorrow of both soldiers and citizens, the Reverend W. H. Gillam of the Christian Commission led the singing of the hymn "There Is a Stream Whose Gentle Flow Supplies the City of Our God," joined by the choir, led by Reverend S. F. C. Garrison, of the 40th Iowa. Post Chaplain Francis Springer said the prayer and pronounced the benediction. General Bussey's gunners fired their heavy pieces every thirty minutes throughout the daylight hours. At noon, twenty-one additional guns "called a great nation at the same time, to pay their last and sad tribute to the memory of the great departed."[3]

Fort Smith played an important role in Southwestern history during the immediate postwar period. Officers and troops from the Belle Point station supervised the surrender and demobilization of local Confederate military units, patrolled the border country for die-hard guerrilla bands, relocated Union refugees living near the posts, and assisted in the process of Reconstruction.

On May 26, 1865, Confederate General Edmund Kirby Smith signed a convention with Union General Edward R. S. Canby surrendering all troops and public property under his control. Smith's area commanders reported to Union officers in Arkansas, Texas, and Indian Territory for purposes of signing formal capitulation commitments. Thus, three days after the Smith-Canby convention, Confederate General Thomas P. Dockery made preparations to surrender to General Joseph Reynolds all Confederate troops in Arkansas south of the Arkansas River. Cherokee Commander Stand Watie, the last Confederate general to surrender, tendered his sword to Union officers at Doaksville in the Choctaw Nation on June

[3] *Fort Smith New Era*, April 22, 1865.

23. The capitulation process required that Confederate soldiers report to Union commanders; after tendering arms, each man received a certificate of parole. Officers at Fort Smith issued several hundred such certificates during the spring and summer of 1865.[4]

The editor of the *Fort Smith New Era* observed that hundreds of demobilized Confederate soldiers and many pro-Confederate families were returning to Sebastian and Crawford counties. On June 17, he wrote that the Confederates "have given evidence of agreeable surprise at the unoffending and polite reception with which they have been greeted by old acquaintancs of the Union faith." Many had approached Union lines with caution, expecting insults or the scaffold. On being greeted "with kindness and cordiality, they seemed transported with delight." The Union seemed to say to them: "Well my dear boys, you have been away on a bad errand and in violation of the rules of my house; but as you have returned repentant, I cheerfully, receive you again to fellowship and confidence. Now behave yourselves handsomely, and it shall be well with you."[5]

Guerrilla bands preyed on Union farmsteads near Fort Smith for several months after General Lee's capitulation. On April 19, while most of the Fort Smith troops were attending the memorial service for President Lincoln, five raiders hit a farm six miles east of Fort Smith, terrorized the household, and made off with a horse, a wagon, and a yoke of oxen.[6]

These guerrillas became so bold and destructive during late April and throughout May that many rural families returned to the protection of Fort Smith. On May 1, Captain G. W. Raymond and a detachment of the 1st Arkansas Cavalry, escorting Union families to Fort Smith, camped for the evening

[4] Grant to Sheridan, May 28, 1865. *Official Records*, Series I, Volume XLVIII, Part Two, 639, 702. *Fort Smith New Era*, June 17, 1865.

[5] *Fort Smith New Era*, June 17, 1865.

[6] *Ibid.*, April 22, 1865.

near Massard Prairie. After supper, as the troopers lounged around the fire, hidden riflemen fired into the camp. Sergeant John J. Laster fell with fatal wounds as the other men scrambled for cover. Raymond rallied his troops, but the bushwhackers slipped away.[7]

Cavalry and infantry patrols from Fort Smith maintained relentless pressure on the partisan raiders, and by June 15 the border violence had ceased. Troops escorted refugees back to their farms, and peace came at last to the troubled Southwestern frontier. Confederate irregulars surrendered at Fort Smith throughout the summer. As late as August 16, a guerrilla band entered Fort Smith for parole, and military and civilian observers alike pronounced them the "hardest"-looking group they had ever seen.[8]

After local Confederate forces had been demobilized, Fort Smith served as a mustering-out center for Union troops. General Reynolds had instructed his subordinates in the Department of Arkansas first to disband the Arkansas militia units. Fort Smith officers were to collect all public arms and accouterments from the "Mountain Federals" before they issued discharge certificates. Local Union troops included the 1st Arkansas Infantry, garrison force at Fort Smith, which was to be relieved by the 57th United States Colored Troops currently at Little Rock.[9]

Several Union units in the Fort Smith area were demobilized in July and early August. On July 5, six companies of the 18th Iowa departed Belle Point on the transport *Randolph*. They were followed by the 2d Kansas Battery and the 40th Iowa, which came from Fort Gibson to check in military gear and await transportation. There was a momentary troop

---

[7] *Ibid.*, May 6, 1865.

[8] *Ibid.*, August 19, 1865.

[9] Levering to Solomon, May 27, 1865. *Official Records*, Series I, Volume XLVIII, Part Two, 632.

buildup at Fort Smith in late August and early September, possibly to intimidate and overwhelm delegates of the Confederate Indian nations gathering at the post to participate in the peace council called by the national government. Military units imported for the occasion included the 3d Iowa Battery from Little Rock, a battalion of the 22d Ohio in from provost duty, three companies of the 9th Iowa, and the 54th Illinois. When the council concluded on September 21, these units were demobilized at Fort Smith and Little Rock. After all wartime units serving in the Fort Smith area had been demobilized, the Belle Point garrison force was to be a Negro unit, the 57th United States Colored Troops, commanded by Colonel Paul Harwood.[10]

One effect of the departure of troops from the Arkansas frontier was to stifle the economy of Fort Smith town. Businessmen complained to the editor of the *New Era* that there seemed to be "no money in the country." Another result of demobilization was a vast buildup of military stores, equipment, and livestock at Fort Smith. Officers organized survey boards and supervised the sale of surplus property at public auction. The sales of horses and mules, held the third week in July at the government stables, attracted a huge crowd and proved highly satisfactory to the government because of the high prices received. One observer said this was easily understood when one realized that between the Jayhawkers and the bushwhackers, the area had been "almost completely stripped of horses and mules." With the return of peace, the farmers wanted to get back to work, to "redeem the land and make it smile in plenty once more." At an auction that continued for several days at the commissary building for the disposal of condemned stores, the bidding was again lively.[11]

[10] Special Orders 171, July 21, 1865. *Official Records*, Series I, Volume XLVIII, Part Two, 1113. *Fort Smith New Era*, August 5, 1865.
[11] *Fort Smith New Era*, July 22, 1865.

Fort Smith buzzed with activity during 1865. Besides pacifying the border country, paroling Confederate troops, and demobilizing Federal units, officers and men at the Belle Point station were also involved in the Reconstruction process. Congress intended that the former Confederate states and their satellites, including Indian Territory, should pay a penalty for secession and war by undergoing a process of political rapprochement. Fort Smith was the site for the grand council conducted by the national government to set forth the terms under which the former Confederate Indian nations could resume their proper relationship with the United States.

The United States delegation at the Fort Smith Council included: D. N. Cooley, commissioner of Indian affairs and chairman of the treaty commission; Elijah Sells, superintendent for the Southern Indians; Thomas Wistar, prominent Pennsylvania Quaker; General William S. Harney, representing the United States Army; Colonel Ely S. Parker, from General Grant's staff; and Charles E. Mix, chief clerk of the Indian Bureau and secretary of the Fort Smith Council.[12]

Officers at Fort Smith set aside rooms in the post buildings for a commission council chamber and offices, and Cooley sent notices to the Indian nations that the council would open on Friday, September 8. Representatives of Union factions from the Creeks, Osages, Quapaws, Senecas, Shawnees, Cherokees, Seminoles, Wyandots, Chickasaws, and Choctaws arrived on opening day; Confederate delegations reached Fort Smith two days later. Cooley called the council to order; Lewis Downing, acting chief of the Cherokee Nation, offered a prayer. Then Cooley spoke to the delegates, telling them that the council's purpose was to permit the Indian nations and tribes who had united "with wicked white men who have

[12] An account of the proceedings of the Fort Smith Council can be found in *Annual Report of the Commissioner of Indian Affairs for the Year 1865*, 296–358.

engaged in war" to renew allegiance to the United States and to settle differences in each tribe arising out of division by war. He assured the Indians that the president was concerned with those Indians "who remain true and who have aided him in punishing the rebels, he is well pleased with you, and your rights and interests will be protected by the United States."

Cooley declared that certain of the Indian nations and tribes represented in the council had "by their own acts, by making treaties with the enemies of the United States . . . forfeited all right to annuities, land, and protection by the United States." By the law of Congress of July 5, 1862, "all the nations and tribes forfeited and lost all their rights to annuities and lands. The president, however, does not desire to take advantage of or enforce the penalties for the unwise actions of these nations. The president is anxious to renew the relations which existed at the breaking out of the rebellion." Cooley went on to say that, to renew their relationship with the United States, the leaders of the former Confederate Indian nations were required to negotiate with the peace commission new treaties containing clauses providing for peace and amity among themselves—each nation and tribe—and with the United States. Each Indian nation had to abolish slavery and incorporate the freedmen into the tribe on an equal footing with the Indian members or to make suitable provision for the former slaves. In addition, the Indian nations were expected to surrender certain parts of their lands to resettle tribes from Kansas and elsewhere; each Indian nation had to commit itself to the ultimate organization of a consolidated government for Indian Territory.

Silas Armstrong, a Wyandot delegate, told the council:

I must confess, council has taken a different course from what I expected . . . we are all in the suds. We thought the government would first make a treaty of peace with us all. Indians are different from whites. They are vindictive;

hatred lasts long with them. Not so with the white. The government must settle this difficulty; the Indians cannot.

Cooley fully expected to conclude comprehensive treaties before he left Fort Smith, but his anticipation of a brief council followed by successful negotiation had not reckoned with the obstructionist talents of certain Confederate Indian spokesmen. Statements made before the council by Elias C. Boudinot, erudite delegate for the Confederate Cherokees, illustrate the tactics as well as the viewpoint of Confederate representatives at the Fort Smith Council. On one of several occasions when he had the floor, Boudinot said:

We have accepted the abolition of slavery as a fact accomplished, and are willing to give such fact legal significance by appropriate acts of council. But we respectfully submit that it would neither be for the benefit of the emancipated negro nor the Indian to "incorporate" the former into the several tribes "on an equal footing with the original members." That the emancipated negro must be "suitably provided for" is a natural sequence of his emancipation; but so serious and delicate a question should not be so hastily considered and acted upon, and we therefore ask further time before deciding upon it, pledging ourselves to acquiesce in good faith in any plan which may be considered reasonable and just.

The consolidation of all the nations and tribes in the Indian territory into one government is open to serious objection; there are so many, and in some instances antagonistic, grades of tastes, customs, and enlightenment that to throw the whole into one heterogeneous government would be productive of inexplicable confusion.

We beg to assure the government that our objections . . . are made in no captious spirit, but with a view solely to the good of our common people; and we announce ourselves willing to yield such objections if, after mature deliberations, no better than can be suggested by us which will be satisfactory to the government.

On September 21, Cooley adjourned the council to meet again at the call of the secretary of the interior. Cooley's lone accomplishment as leader of the United States delegation was a treaty of peace and amity "pledging anew, on behalf of the Indians, allegiance to the United States, and repudiating all treaties with other parties; and on the part of the United States agreeing to re-establish peace and friendship with them."[13]

At the conclusion of the Fort Smith Council, the demobilization process resumed for troops assigned to the Belle Point area. The 3d Iowa Battery and the 54th Illinois boarded transports for Little Rock, where they were mustered out. In February, 1866, the 3d United States Cavalry reached Fort Smith to relieve the three companies of the 9th Iowa. Before departing Fort Smith for home, the Iowa men turned their horses and equipment over to the post quartermaster.[14]

Negro soldiers of the 57th United States Colored Troops, Fort Smith's garrison force, aroused mixed reaction among local citizens. The *New Era* reported that people at Fort Smith town were surprised to learn that one-third of the enlisted personnel could read. According to the unit chaplain, the men would probably be completely literate before another year passed. The editor of the *New Era* wrote, "Their [the Negroes'] desire for self improvement is remarkable and notwithstanding the heavy guard and fatigue duties they have to perform, [they] are making rapid strides toward the attainment of knowledge and knowledge is power."[15]

[13] *Ibid.*

[14] *Van Buren Press*, February 24, 1866. *Roster and Record of Iowa Soldiers in the War of the Rebellion together with Historical Sketches of Volunteer organizations, 1861–1866.* Vol. IV, 1654; Vol. V, 1756. *Report of the Adjutant General of the State of Illinois.* Vol. III, 691.

[15] *Fort Smith New Era*, August 26, 1865.

Early in 1866, officers at Fort Smith were ordered to make preparations for an expedition to New Mexico. The column was to include a battalion of the 3d United States Cavalry and the 57th United States Colored Troops. It was reported that the Negro troops did not look with favor on the march to New Mexico and that, when informed of their assignment, they became mutinous and refused to go. Officers ordered out the men of the 3d Cavalry, who surrounded the garrison and disarmed the Negroes. Colonel Marshal S. Howe, 3d Cavalry officer, ordered the Negro troops to Little Rock. Department Commander General Reynolds sent the mutinous 57th back to Fort Smith aboard the *Argos* and *Pilgrim* with instructions for the "previous orders to march to New Mexico to be carried out to the letter." Thereupon, Colonel Howe assured the Negroes that any further disobedience would "result seriously to those engaged." Before Howe's column left for New Mexico, two companies of the 19th United States Infantry reached Fort Smith with orders to serve as the garrison force. Captain Robert W. Barnard, of the 19th Infantry, became post commander.[16]

Many other changes in command occurred at Fort Smith after the war. On September 21, 1865, General Henry J. Hunt was assigned to Fort Smith to replace General Bussey as commander of the Frontier District. Hunt had been at Fort Smith in the 1850's as an artillery captain. Early in 1866, General Grant appointed Hunt to the War Department's Artillery Board. On March 24, 1866, a general order discontinued the Frontier District, which included the Fort Smith area. In a subsequent shuffling of military jurisdictions, the War Department created the 7th Military Department, including Arkansas and Indian Territory, under the command of General Edward

[16] Inspection Returns for Companies F and G, 19th Infantry, June 30, 1866. National Archives, War Department, Reports Received File. *Van Buren Press*, April 14, May 12, 19, 26, June 9, 23, 30, 1866.

O. C. Ord, with headquarters at Little Rock. In December, 1866, Ord transferred the headquarters of the 7th Military Department to Fort Smith, but subsequently moved them back to Little Rock.[17]

The emerging Reconstruction program brought additional changes to Fort Smith. The 1867 Reconstruction Acts returned ten of the eleven former Confederate states to military government. Fort Smith figured in the enforcement of the Reconstruction program as a military post in the 4th Military District, consisting of Arkansas and Mississippi. General Ord was assigned to command this district, with headquarters at Vicksburg. The *Van Buren Press* predicted that Arkansas could expect a just and mild Reconstruction administration under Ord. On April 6, 1867, Ord issued a general order establishing the subdistrict of Arkansas, commanded by Colonel Charles H. Smith of the 28th Infantry, with headquarters at Little Rock.[18]

Fort Smith, as an outpost in the subdistrict of Arkansas, was a local administrative center in the Reconstruction process. During 1867, four additional companies of the 19th Infantry were assigned to Fort Smith. Lieutenant Colonel DeLancey Floyd-Jones, new garrison commander, distributed most of his men among the small towns peripheral to Fort Smith to maintain surveillance over this former Confederate area and to enforce Reconstruction regulations, including the observance of the new rights of freedmen. Floyd-Jones served also as supervisor of registrations for a Reconstruction district which included Sebastian, Crawford, Scott, Franklin, Johnson, Washington, Madison, Carroll, and Benton counties. Fort Smith was designated headquarters for this registration district.[19]

[17] Parker to Bearss, May 19 and 22, 1963. *Van Buren Press*, December 7, 1866.

[18] Parker to Bearss, May 31, 1963. *Van Buren Press*, March 1 and April 12, 1867.

In 1868, Arkansas and Fort Smith became part of the Department of Louisiana; a year later, the post was transferred to the Department of the Missouri. Garrison changes at Fort Smith grew out of a War Department decision in 1869 to reduce its forty-five infantry regiments to twenty-five. Fort Smith's garrison force, the 19th Infantry, was to be consolidated with the 28th Infantry stationed at Little Rock. Consolidation took place at Fort Smith on March 31, 1869; after the merger, the reorganized 19th Infantry was ordered to Louisiana. Before leaving Fort Smith, the 19th regimental band gave a farewell concert. The last piece played was "The Girl I Left behind Me." The editor of the *Weekly Herald*, speaking on behalf of the girls at Fort Smith town, said that this song would ring in "the ears of many, and cause some sleepless, dreamless hours to pass quite heavily." To such young ladies, he sent his "condolences." After the regiment departed on April 10 and 13, 1869, a detachment was left at Fort Smith to guard the buildings and supplies until the new garrison—the 6th Infantry—arrived from Fort Gibson.[20]

Two 6th Infantry companies reached Fort Smith by steamer on April 26, and Captain John J. Upham became garrison commander. Other military occurrences of consequence for Fort Smith during 1869 included orders issued by the commander of the Department of the Missouri discontinuing the subdistrict of Arkansas and reassigning Colonel William B. Hazen, superintendent of Indian affairs, from western Indian Territory to Fort Smith. Fort Smith was designated headquarters for Hazen's command, described as the Lower District of Arkansas.[21]

[19] Parker to Bearss, May 29, 1963. *Van Buren Press*, June 21, 1867.

[20] *Fort Smith Weekly Herald*, March 27, April 17, 1869.

[21] Easton to Meigs, February 5, 1870. National Archives, War Department, Quartermaster General, Letters Received File. *Van Buren Press*, April 30, 1869.

A disaster struck Fort Smith in 1870 which led to the final abandonment of the post by the War Department. Soon after the close of the war, one building of officers' quarters burned. Then, on December 19, 1870, the other building of officers' quarters was destroyed by fire, which broke out in a flue on the second floor. A board of inquiry placed the cause of the fire as the accumulation of soot in a defective flue.[22]

When the report of the fire reached the War Department, Secretary of War William W. Belknap and General William T. Sherman decided that Fort Smith should be abandoned and sold. Earlier, Belknap had recommended to Congress that Fort Smith "be included in the pending bill for the disposition of useless Military reservations." Congress passed this measure on February 11, 1871, and President Ulysses S. Grant signed it two weeks later. The bill empowered the secretary of war to transfer to the secretary of the interior various military reservations—including Fort Smith—for disposition for cash according to existing federal laws relating to public lands "after appraisement to the highest bidder, and at not less than the appraised value, nor less than one dollar and twenty-five cents per acre."[23]

In the spring of 1871, Belknap transferred Fort Smith to Secretary of the Interior Columbus Delano with the proviso that the War Department retain custody of the post's national cemetery. In July, orders from headquarters of Department of the Missouri, directed that Fort Smith's 6th Infantry garrison force proceed to Fort Gibson. A detachment would re-

[22] Thibaut to GHQ, Department of Missouri, December 20, 1870. Report of "Board of Citizens," December 29, 1870. National Archives, War Department, Quartermaster General, Letters Received File. *Van Buren Press*, December 27, 1870. "Record of Events" Post Return Fort Smith, Arkansas, November, 1865. National Archives, Post Returns.

[23] Townsend to Pope, February 11, 1871. National Archives, War Department, Quartermaster General, Letters Received File. General Order 19, March 9, 1871. National Archives, War Department, Adjutant General's Office, Letters Sent File.

main at Belle Point to guard public property until the Department of the Interior could take charge. Fort Smith's last garrison force marched out on July 19. The 6th Infantry guard detachment remained at Fort Smith until November 10, 1871, when the United States marshal for the Western District of Arkansas assumed responsibility for the station property.[24]

Almost two years passed before Secretary of the Interior Delano appointed three commissioners—Edward M. McCook, A. H. Van Vorhes, and James R. Laffery—to appraise the lands and buildings at Fort Smith. Their report, submitted on October 21, 1873, disclosed that the military reservation consisted of 296.84 acres, which they valued at two hundred dollars an acre. They appraised the buildings at $22,855, making the aggregate appraised value $82,223.[25]

Before the Fort Smith buildings and land were sold, the federal government found another use for the old post, extending its life as a frontier service center to 1896 and providing a macabre epilogue for the Belle Point outpost. The Civil War on the Western frontier spawned a bumper crop of wild, lawless men and women. After the war, many renegades used Indian Territory as a sanctuary for raiding banks, stagecoaches, trains, and businesses in adjacent states. They drove herds of cattle and horses, gathered from Texas ranches, into Indian Territory for resale to dealers who had no compunctions about brand registrations and bills of sale. These desperadoes even robbed and killed ordinary citizens. After 1870, railroad construction across Indian Territory

[24] Inspection Returns, Company D, 6th Infantry, August 31 and October 31, 1871. National Archives, War Department, Reports Received File. Roots to Akerman, November 10, 1871. National Archives, General Land Office, Fort Smith, AMR File.

[25] Commissioners to Delano, October 21, 1873. National Archives, General Land Office, Fort Smith, AMR File. Smith to Bearss, May 31, 1963.

brought additional disorders. Each railhead and construction camp became a kind of Satan's paradise. These migrant communities included, in addition to the rough-and-ready, brawling construction crews, a wide assortment of tinhorn gamblers, thieves, prostitutes, whisky sellers, and other hoodlums. Gibson Station, a typical rail camp, was reputed to have had at least one killing each night. The criminal population of Indian Territory was increased by lawless Indians and freedmen whose depredations on life and property rivaled those of white intruders. The reputation of Indian Territory spread far and wide as "Robbers' Roost" and "Land of the Six-gun" and was epitomized in the tag "There is no Sunday west of St. Louis—no God west of Fort Smith." Indian tribal governments, weakened by the war and its aftermath, were unable to cope with this crisis in crime, and their leaders appealed to the federal government for help in removing this torment. They pointed out that no traveler was safe, that even the tribal treasuries had been robbed by white intruders; for example, at Caddo, a railroad town on the M. K. and T. Railroad in the southern Choctaw Nation, fifteen murders had been committed with impunity in less than a year.

On March 3, 1871, Congress responded to these pleas with an enactment which moved the Western Arkansas Federal District Court from Van Buren to Fort Smith. The court for the Western District would continue to have jurisdiction over Indian Territory. Court officials rented the second floor of the Rogers' Building in Fort Smith town, used as a meeting place by Masons and Odd Fellows, as a federal district courtroom. On May 8, 1871, Judge William Story opened the first session of what would soon become the world's most notorious court.[26]

The editor of the *Tri-Weekly Herald* was impressed by the

26 *Fort Smith Tri-Weekly Herald*, May 9, 1871.

large number of attorneys from other counties in attendance. "The town is jammed with strangers from all parts, some in office, some hunting for office, and a vast number that have been in, and now out, and some who do not want pap, though they are scarce; altogether the U. S. Court adds considerably to the life of the city."[27]

The editor of the *Van Buren Press* sat in on a session and re-flected the resentment of his townspeople at losing the court by writing that he found the United States court at the "Hole in the Wall" at Fort Smith. The room was "gloomy and dark and rank with nigger and Indian." The *Fort Smith Herald* did not appreciate the allusion to the "Hole in the Wall" court, and countered that "nigger and Indian" were "certainly no more 'rank' now, than they were" when the court sat at Van Buren.[28]

On June 17, the court adjourned until the next regular term. Judge Story had disposed of 132 cases, of which eighty-seven were criminal. The juries had voted twenty-three con-victions and twenty-four acquittals; the rest of the criminal cases were continued, quashed, or disposed of in some other manner. The criminal docket included four murder indict-ments and twenty-five larceny cases; twenty-four men were accused of introducing whisky into Indian Territory, and six-teen were charged with assault with intent to kill. Story's most severe sentence at this term was a two-and-one-half year term for assault with intent to kill. Western celebrity Wyatt Earp, arrested for horse theft in Indian Territory and out of bail, jumped his bond and fled for parts unknown. Altogether, Story's first session at Fort Smith was a tame one.[29]

[27] *Ibid.*
[28] *Ibid.*, May 18, 1871. Two doors away from the Rogers' Building was a back-room saloon—the "Hole in the Wall"—reached by a long, narrow hallway. See S. W. Harmon, *Hell on the Border: He Hanged Eighty-eight Men*, 700.
[29] *Fort Smith Tri-Weekly Herald*, June 10, 1871.

From the beginning of the federal district court at Fort Smith, the adjacent military post played a role in the administration of justice for Indian Territory in that a log building on the original Belle Point site was used as a federal jail. By August 30, 1871, deputy marshals had delivered to the federal jailer and his four guards nine white prisoners, seven Negroes, four Indians, and a Mexican. Tacked to the prison wall was a list containing the names of sixty-seven attorneys, which outnumbered the prisoners by three to one. One inmate said, "If there were fewer lawyers their hope of delivery would be better."[30]

On November 14, 1872, fire destroyed the Rogers' Building. Story moved his court to the Sebastian County Circuit Courtroom and held a two-day session. Meanwhile, United States Marshal Logan Roots received permission from the Department of the Interior to open the large brick building within the walls of Fort Smith known as the Soldiers' Quarters. On November 18, Story called court to order in this building. The northeast room of the first floor was taken over as a courtroom. The southwest room was converted to offices for the United States marshal, clerk, and other officials. The full basement, used by the military as kitchens, was turned into a federal jail.[31]

Judge Story's most famous case at Fort Smith was the murder trial of John Childers. Childers, a tall, muscular Cherokee half-blood from Cowskin Creek, had no previous criminal record. His troubles began with Rayburn Wedding, an itinerant peddler from Kansas who owned a handsome black horse. Childers was alleged to have joined Wedding on the morning of October 14, 1870, as Wedding drove up Caney Creek in the northern Cherokee Nation. Childers tried to

30 *Ibid.*, August 31, 1871.
31 Harmon. *Hell on the Border*, 71-72. *Fort Smith Western Independent*, November 21, 1872.

trade for the horse, but Wedding refused. Later, Wedding was found, his throat cut, in Caney Creek. At Broken Arrow in the Creek Nation, a deputy marshal recognized Childers and the black horse and arrested the Cherokee on a charge of murdering Wedding. Childers escaped, was again arrested, and again escaped. He was said to be enraptured by a whore at Fort Smith. United States marshals gave her ten dollars to lure Childers out of hiding. Marshals watched her house, and when Childers finally came to her they sprung the trap. Continuances by his attorneys delayed action until November, 1872, when a federal jury at Fort Smith returned a verdict of guilty. Judge Story ordered Childers to be executed on Friday, August 15, 1873.[32]

Workmen erected a gallows near the jail. Until a few hours before the execution, Childers expected to be pardoned or to have his sentence commuted. His attorneys had forwarded petitions for executive clemency to President Grant. These hopes were crushed by a telegram from Attorney General George H. Williams informing the lawyers that it was believed in Washington that Childers was guilty and that consequently the president would not intervene. Heavy pressure to let the law take its course was said to have been exerted by persons living in southern Kansas who had been friends of Wedding.

The day of the execution dawned bright and clear, and a large crowd turned out to watch. As the fatal hour approached, the multitude grew restless. Finally, at one in the afternoon, there was a shout. Childers, guarded by six deputy marshals led by Marshal John Sarber and Jailer Charles Burns, had left the jail. As the execution party approached the scaffold, a small black cloud was sighted bearing in from the

[32] Records of Disposition of Cases, 1872–73, United States Court for the Western District of Arkansas. *Western Independent*, November 21, 1872, May 22, 1873.

southwest. By the time the group reached the steps leading to the gallows, rain began. Marshal Sarber faced the prisoner, who puffed a cigar with "as much noncholance as if the affair was none of his." When given an opportunity, Childers spoke for sixteen minutes, admitting that he had killed Wedding but asserting that there should have been a mistrial because the date of the murder named in the indictment and in the testimony was wrong. He cautioned young and old to avoid evil companions and bad practices. He said that he had no regret, except at leaving his sister and friends, and asked that his body "be not given for dissection, but that his sister be permitted to give it burial in the Cherokee Nation." He waved farewell with a general sweep of his hand. To the marshal, he said in a firm, clear voice heard by all, "Didn't you say you were going to hang me?" Sarber replied, "Yes." Childers coldly responded, "Then why in hell don't you do it!" After Childers had finished speaking, Reverend Harrell offered a prayer which brought tears to many eyes. Jailer Burns read the death sentence. The rope was adjusted and the black cap fitted. At two o'clock, Sarber gave the signal, and a deputy pulled the lever which sprung the trap. Childers' neck jerked to one side as he shot down to the end of the rope. At the same moment, there was a flash of lightning and a loud clap of thunder. Minutes later, the work was done, the cloud vanished, and Childers' body hung limp and quivering.

The hanging and the storm filled many of the spectators with awe. A Negro woman screamed, "John Childers' soul has gone to hell; I done heard de chains clankin!" Others believed that Childers was never executed, that the man on the scaffold that day was "the devil in human disguise." Others may have thought of the thunder and lightning as God's condemnation of the evil in Indian Territory—the Armageddon of the West. John Childers was only the first of eighty-seven convicted felons to die on the Fort Smith gallows.[33]

In 1873, Judge Story sentenced three Cherokees—Young Wolf, Tun-ne-ha, and Six Killer—to hang after their conviction on a charge of murdering two white trappers on Grand River. The next year, he sent to the Fort Smith gallows three more men—John Billy, a Choctaw; Pointer, an eighteen-year-old Seminole; and Isaac Filmore, a Choctaw—convicted of murdering white men in Indian Territory.[34]

Billy, Pointer, and Filmore were the last men to be sent to the gallows by Judge Story. He was called to Washington to explain to Congress the expenditure of $724,000 in his judicial district during a three-year period. Congressional investigators charged that this sum expended in a judicial district serving three hundred thousand persons exceeded the amount spent for the same period for judicial purposes in the New England states, New Jersey, Pennsylvania, and Ohio. The Committee on Expenditures by the Department of Justice found that Story's United States marshal had organized a national bank at Fort Smith; that he owned three-quarters of the bank's stock; that he forwarded to this bank for payment vouchers of witnesses, jurors, and marshals; and that these vouchers were paid at a "tremendous discount." Investigators declared that there "was a most lamentable state of morals among the court officials in the district." They charged that Story allowed bail for felons convicted on a capital offense and while they were awaiting sentence. Story's explanations were characterized as "lame, disconnected, and unsatisfactory." The committee recommended that Congress abolish the court at Fort Smith, to assure that "every door to fraud will be closed, and the administration of justice can be more successfully maintained." In the spring of 1874, a bill was introduced in Congress to abolish the federal court at Fort Smith; when

[33] *Ibid.* Harmon, *Hell on the Border,* 187–95.
[34] *Western Independent,* April 9, 1874 and Harmon, *Hell on the Border,* 196.

Story resigned to escape impeachment, the Senate failed to pass the measure.[35]

Pending appointment of a new judge at Fort Smith, Henry J. Caldwell presided over the court. He sentenced one man to the gallows, making a total of eight executed before President Grant appointed Isaac Parker judge of Western District of Arkansas.

Parker arrived with his family from Missouri on May 2, 1875. Eight days later, he opened his first term of court for the Western District, a jurisdiction he presided over for twenty-one years. Parker was soon widely known as "the hanging judge of Fort Smith."

The physical setting of Parker's court was as grim as the proceedings there. The courtroom in the old Soldiers' Quarters was fitted with a jury section; tables and chairs for attorneys, witnesses, and prisoners; and a gallery for spectators. Parker sat behind a huge cherry-paneled desk in an exceedingly high-backed leather-bottomed chair. An armed escort brought the prisoners in leg shackles up from the basement jail. Inside each basement entrance to the jail was a small vestibule of rough timber, eight feet by ten feet, where prisoners were permitted to confer with their attorneys. Judge Parker established an office and library in the old commissary storehouse.[36]

Parker's first murder trial was that of Daniel Evans, charged with killing a nineteen-year-old youth near Eufaula in the Creek Nation. The judge's charge to the jurors was lengthy. In effect, he led the jury—he believed that Evans was guilty and that the guilty must be punished. The jury, out only a few minutes, returned with a verdict of guilty. On June 26,

[35] Fort Smith Tri-Weekly Herald, June 13, 1874. Story's troubles are detailed in "Western District of Arkansas," House Report No. 626, 43rd Congress, 1st Session.

[36] Fort Smith Elevator, January 15, 1886. Also Harmon, Hell on the Border, 71–72.

Parker pronounced sentence, and delivered a long, bitter harangue denouncing Evans in a cold, harsh voice. Then, instead of saying that the prisoner was to be hanged "until dead," the judge repeated the dread word three times—"I sentence you to hang by the neck until you are dead, dead, dead!"[37]

During Parker's first term at Fort Smith, eighteen persons were charged with murder, of which fifteen were convicted and eight sentenced to hang. One condemned prisoner died in an escape attempt; another had his sentence commuted to life imprisonment. There remained on death row, besides Evans: Heck Campbell (a Negro), Sam Fooy, James H. Moore, William J. Whittington, and Smoker Man-Killer (a Cherokee). Parker had decided that all six should be hanged together to warn the lawless that law had come to Indian Territory.

A scaffold was erected at the south side of the garrison against the front of the magazine. A reporter from St. Louis wrote:

> The structure is built of rough timbers. The crossbeam is a stout piece of hewed oak, supported on two upright posts, very strongly braced. The platform is about seven feet from the ground. The distance between the supporting posts is about twelve feet, giving nearly two feet space for the fall of each victim. The trap extends across the breadth of the platform, and consists of two pieces strongly hinged to the flooring of the platform so that they form a connection in the nature of a double door when closed from below. These are held in place when brought up by a stout beam of oak, extending in the direction of the gallows' beam on which rest two arms firmly fastened to one flap of the door below. To this beam about the middle is secured an iron trigger bar which passes up through a place provided in the trap doors and is secured by a knee in a strong iron lever about three feet long, well secured on the facing of the plat-

[37] St. Louis Republican, September 4, 1875. Also Western Independent, September 8, 1875.

form floor. By a movement of this lever back, the trigger bar which holds the trap in position is released and the doors drop down. On this door the condemned men will stand. Six ropes at this moment are tied over the beam, and six bags of sand of 200 pounds in weight each have been thrice dropped to test the further working of this awful enginery of death.[38]

The execution was well reported. All local newspapermen were present, along with correspondents from Little Rock, St. Louis, and Kansas City. In the crowd which gathered inside the walls of old Fort Smith on September 3, 1875, were whites, Negroes, Indians, farmers in working clothes, well-dressed city people, and rough-clad frontiersmen. Hangman George Maledon tested each rope. At nine-thirty, the prison door swung open, and out marched the prisoners, two abreast, toward the waiting gallows. Each man wore a leg iron and handcuffs. Four clergymen marched with the procession; armed guards fell in at the sides and rear. The prisoners climbed the steps and took their seats on rough benches. Each was permitted last words. Campbell, the Negro, bade the multitude "farewell and hoped they would all meet in heaven." Smoker Man-Killer spoke in Cherokee—an interpreter translated, "I am prepared to die"—declared his innocence, and said, "My conviction was caused by prejudice and false testimony." Moore, a giant of a man feared as a gunfighter, looked down and in clear, crisp tones said, "I have lived like a man, and I will die like a man." Evans held his poise and silence. The warrants were read, followed by prayers, hymns, and benediction. Maledon stepped forward and lined the felons up with "their feet squarely across the line where met the two planks forming the death-trap." One by one he placed black hoods over the men's heads and adjusted the nooses. Then he took his position and pulled the lever which sprung the trap.

[38] *St. Louis Republican*, September 4, 1875.

The bodies dropped. Maledon had done his work well. Every neck was broken by the fall, and six lifeless bodies dangled from the end of the ropes. Guards placed the corpses in coffins. Friends and relatives called for four of the bodies. Whittington and Campbell's remains were buried in a small plot on the military reservation set aside for that purpose. The most melancholy sight was that of Smoker Man-Killer's Cherokee wife and mother. His mother claimed his remains, placed the coffin in a little wagon, and started back to the Cherokee Nation, with the widow, softly sobbing, walking alongside carrying a baby.[39]

Accounts of the mass hanging appeared in newspapers across the country. The macabre doings at Fort Smith had caught the public fancy, and widespread editorial notice gave rise to Parker's being called—"the hanging Judge." Executioner George Maledon, who became a celebrity almost as famous as the judge, took great pride in his work. Parker's heavy docket saw 160 men sentenced to the Fort Smith gallows; on review, many sentences were commuted to long prison terms, usually for life. Maledon hanged a total of sixty of the seventy convicted criminals executed at Fort Smith during Parker's term as presiding judge. He conscientiously selected handwoven hemp rope from St. Louis, specifying that each rope be impregnated with pitch to prevent slippage. The Fort Smith gallows carried the sign: "The Gates of Hell."

For years, the attraction that drew the largest crowds on the Southwestern frontier was the annual mass execution on the gallows at Fort Smith. In April, 1876, more than seven thousand gathered to watch the hanging of five Indian Territory criminals. By 1880, Parker, embarrassed by the carnival-like atmosphere these executions generated, decided to restrict attendance. For the September, 1881, execution, only about

[39] *Western Independent*, September 8, 1875. Also *St. Louis Republican*, September 4, 1875.

fifty newspapermen, attorneys, clergymen, and court officials were permitted to witness the hanging of five convicted murderers.[40]

Although the executions were the most conspicuous feature of Parker's administration of justice on the Southwestern frontier, most of the court's time was taken up with less dramatic matters. Nearly nine thousand persons were tried for various crimes during Parker's twenty-one years at Fort Smith. A random sampling of judicial business indicates that for the year November 1, 1882, to November 1, 1883, the court was in session for 291 days. The sessions began at seven-thirty in the morning and usually adjourned about five in the afternoon, although night sessions often ran until nearly midnight. During this year, twenty-six persons were charged with murder; one, arson; five, rape; forty-four, assault with intent to kill; three, perjury; 230, introducing whiskey into Indian Territory; sixteen, moonshining; three, embezzlement; two, counterfeiting; two, cutting timber on government land; one, intimidating witnesses; twenty-eight, contempt; one, selling patent medicine. Convicted persons given prison terms were sent to the Detroit House of Correction, Little Rock Penitentiary, Albany (New York) Prison, Washington, (D. C.) Reform School, and Menard Penitentiary at Chester, Illinois.[41]

Prisoners were said to dread commitment to the federal jail in the basement of the old Soldiers' Quarters almost as much as they did Parker's stern pronouncements. Some inmates likened this jail to the Black Hole of Calcutta. During a nine-month period in 1884, 522 persons served some time there. The *Fort Smith Elevator* reported that on October 13, 1888, the 170 prisoners in the federal jail at the military post represented "the largest number ever incarcerated at one time in

40 *Western Independent*, April 26, 1876, and September 7, 1881. Also *Fort Smith Elevator*, September 9, 1881.

41 *Fort Smith Elevator*, January 25, 1884.

the history of the court." Female prisoners were lodged in the old brick guardhouse constructed at Fort Smith before the Civil War.[42]

A new federal jail, constructed next to the old courthouse, was completed in 1888 and was occupied sooner than the United States marshal had anticipated. On March 17, the prisoners attempted a mass escape. They had just received a large number of religious tracts and Sunday-school pamphlets from local clergymen, and they stuffed these into cracks in the ceiling of the old jail and set them afire. Guards discovered the fire, put it out, and checked the escape. On March 19, 1888, the United States marshal moved the prisoners to the new federal jail. Additional improvements in the federal court establishment at Fort Smith included construction of a new courthouse in 1889. The February, 1890, term opened in the new building. Thereafter, the old Soldiers' Quarters was used to house officers for the jailer, the United States commissioner, and the marshals, as well as a hospital for the prisoners.[43]

United States deputy marshals brought in most of the persons tried in Parker's court. Citizens' posses and light-horse police companies from the Indian nations also assisted in apprehending fugitives. On one occasion, a murder suspect was delivered to the court by the father of the victim. William Brown, a cowboy in the Chickasaw Nation, shot seventeen-year-old Ralph Tate. Brown fled when he learned that the father of the slain boy was after him. The elder Tate trailed Brown for six hundred miles through Indian country into Texas. After twenty-eight days of hard travel, he captured his son's killer near Henrietta. Tate manacled Brown, padlocked a heavy trace about his neck, and led him all the way to federal jail at Fort Smith. Not until the jury found Brown

[42] *Ibid.*, October 19, 1888.

[43] Foster to Attorney General, December 16, 1889. National Archives, Department of Justice File 4-779-1889. Also *Fort Smith Elevator*, March 23, 1888.

guilty and Parker sentenced him to hang did the father return home.[44]

Many Western celebrities felt the stern justice of the federal court at Fort Smith. One of the most colorful figures to appear before Judge Parker was David L. Payne, the Boomer leader. On August 13, 1880, federal troops reached Fort Smith with Payne and five followers, whom they had arrested in the Indian country near Fort Reno on a charge of trespass on Indian lands. Payne claimed that he was merely seeking a home on land belonging to the United States, exercising his rights under the Homestead Act. Much interest in the Payne trial was aroused among the Indian nations. Tribal leaders feared that if the court upheld the Boomer leader's contention, it would "legalize the overwhelming of our whole territory," and they contributed money to assist the prosecution. At the preliminary hearing, Parker said that there were no criminal charges against Payne and his comrades, and he set them at liberty and ordered them to appear at the February term "to answer charges of going, the second time, into the Indian Territory."[45]

Payne used the Fort Smith court as a forum to forward his contentions, speaking to large audiences and having a good press. At his 1881 trial, he and his attorneys argued that the central part of Indian Territory, at two-million-acre tract known as the Unassigned Lands, was properly a part of the public domain and open to homestead entry. Parker said that he would take the matter under advisement. On May 2, 1881, Parker ruled against Payne in that although the lands in question were unassigned, they were clearly a part of the Indian country. Federal laws to protect the Indian nations obligated the United States to expel intruders for first offenses and to

[44] *Western Independent*, March 9, 1881. Also *Fort Smith Elevator*, March 11, 1881.
[45] *Fort Smith Elevator*, August 20, 1880.

fine them for second offenses. Parker declared that the Boomers must stay out of Indian Territory, and fined Payne one thousand dollars. The Indian nations were jubilant over this decision.[46]

One of the most colorful and notorious characters to appear in Judge Parker's court was Belle Starr, famous as a lover, horse thief, and bandit queen. A product of the border guerrilla wars, Myra Belle Shirley had married Jim Reed, a renegade who operated between the Missouri settlements and Texas. Belle's marriage into the Starr family brought her the professional name by which she is known in history. In 1882, she was arrested near the Osage line on a charge of stealing several horses in the Cherokee Nation with the intent of selling them on the McAlester market. The following February, Parker's courtroom was jammed for the Belle Starr trial. One observer said she lacked grace of carriage and looked much older than she was. But Belle was active. She refused to take the stand, she dashed off notes to her attorneys, she cried when someone mentioned Jim Reed, and she looked up at Judge Parker with a "bold and fearless glance." None of these wiles helped—she was found guilty of horse theft and sentenced to one year in prison.[47]

Other dramatic trials involving women at Fort Smith were those of Elizabeth Owens and Fanny Echols. Mrs. Owens was charged with the murder of Ezekiel Hurd. The Owens and Hurds were farm neighbors in the Choctaw Nation—their dwellings were about two hundred yards apart, and they used the same well. Hurd accused the Owens family of abusing his stock when the animals wandered into the Owens yard, and he sent word that if they did not stop he would "stomp" them "into the ground." On another occasion, he threatened to "come down and kill the whole damned outfit." As Hurd

---

[46] *Ibid.*, March 18 and May 4, 1881.
[47] *Ibid.*, February 23 and March 16, 1883.

rode past the Owens house on May 26, 1877, Elizabeth walked into the road and demanded to know if he planned "to carry his threat into effect." Hurd shouted for the woman to "go to hell," and rode on. When he returned, Elizabeth Owens picked up a shotgun, walked into the road, and asked Hurd, "Are you going to do what you said you was?" Hurd replied, "If you are willing to drop it, I am." Mrs. Owens snapped, "See that you do it," and turned toward the house. Hurd leaped off his horse, seized her by the hair with one hand, and caught the shotgun with the other. Throwing Mrs. Owens to the ground, Hurd began "stomping" her. Elizabeth's husband Obediah was on the porch skinning a raccoon. He heard his wife's screams, rushed to the road, and three times told Hurd to release his wife. Hurd refused, and Owens stabbed him in the chest with a barlow knife. Hurd staggered back several steps, collapsed, and died within a few minutes. Both Obediah and Elizabeth Owens were arrested and brought to Fort Smith. At the close of Elizabeth Owens' trial, the jury deliberated for one hour before returning a verdict of not guilty. Much interest was manifested in her trial, for this was the first time that a woman had been tried for murder in Parker's court. Apparently, the verdict was popular because it was followed by "general applause."[48]

Fanny Echols was a bright-looking, well-proportioned, neat, and attractive Negro girl of twenty. She and John Williams worked for Mrs. Crabtree at Eufaula in the Creek Nation. Though not married, Fanny and John lived together. One day when an admirer came to see Fanny, John fired five shots at him, drove him off, and then tried to kill Fanny. She escaped with a severe beating. Later, a friend gave her a pistol; the next time Williams beat her, she shot him. A deputy marshal arrested Fanny and took her to Fort Smith federal

[48] *Western Independent*, February 27, 1878.

jail.[49] At her trial before Judge Parker, she was "plainly though neatly dressed, and wore a nicely laundried sun bonnet." She informed the court that "if she had not done what she did, she would have been killed herself." The jury found her guilty. When the "hanging judge" sentenced her to the Fort Smith gallows, she stood and listened with no show of emotion; but when the guards took her from the courtroom, she broke down and was removed weeping to her cell.[50] On July 11, 1884, Fanny Echols was to die with five other condemned killers. According to the editor of the *Fort Smith Elevator*, none of the six "seem to be making any great preparations for their departures unless it is Fanny Echols, who was baptized in the river" on the last day of June by the minister of the Negro Baptist Church. Happily for Fanny, a telegram from Washington arrived in Fort Smith on July 3, advising that President Chester A. Arthur had commuted her sentence to life imprisonment.[51]

Even the Fort Smith executioner, George Maledon, expressed relief when the president commuted Fanny Echols' death sentence—he dreaded the thought of hanging a woman. Another time when Maledon showed sentiment was at the Busby execution. Shep Busby, a Kentuckian, served in the Civil War with the 56th Illinois and the 50th Missouri. After the war he settled in the Cherokee Nation fifteen miles northwest of Fort Smith. At one time he served as a deputy marshal for the Fort Smith court. About 1891, Shep's wife left him, and he took in two Indian women. The United States commissioner at Fort Smith swore out a writ accusing Busby of adultery, and Deputy Marshal Barney Connelley rode with the warrant to Busby's cabin. Busby saw Connelley coming and killed him from an ambush. Busby hid in the wilderness

[49] *Fort Smith Elevator*, August 24, 1883.
[50] *Ibid.*, May 2, 1884.
[51] *Ibid.*, July 4 and 11, 1884.

for several weeks, finally surrendering to a posse. At his Fort Smith trial, he claimed self-defense, saying that he did not know that Connelley was an officer of the law. The jury found Busby guilty, and Parker sentenced him to die. As the day set for Busby's execution approached, Maledon called on Parker and asked to be excused from his usual duty. Never before had Maledon done this, and Parker was puzzled. When Maledon explained that he could not execute Busby "because he is a Union soldier," Parker assigned Deputy Marshal G. S. White as Busby's executioner.[52]

James C. Cashargo was the last man to die on the Fort Smith gallows. Born in Arkansas, son of an Italian immigrant farmer, Cashargo had a long record of crimes, including forgery, larceny, and jailbreak. In May, 1895, he was arrested on a charge of killing Zacharia W. Thatch in the Creek Nation and taking the slain man's team, wagon, and valuables. A jury found him guilty, and Parker sentenced him to hang on July 30, 1896.[53]

Between 1883 and 1896, various federal laws nibbled away at the jurisdiction of Parker's Fort Smith court. An 1889 law reassigned the Chickasaw Nation and the greater part of the Choctaw Nation to the Eastern Judicial District at Paris, Texas. Other sections of Indian Territory were assigned to federal courts at Wichita and Fort Scott, Kansas. Then, on September 1, 1896, Parker's court lost its remaining jurisdiction over the country west of Arkansas. Indian Territory was divided into three judicial districts, each with its own court with original and exclusive jurisdiction.[54]

Parker died on November 17, 1896. The news caused loud rejoicing among the prisoners in the Fort Smith federal jail. Word quickly passed from cell to cell like "a signal for jubilee." "The devil's shore got de ole cuss dis time!" sang out one

[52] *Ibid.*, August 21, 1891, December 18, 1891, February 5, 1892, and April 29, 1892.
[53] *Ibid.*, June 7, 1895, and July 31, 1896.
[54] *United States Statutes at Large*, XXVIII, 693.

prisoner. "Is he dead? Whoopee!" yelled another. "Almost in a twinkling, those prisoners nearest the ones first learning of Judge Parker's demise, took up the refrain, and for a brief period it looked as if pandemonium was about to break loose."[55]

After the 1896 judicial reorganization act went into effect, the federal government stepped up its program, initiated in 1871, of liquidating the Fort Smith property. An 1884 act had granted certain military reservation lands to the city of Fort Smith for the erection of public buildings. The rest of the reservation—except for the national cemetery, the area within the garrison walls, and a site to be selected by the secretary of the treasury for a public building—was given to the city of Fort Smith for public schools.[56]

In 1897, Congress made provision for the sale of part of the land within the fort walls, but reserved the federal jail and barracks and the land these buildings occupied. During World War I, the Department of Justice authorized the Arkansas National Guard to use these buildings as temporary quarters. In 1925, the federal government transferred the remaining post property to the city of Fort Smith.[57]

Shortly thereafter, paved streets formed perimeters around a cluster of businesses, largely warehouses, constructed on the old post grounds. The tracks of two railway companies (Frisco and Missouri Pacific) separated Belle Point from the second Fort Smith. Belle Point, isolated from the town by the railroad tracks, became a neglected weed patch on the river bank, overgrown with trees and brush. Town derelicts and vagabonds traveling on the freight trains squatted in this hobo jungle, called "Coke Hill" by townspeople because of the

[55] Harmon. *Hell on the Border*, 100–101.
[56] *United States Statutes at Large*, XXIII, 19.
[57] *Ibid.*, XXIX, 596.

wide use of narcotics, canned heat, and moonshine whisky by its denizens.

Restoration and preservation of Fort Smith began when a group of local women formed the Old Fort Museum Association and, in 1911, occupied the commissary building in order to display military and pioneer artifacts. Finally, in 1957, general citizen interest in the historic post caused town leaders to restore the barracks, built in 1851 and used as a courtroom and jail by Judge Parker, and to clear Belle Point of its hobo hovels and sponsor excavation of original fort foundations by archaeologists. There followed a move by city officials to urge incorporation of Fort Smith into the National Park System. Thus when Congress, on September 13, 1961, adopted legislation designating Fort Smith a National Historic Site, the city of Fort Smith assigned its properties on the old military reserve to the United States.

National Park Service personnel working at Fort Smith initially were custodians for Belle Point, containing the excavated foundations of the first Fort Smith, and scattered parcels of land on the site of the second Fort Smith, including the commissary building (1846) and a barracks (1851), the latter in 1872 converted to a courthouse and basement jail, to which a jail wing had been added in 1887. In 1963 they formulated a master plan to guide the restoration and the development of these properties. They gradually acquired title to most of the properties situated within the historical site and removed several business buildings. And they conducted extensive archaeological surveys and historical research in order to authenticate their work at both post sites.

Fort Smith as a National Historic Site became a popular visitor center, but National Park Service personnel acknowledged its limited restoration, and they believed the facilities could be substantially improved. Therefore, during the early 1970's, they revised the 1963 master plan for Fort Smith with what they called the General Management Plan. It contains a long-range scheme for development and management of the area's resources and for visitor use which will guide their restoration work into the 1980's. The plan objectives are to preserve, protect, and restore Fort Smith's historic resources, and to perpetuate the natural landscape qualities that contribute to their significance in a manner consistent with historic preservation law and current National Park Service management policies. This commits the National Park Service to preserve the historical setting of the entire site; to restore the interiors and exteriors of existing historical structures compatible with the historical periods; to reconstruct significant structural elements (buildings, walls, walks) where technical knowledge is sufficient and policy and legal considerations allow; to adjust boundaries to include lands adjacent to the historic site that are critical to site integrity and interpretation; to encourage public use by providing appropriate access to the park's cultural resources; and to regulate such use in a reasonable manner that ensures long-term preservation of park resources. While early emphasis at Fort Smith under National Park Service management was upon the post's role in law and order on the border, under the revised plan the emphasis will be upon Indian removal, highlighting resources that illustrate various aspects of this theme and stressing the three historical Fort Smith periods that relate to the settlement of the eastern tribes in the Indian Territory.

On October 21, 1976, Congress adopted legislation implementing the General Management Plan for Fort Smith. It permits National Park Service personnel to recover up to seventy-five acres for the site. Besides purchasing properties within the National Historic Site area, they have formulated specific restoration projects. For the first Fort Smith they plan to maintain the foundations of the original post buildings and to restore the Belle Point environment. No attempt will be made to restore or reconstruct any part of the original post structure. For the second Fort Smith they plan, after acquiring essential properties, to remove business buildings, obliterate present city streets and parking lots, and then to conduct intensive archaeological investigations to determine precise locations of historic walls and buried foundations. They will restore grounds of the second fort, including landscaping and walkways, reconstruct portions of the second post wall, and restore the cistern and the commissary building. National Park Service personnel expect to furnish the commissary building with period pieces and exhibits. The barracks-courtroom-jail will be restored, the first floor divided into marshal and clerk offices and the courtroom, the basement into the original jail, and the added wing furnished to reflect the 1880's period. And the gallows will be moved to the original location on the post grounds.

Fort Smith's restoration as a National Historic Site is a latter-day reassertion of the old post's refusal to die. Deliberate federal liquidation nearly did it in between 1896 and 1925, but Fort Smith's phoenix-like quality asserted itself, and a new role was found, happily in this instance, to provide a tangible reminder of its colorful past.

The restored Fort Smith is an enduring tribute to the resourcefulness of border folk who labored mightily to keep this federal income-producing installation in operation. But above all else, Fort Smith resurrected serves as a monument to the soldier. He pacified this bloody frontier, built its first roads, and opened it to settlement. His presence at the Belle Point outpost marked the vanguard of Anglo-American civilization in the Southwest.

# Bibliography

## Manuscripts

Arkansas History Commission
  Nicks-Rogers Sutler Account Book, Fort Smith, 1821–22
Library of Congress
  Andrew Jackson Papers
  Zachary Taylor Papers
Missouri Historical Society (St. Louis)
  Thomas A. Smith Papers
National Archives
  General Land Office Records, Fort Smith, AMR File
  Justice Department Records
    Disposition of Cases, 1872–96, United States Court for the Western District of Arkansas
  Office of Indian Affairs
    Letters Sent and Letters Received Files
    Southern Superintendency Letters Received File
    Treaty File
  War Department
    Adjutant General Letters Sent and Letters Received Files
    Judge Advocate General Files
    Plans and Sketches of Early Posts and Harbors File
    Post Returns—Fort Smith, 1818–1870
    Quartermaster General Letters Sent and Letters Received Files

Second Military Department, Western Division Order
Book
Secretary of War Letters Received File
Seventh Military Department Order Book
Western Department Letters Sent and Letters Received
Files
Western Department Reports Received File

PUBLISHED DOCUMENTS

*American State Papers, Indian Affairs*, Volume II. Washington, 1834.

*American State Papers, Military Affairs*. Volumes V, VI and VIII. Washington, 1832–34.

Carter, Clarence E. (ed.). *Territorial Papers of the United States: Territory of Louisiana-Missouri, 1815–1821*. Volume XV. Washington, 1951.

———. *Territorial Papers of the United States: Territory of Arkansas, 1819–1836*. Volumes XIX, XX, and XXI. Washington, 1953–54.

Heitman, Francis B. *Historical Register and Dictionary of the United States Army*. Volumes I and II. Washington, 1903.

Kappler, Charles J. (comp. and ed.). *Indian Affairs: Laws and Treaties*. Volume II. Washington, 1904.

*Report of the Commissioner of Indian Affairs for the Year 1865*. Washington, 1865.

United States Congress. *House Report No. 263*. Twenty-third Congress, First Session.

———. *House Report No. 626*. Forty-third Congress, First Session.

———. *House Document No. 278*. Twenty-fifth Congress, Second Session.

———. *House Journal*. Twenty-third Congress, First Session.

*United States Statutes at Large*. Volumes IV, V, XXIII, XXVIII, XXIX and LXXV. Boston, 1846, and Washington, 1885–1961.

*War of Rebellion: A Compilation of the Official Records of the Union and Confederate Armies.* Series I, Volumes I, III, VIII, XIII, XXII, XXXIV, and XLI; Series IV, Volume I. Washington, 1880–1900.

## Books

Beers, Henry P. *The Western Military Frontier, 1815–1846.* Philadelphia, 1935.

Bell, John R. *The Journal of Captain John R. Bell.* Volume VI of *Far West and Rockies Series*, ed. by Harlin M. Fuller and LeRoy R. Hafen. Glendale, 1957.

Britton, Wiley. *The Civil War on the Border.* Volumes I and II. New York, 1899.

———. *Memoirs of the Rebellion on the Border.* Chicago, 1882.

Callan, John F. *The Military Laws of the United States.* Philadelphia, 1863.

Debo, Angie. *Rise and Fall of the Choctaw Republic.* Norman, 1934.

Dupuy, Richard E. *The Compact History of the United States Army.* New York, 1957.

Foreman, Grant. *Advancing the Frontier.* Norman, 1933.

———. *The Five Civilized Tribes.* Norman, 1934.

———. *Indians and Pioneers: The Story of the American Southwest before 1830.* New Haven, 1930.

———. *Pioneer Days in the Early Southwest.* Cleveland, 1926.

Fraser, Robert W. *Forts of the West.* Norman, 1965.

Ganoe, William A. *The History of the United States Army.* New York, 1924.

Gordon-Miller, William L. *Recollections of the United States Army.* Boston, 1845.

Graves, William W. *The First Protestant Osage Missions, 1820–1837.* Oswego, Kansas, 1949.

Harmon, S. W. *Hell on the Border: He Hanged Eighty-eight Men.* Fort Smith, 1898.

Harrell, John M. *Confederate Military History of Arkansas.* Atlanta, 1889.

Hart, Herbert M. *Old Forts of the Southwest.* Seattle, 1964.

Hollon, W. Eugene. *Beyond the Cross Timbers: The Travels of Randolph B. Marcy.* Norman, 1955.

James, Edwin. *Account of an Expedition from Pittsburgh to the Rocky Mountains.* Volumes XIV, XV, XVI, and XVII of *Early Western Travels, 1748–1846,* ed. by Reuben G. Thwaites. Cleveland, 1905.

Lang, Walter B. *The First Overland Mail: Butterfield Trail.* Volumes I and II. Washington, 1940.

McAfee, Josiah B. (comp.). *Official Military History of Kansas Regiments during the War for the Suppression of the Great Rebellion.* Leavenworth, 1870.

Morrison, William B. *Military Camps and Posts in Oklahoma.* Oklahoma City, 1936.

Nuttall, Thomas. *A Journal of Travels into the Arkansas Territory during the Year 1819.* Volume XIII of *Early Western Travels, 1748–1846,* ed. by Reuben G. Thwaites. Cleveland, 1905.

Richardson, Rupert N. *The Frontier of Northwest Texas, 1846–1876.* Glendale, 1963.

Risch, Erna. *Quartermaster Support of the Army, A History of the Corps, 1775–1939.* Washington, 1960.

Tunnard, W. H. *A Southern Record: The History of the Third Regiment, Louisiana Infantry.* Baton Rouge, 1866.

Utley, Robert M. *Frontiersmen in Blue: The United States Army and the Indian, 1848–1865.* New York, 1967.

Wardell, Morris L. *A Political History of the Cherokee Nation.* Norman, 1938.

Webb, Walter P. *The Texas Rangers.* Boston, 1935.

Weigley, Russell F. *History of the United States Army.* New York, 1967.

Woodward, Grace S. *The Cherokees.* Norman, 1963.

PERIODICALS

Bearss, Edwin C. "Fort Smith Serves General McCulloch as a Supply Depot." *Arkansas Historical Quarterly*, XXIV (Winter, 1965), 315–47.

Haskett, James N. "The Final Chapter in the Story of the First Fort Smith." *Arkansas Historical Quarterly*, XXV (Autumn, 1966), 214–28.

"2nd Infantry Regiment." *Military Collector and Historian* (March, 1951), 16–17.

Wright, Muriel H., and George Shirk (eds.). "The Journal of Lt. A. W. Whipple." *Chronicles of Oklahoma*, XXVIII (Autumn, 1950), 235–83.

NEWSPAPERS

*Fort Smith Herald* (1848–49).

*Fort Smith New Era* (1864–65).

*Fort Smith Tri-Weekly Herald* (1871–74).

*Fort Smith Weekly Herald* (1850).

*Fort Smith Western Independent* (1872–78).

*Little Rock Arkansas Gazette* (1820–36).

*Niles Register* (1817–24).

*St. Louis Republican* (1875).

*Van Buren Arkansas Intelligencer* (1858).

*Van Buren Press* (1861–65).

# Index

280, 282, 290, 305, 309, 313, 321,
323, 326, 330
Infantry: 79, 84, 209, 267, 303
Inspections: 79, 87
Intemperance: 29, 79, 87
Irwin, James R.: 186
Izard, George: 100, 107

Jackson, Andrew: 13, 19, 50, 115,
132
Jackson, Claiborne F.: 247
James, Edwin: 34
Jefferson Barracks: 190, 222
Jefferson, Thomas: 9
Jesup, Thomas: 68, 73, 103, 105,
145, 175–76, 179, 181, 183,
188–89, 193, 196–98, 205, 211,
220
Johnson, James: 36
Johnson, Robert D.: 138
Johnson, R. W.: 212–13
Johnston, Albert S.: 258
Jolly, John: 23, 26
Jones, Robert M.: 245
Jones, Roger: 201
Judson, William R.: 279, 281
Jumper, John: 289

Kansas Territory: 216, 232
Kearny, Stephen W.: 146, 149
Keelboats: 15, 19, 32, 36, 53, 157,
162, 218, 227
Kiamichi mountains: 17, 33
Kiamichi River: 6, 17, 39, 60, 89
Kimball, Nathan: 285
Kiowas: 6, 230
Kirby, Edmund: 301

Laffery, James R.: 313
Land warrants: 29
Lane, Jim: 280
Lansing, Arthur B.: 194, 205
Laster, John J.: 303
Lawlessness: 7, 313, 323
Lawson, Thomas: 51, 55, 70, 74

Lear, William: 184
Leased District: 230, 232
Leavenworth, Henry: 90
Lee, Robert E.: 298, 302
Lee's Texas Battery: 284
Leftwich, Granville: 55, 64, 73
Lewis, Reuben: 11, 23, 25, 39
Lighthorse police: 325
Lincoln, Abraham: 293, 296, 300
Little Rock, Arkansas: 17, 61, 104,
113, 115, 119, 171, 238, 241, 243,
247, 263, 271, 279, 285, 291, 294,
297, 303, 310, 311
Little Rock and California
Association: 207
Log Raft (Red River): 211
Log, Stephen H.: 14, 16, 19, 20,
33, 35, 53, 97
Louisville, Kentucky: 30, 90
Lovell, Joseph: 140
Lovely, William L.: 9–11
Lovely's Purchase: 11, 24, 39, 45,
88, 92, 109
Lyo, Nathaniel: 248–49

McAlester, Indian Territory: 327
McClellan, George B.:236
McClellan, William: 100, 102, 107
McCook, Edward M.: 313
McCulloch, Ben: 246–49, 253, 255
McCurtain, Jack: 283
McGrannie, Danniel: 86
McIntosh, James: 253
McKenney, John: 173
McKenney, Thomas L.: 103, 108,
110
McNamara, Thomas: 95
McNeil, John: 273
McRee, Samuel: 183

Macomb, Alexander: 188
Magazines: 281
Mails: 108
Maledon, George: 322, 329, 330